COMMUNICATING

IN CHINESE

an interactive ... ing Chinese

Speaking

Cynthia Ning
University of Hawai'i

Far Eastern Publications
Yale University

Library of Congress Cataloging in Publications Data:

Ning, Cynthia
       COMMUNICATING IN CHINESE: STUDENT'S BOOK FOR
       LISTENING AND SPEAKING

       1. Chinese language-Grammar
       2. Chinese language-Textbooks for foreign speakers-
          English

       ISBN 0-88710-175-5

Printed in the United States of America

10 9 8 7 6 5 4 3

Preface

Communicating in Chinese (CIC) was inspired by Mrs. Hope Staab, a Chinese language teacher at Punahou, a private secondary school in Hawaii, who agitated at length for an interactive, task-based curriculum in Chinese, similar to volumes already available in Spanish, French, and other more commonly taught languages. *CIC* was supported from beginning to end by the US Department of Education, first with three consecutive grants from the Mathematics, Science and Critical Foreign Languages program, and finally through funding to the University of Hawaii's National Foreign Language Resource Center (NFLRC).

CIC is not a self-study curriculum. Rather, it consists of materials to support language-focused interaction between teachers and students, and among students themselves.

This Listening and Speaking volume is written in English and *pinyin*, the form of romanized Chinese currently in use in the People's Republic of China (PRC). Since this volume aims to develop students' listening and speaking skills, romanization is used in place of Chinese characters to represent spoken Chinese, *pinyin* being a far better guide to pronunciation than characters, which are unnecessary at this stage but will appear in the Reading and Writing volume. The choice of *Hanyu pinyin*, as opposed to other forms of romanization available in Taiwan, Hong Kong, or overseas, was made strictly on grounds of expediency, since *pinyin* is the form of romanization most widely used in contemporary media. Orthographic rules laid out in *Chinese Romanization: Pronunciation and Orthography* (1990) by Yin Binyong and Mary Felley were the basis of romanization here; the 1989 edition of *Hanyu Pinyin Cihui* was an additional guide. In those rare instances where these two sources are in conflict, *CIC* has followed the *Cihui*.

The short dialogues that appear in the text are not set in a specific location: most are equally applicable to any Chinese locale. Some even imply a Chinese enclave overseas.The type of language used is similarly unaligned by intent. Consultants to this curriculum have come from the PRC, Hong Kong, Taiwan, and the U. S. Under their scrutiny, the language models that have survived in this text are those that are largely non-dialectal, and generally acceptable as modern standard Chinese.

The ten topics covered in this Listening and Speaking volume roughly correspond to the topics suggested by the proficiency levels detailed in the Introduction which follows.

The members of the original teams that began curriculum writing projects in 1986 include David Ashworth, Hazel Hasegawa, Susan Hirata, Nobuko Kawaura, Yutaka Sato, and Margaret Yamashita, all (at the time) of the University of Hawaii, except for Ms. Hasegawa, who was released to us by the Hawaii Department of Education. I am particularly grateful to David Ashworth and Hazel Hasegawa for their continuing support. Three teachers in Honolulu have tested the curriculum over the course of three years, have provided very valuable feedback, and have had to put up with having to depend upon materials that were just barely being produced in time for class—Hope Staab, Maylani Chang, and Yao Wheeler. Hope Staab in particular was instrumental in getting this project started and keeping it going in the early days. Additionally, Lisa Lin (Ohio) and Kathy Chen (Connecticut) used the draft forms of the materials and suggested modifications. David Hiple, Richard Chi, Ying-che Li and Ronald Walton reviewed draft versions of the curriculum and provided suggestions and encouragement. My first intern in the NFLRC, Stephen Fleming, later a regular, full-time instructor with the Department of East Asian Languages and Literature, test-used the curriculum in experimental sections of beginning Chinese at the University of Hawaii. He provided extensive input, particularly on the grammar notes, which is reflected in the current version of the curriculum. Five teachers who participated in the 1991 Summer Intensive Teacher Training Institute in Foreign Languages at the University of Hawaii, sponsored by the NFLRC, utilized the near-final draft of the curriculum and offered critique and additional instructional ideas. They are Hazel Hasegawa, Wenchao He, Yvonne Swun, Eugenia Wu, and Rina Wu. I also thank a number of people who assisted with the production of the curriculum: illustrators Kasumi Ochiai, Natalie Kikkawa, Pepito Galvez, Randy Fagaragan, and Xiaolin Wang, calligraphers Rosa Chiang and Peter Kobayashi, language editors Xu Huang, Rosa Chiang, Meiling Ng, Xia Chen, Yuqing Bai and Lei Ye, proof-reader and word-processor Debbie Sharkey, computer specialists James Herman III, who created the tone-marks for the word-processing program, and Jon Ciliberto, who helped with printing various drafts. Daniel Cole of the Center for Chinese Studies designed the templates that generated the final version of the book, and assisted with each step of the desk-top publication process. The Chinese-English/English-Chinese indexes were developed by Daniel Cole and Yuqing Bai, with help from student assistants Woei Ang and Ip Hung Mar. Allen Awaya, a high school teacher who made numerous trips to Taiwan and the PRC, contributed many of the photographs that appear in the book. Other photographs were provided by William Crampton, a graduate student in Chinese Studies at the University of Hawaii and frequent sojourner in the PRC. The photograph of a Chinese dorm-room in Unit Eight was obtained by Ping Hao, the University of Hawaii's 1991–92 exchange professor from Peking University, from his home institution. John Montanaro of Far Eastern Publications wrote copious lists of suggestions to improve late drafts of the book, most of which have been incorporated. Finally, I am grateful to the University of Hawaii's College of Languages, Linguistics, and Literature; School of Hawaiian, Asian, and Pacific Studies; and the Centers for Chinese and Japanese Studies, for monetary, staff, and moral support over many years.

CONTENTS

Introduction

Communicating in Chinese is intended to facilitate a proficiency- (or performance-) based curriculum. The notion of "proficiency-based" foreign language education derives from current perspectives on standardized testing of learner performance using the foreign language.

It is projected that in a natural language environment, you would acquire control of functions involving the use of language in a rough order. You begin by gaining control of simple, high-frequency tasks (greeting, asking and stating personal information, decoding street signs) that are required of all language users, and eventually attaining control of more complex, higher level tasks that are less commonly required of a smaller subset of users (hypothesizing, abstracting, reading a technical journal).

Tests of your proficiency in the foreign language place your level of accomplishment somewhere along this hypothetical continuum. Can you accomplish simple communicative tasks, pertaining to personal needs? Can you meet progressively more challenging demands in general social interaction (state, reiterate, describe, narrate)? Can you meet professional needs (negotiate, state and defend a position, explain a technical issue)?

Following are simplified proficiency level descriptions for listening and speaking, based on generic and Chinese-specific descriptions promulgated by the American Council on the Teaching of Foreign Languages (ACTFL).

Listening

Novice Level Able to recognize learned material and isolated words and phrases when these are strongly supported by context.

Intermediate Level Able to understand main ideas and some facts from interactive exchanges and simple connected aural texts.

Advanced Level Able to understand main ideas and most details of connected discourse on a variety of topics beyond the immediacy of the situation, including some topics where comprehension is complicated due to an unexpected sequence of events.

Superior Level Able to understand concrete and abstract topics in extended discourse offered by speakers using native-like discourse strategies.

Speaking

Novice Level Able to communicate minimally, using memorized words and phrases.

Intermediate Level Able to create with the language by combining and recombining learned elements; initiate, minimally sustain, and close in a simple way basic communicative tasks; and ask and answer questions.

Advanced Level Able to converse in a clearly participatory fashion; initiate, sustain, and bring to closure a wide variety of communicative tasks, including those that require an increased ability to convey meaning with diverse language strategies due to a complication or an unforeseen turn of events; satisfy the requirements of school and work situations; and narrate and describe with paragraph-length connected discourse.

Superior Level Able to participate effectively in most formal and informal conversations on practical, social, professional, and abstract topics; and support opinions and hypothesize using native-like discourse strategies.

(Novice and Intermediate levels are further divided into Low, Mid, and High subranges, and Advanced is further divided into Advanced and Advanced High subranges. Reading and Writing guidelines are described in *Communicating in Chinese, Student's Book for Reading and Writing.*)

Communicating in Chinese, Listening and Speaking, aims to help you attain the **Intermediate Level** in both listening and speaking. Specifically, we hope that you will be able to handle everyday situations that involve asking and answering questions, making and responding to simple statements, and maintaining uncomplicated face-to-face conversation. Topics will be limited to personal background, basic needs such as getting meals, shopping, and transportation, and routine social functions.

Some advice to the learner

This student text is a reference volume/workbook, mostly to use outside of class to prepare for and to review classwork. Ideally, you will not refer to it very much during class sessions. The instructor will conduct a variety of activities during class, which are intended to familiarize you with the various structures and usages of Chinese, and to provide you opportunities to use them to express what you wish.

Do not expect to gain full control over every item in every lesson: some information has been provided as a preview, to afford you some familiarity with a new concept (particularly in the "slice of life" conversations that precede the *Culture Notes* in each lesson). You will require many encounters with the material in many different forms before you will be able to use it freely and accurately. Do your best to become as comfortable with as much of the lesson as you can, but expect that you will come to know some of the material very well, some of it only partially, and some of it hardly at all. As the course proceeds, much of what was murky in one lesson will become clearer after subsequent lessons.

Do feel free to take risks. If you do not understand something, try to **guess** at what it means, using whatever contextual clues you can to assist you. Some lessons contain items that have are not formally introduced anywhere, with the expectation that you can use contextual information to interpret them, even if incorrectly at first. In the long run, it is as important for you to develop **strategies** for extracting meaning from unknown language in context as it is to memorize the meaning of that language.

Please try to **understand and to express yourself fearlessly** in Chinese, without undue concern for "sounding foreign" or for maintaining absolute accuracy at this stage (you cannot). Of course, you should **aim** to be accurate, but do not sacrifice an opportunity to communicate because you are afraid that what you think you understand or what you are about to say might not be quite right. You will have to make many mistakes in the course of learning any language, foreign or your own, initially. As long as you can detect that there are discrepancies between your own performance and the language modelled by your teacher and other live or recorded sources, you stand a good chance of self-correcting in time to keep your progress on track.

If you accept that language learning is the process of acquiring SKILLS rather than of memorizing a body of knowledge, you will realize that foreign language is not a subject for which you can cram successfully. Practice and study sessions **at regular intervals over a long period of time** will be more useful in building up your foreign language stamina and competence than occasional, extended bouts with the material. An athlete trains daily over the course of months and years; similarly, a successful language learner disciplines him/herself to work steadily with the material for an extended period of time. If you allocate yourself five hours a week of study for this class, it is better to distribute the time evenly, say an hour a day, rather than five hours the night before the test.

Each lesson in the book begins with a reference **list of key terms and expressions** pertinent to the skill described for that lesson. Through your classroom activities, you will become familiar with these terms, and will begin to experiment with using them to accomplish tasks that your teacher will set. Following the list are brief **dialogue puzzles** that you have to solve, which then will provide you models of simulated native-speaker interaction. These dialogues are *more or less* limited to the vocabulary and structures you have been exposed to in this and previous lessons, although on rare occasion you will encounter a term that you might not have seen before, but likely can decipher from context. Next is a "slice of life" **contextualized conversation** based on the theme of the lesson, but NOT limited to its language. English translations are provided. These conversations are intended to impart a "flavor" of more natural interactions in a Chinese setting, and to help you build up a tolerance for language that is not strictly tailored to your level of competence. Similarly, **photograph captions** are not strictly limited to language you know: guess at their meaning given the context in which they occur. The **structure and culture** notes are for you to read at your leisure, at home, to give you some background information about the language you are using in class. The **structure exercise** should be completed at home and checked in class; it is intended to help you develop the ability to monitor the grammatical accuracy of your own speech.

Foreign language is the key to a new universe: a different people, culture, social system. It is possible for you to become sufficiently competent to navigate in that universe, an accomplishment which will surely bring you reward enough to compensate for the innumerable hours you will have invested in learning the language. Even if you never attain the upper reaches of competence, if you never become a Superior, or an Advanced, or even a higher Intermediate level performer, the glimmers of understanding enjoyed by a Novice Mid or High are illuminating when compared with the darkness that surrounds someone who isn't even on the scale— a zero.

CREDITS

Cover

Upper left: (Allen Awaya, 1990) Karen Ward, American high school English teacher, posing with a participant in the Shanghai Children's Palace.

Upper right: (Allen Awaya, 1990) Kathryn Safsten and Myra Hulama, American students, on the Beijing to Xi'an train.

Bottom left: (Allen Awaya, 1991) Teachers in Xinxiang, Hebei.

Bottom center: (Allen Awaya, 1991) Man lunching on fried dough in Shanghai.

Bottom right: (Allen Awaya, 1991) Child out strolling with her grandparents in Beijing.

Cover calligraphy provided by Charles Chu of New London, Connecticut.

Page 17

(Allen Awaya, 1990) Child on a Shanghai playground.

Page 36

Top: (William Crampton, 1991) Baby in a bamboo carriage in Linfen, Shanxi.

Bottom: (Allen Awaya, 1991) A *Taijiquan* master and student in Zhengzhou pause to talk to American students.

Page 38

(Allen Awaya, 1991) Primary school student completing a class assignment, Xinxiang, Hebei.

Page 47

(Li Dianping, 1991) William Crampton and his wife Sachi Matsuoka in a stationery shop in Linfen, Shanxi.

Page 48

Top: (William Crampton, 1991) Peasant woman returning from the fields in Taiyang village, Shanxi.

Bottom: (Allen Awaya, 1991) Card game on a sidewalk in Beijing.

Page 49

(Cynthia Ning, 1991) Robyn Ning Yee, 9, meets the guard at the entrance to the gardens of the National Palace Musuem, Taipei.

Page 57

(Chungfong Ning, 1954) *Left to right:* Robert Ning, Cynthia Ning, Grace Chen Ning, Samuel Ning, Pauline Ning, and Chungfong Ning outside the Punjab Vegetable Ghee Mills in Lahore, Pakistan.

Page 66

Top: (William Crampton, 1991) A peaceful moment in mid-afternoon, at the West Gate of Tiantan park in Beijing.

Bottom: (William Crampton, 1991) Eating popsicles on Wangfujing, a busy shopping street in Beijing.

Page 67

(Allen Awaya, 1991) A peasant woman along the road between Shanghai and Hangzhou takes a rest from gathering twigs for fuel.

Page 73

(William Crampton, 1991) Napper on the grounds of Huaqingchi in Xi'an, Shaanxi Province.

Page 88

Left: (William Crampton, 1991) Kindergarten boy of the Qiao family, playing the part of a People's Liberation Army soldier in Linfen, Shanxi.

Right: (William Crampton, 1991) Kindergartener preparing to perform a disco dance in Linfen, Shanxi.

Page 95

(Cynthia Ning, 1991) Robyn and other on-lookers enjoying a swan and carp in the gardens of the National Palace Museum, Taipei.

Page 105

(William Crampton, 1991) Kindergarten girls dressed to perform a dance entitled "Happy Minority Women give Scarves of Friendship to People's Liberation Army Troops" in Linfen, Shanxi.

Page 108

Top: (William Crampton, 1991) Periodic market in Taiyang village, Shanxi Province.

Bottom left: (William Crampton, 1991) A peddlar's stall in Dali, Yunnan.

Bottom right: (William Crampton, 1991) Shopkeeper guarding his store in Hohhot, Inner Mongolia.

Page 114

Top: (Allen Awaya, 1991) Card-players on the Great Wall, outside Beijing.

Middle: (Allen Awaya, 1991) Young dancer on Tian'anmen Square, in Beijing.

Bottom: (Allen Awaya, 1991) Peddlar on a street in Beijing.

Page 142

Top: (William Crampton, 1991) Chinese businessman Li Dianping and family friend in the living room of a peasant home in Taiyang, Shanxi.

Bottom: (William Crampton, 1991) American visitor Sachi Matsuoka holding a Chinese baby in a peasant home in Taiyang, Shanxi.

Page 145

(Student Services Department, Peking University, 1993) Graduate students in a men's dormitory at Peking University, late in the spring semester.

Page 148

(William Crampton, 1991) Li Kerui (2, in lap), with aunt's family in Hongtong, Shanxi.

Page 174

(William Crampton, 1991) Chef cooking hand-made noodles in Rong Rong's Restaurant of Linfen, Shanxi.

Page 191

(Allen Awaya, 1989) Limestone cliffs on the southern seacoast, Taiwan (Republic of China).

Page 196

Top left: (Cynthia Ning, 1991) Shopping district in Taipei.

Top right: (Allen Awaya, 1990) Buses and bicycles stopped at a traffic light in Beijing near Tian'anmen Square.

Bottom: (William Crampton, 1991) Hong Kong skyline from the Star Ferry.

Page 206

(William Crampton, 1991) Entrance to the Beijing Railway Station.

Page 207

(Allen Awaya, 1990) Bus-rider in Beijing who did not make it all the way into the bus before the doors closed.

Page 211

Top: (Allen Awaya, 1990) Chinese travelers fighting to board a train in a market town on the Beijing–Xi'an line.

Bottom: (William Crampton, 1991) The entrance to the Great Wall at Badaling, with merchants offering photo opportunities on a horse and camel.

Page 212

(William Crampton, 1991) Basket merchant in Dali, Yunnan.

16

UNIT ONE: *HELLO!*

Skill: To handle basic courtesy expressions in social interactions.

Zǎo.	*Good morning.*
Nǐ hǎo.*	*Hello.*
Nǐ hǎo ma?	*How do you do?*
Hǎo.	*Fine. (I'm fine.)*
Hěn hǎo.	*Fine. (I'm very well.)*
Nǐ ne?	*How about you?*
Bú cuò.*	*I'm not bad.*
Wǒ yě tǐng hǎo.	*I'm pretty well too.*
Wǒ hái kěyǐ.	*I'm okay.*

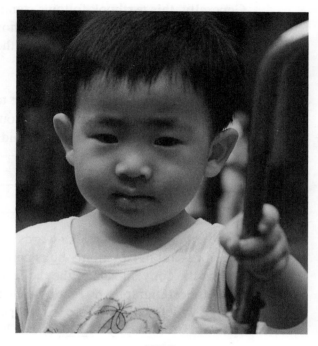

Nǐ hǎo.

Qǐng...	*Please..., go ahead..., help yourself.*
Xièxie.	*Thanks.*
Duō xiè.	*Thanks a lot.*
Fēicháng gǎnxiè.	*I'm extremely grateful.*
Bú xiè.	*You're welcome. (You don't have to thank me.)*
Bié kèqi.	*Don't be (so) polite. You're welcome.*

Duìbuqǐ.	*I'm sorry.*
Zhēn duìbuqǐ.	*I'm really sorry.*
Méi guānxi.	*It's alright, it doesn't matter.*
Méiyǒu guānxi.	*It's alright, it doesn't matter.*

Zàijiàn.	*Good bye.*
Yìhuǐr jiàn.*	*See you in a while.*
Huíjiàn.	*See you in a bit. (PRC)*
Míngtiān jiàn.	*See you tomorrow.*

* A note on pronunciation vs. orthography

Generally, this textbook follows standard *pinyin* orthography (see Preface, p. 7). In some cases, however, the orthography can be misleading to the learner, due in most cases to one of the following reasons.

1) Some Chinese words change tone to accord with their environment. Bù and yī, for instance, are said in the fourth tone when the subsequent word is first, second or third tone, but are said in the second tone when the subsequent word is fourth tone. Thus:

> bù gāo, bù máng, bù hǎo— bú lèi;
>
> yì zhāng, yì máo, yì duǒ— yí lì.

Standard orthography marks words such as bù and yī with the tonal value of the word said in isolation—bù is consistently bù and yī is consistently yī—but for the convenience of the the learner, **this textbook will deviate from standard orthography by marking the actual spoken values of the tones on bù and yī**, which will therefore vary depending upon environment. Thus, standard orthography's bù lèi and yì lì will be bú lèi and yí lì here.

2) A third tone that precedes another third tone becomes a second tone. (See appendix "The *pinyin* romanization system" p. 216.) Thus nǐ + hǎo is pronounced ní hǎo.

Standard orthography retains the original third tone on both words (nǐ hǎo, hěn hǎo, kěyǐ). Since it is useful for the learner to know the basic tonal value of new vocabulary items, **this textbook will conform to standard orthography by marking two adjacent third tones as third tones** (nǐ hǎo rather than ní hǎo), and expect that students will in time learn to shift the first third tone into a second tone (nǐ + hǎo = ní hǎo, kě + yǐ = kéyǐ).

3) A small number of words (such as huì) have a basic tonal value, but are commonly said with a different value in a limited number of set expressions (yìhuǐr jiàn). In such cases, **this textbook will mark the actual spoken value of the phrase, but will asterisk the first occurrence of the expression** and provide standard orthography in a note. Please note, therefore, that what is generally pronounced yìhuǐr jiàn is properly written yīhuǐr jiàn.

Dialogue Practice

The following sets of dialogues presume normal behavior, no unusual circumstances, and no misunderstandings in the contexts indicated. "A" begins the dialogue, "B" responds, "A" responds to "B," etc. Where there is a choice of responses available, please circle the one which is more appropriate.

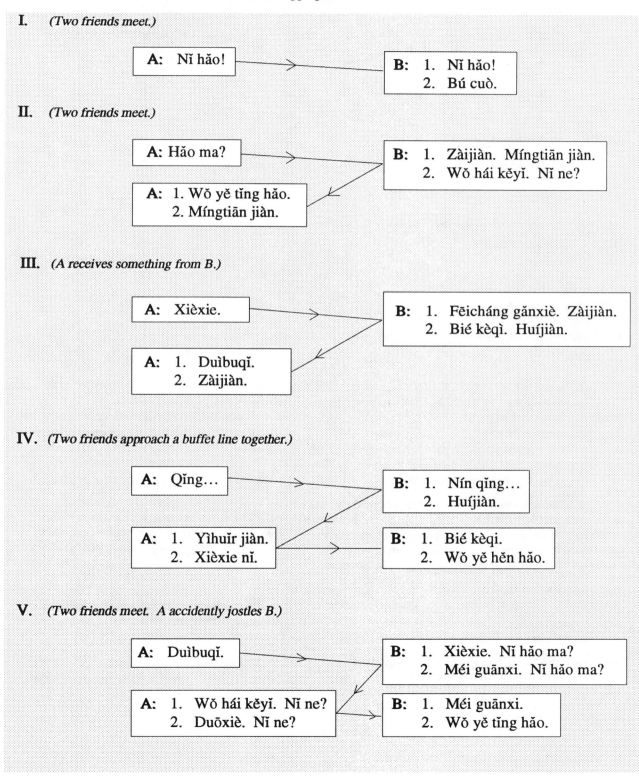

I. *(Two friends meet.)*

A: Nǐ hǎo!

B: 1. Nǐ hǎo!
    2. Bú cuò.

II. *(Two friends meet.)*

A: Hǎo ma?

B: 1. Zàijiàn. Míngtiān jiàn.
    2. Wǒ hái kěyǐ. Nǐ ne?

A: 1. Wǒ yě tǐng hǎo.
    2. Míngtiān jiàn.

III. *(A receives something from B.)*

A: Xièxie.

B: 1. Fēicháng gǎnxiè. Zàijiàn.
    2. Bié kèqì. Huíjiàn.

A: 1. Duìbuqǐ.
    2. Zàijiàn.

IV. *(Two friends approach a buffet line together.)*

A: Qǐng…

B: 1. Nín qǐng…
    2. Huíjiàn.

A: 1. Yìhuǐr jiàn.
    2. Xièxie nǐ.

B: 1. Bié kèqi.
    2. Wǒ yě hěn hǎo.

V. *(Two friends meet. A accidently jostles B.)*

A: Duìbuqǐ.

B: 1. Xièxie. Nǐ hǎo ma?
    2. Méi guānxi. Nǐ hǎo ma?

A: 1. Wǒ hái kěyǐ. Nǐ ne?
    2. Duōxiè. Nǐ ne?

B: 1. Méi guānxi.
    2. Wǒ yě tǐng hǎo.

A brief encounter

A is walking down a path on campus and runs into B. B drops some things he is holding.

A: Ou, zhēn duìbuqǐ.   *Oh, I'm very sorry.*

B: Méiyǒu guānxi.   *It's alright.*

A & B both stoop down to pick up the things. A hands them to B.

A: Na…   *Here…*

B: Xièxie, xièxie nǐ.   *Thanks, thank you.*

A: Bié kèqi.   *You're welcome.*

They nod at each other and continue on their separate ways.

Culture notes

Early childhood training in Chinese families used to include the following admonition:

"Lì rú sōng; zuò rú zhōng." *"Stand like a pine tree and sit like a bell."*

For proper posture, in other words, stand straight with arms and legs close to the body, and sit up straight with elbows in, and heels and knees close together. Both the pine tree and the bell have upright, symmetrical outlines. In emulation of these idealized outlines, one Chinese rule of ettiquette urged that hands and feet be kept to oneself, and that, in public, one not take up unneccesary space by placing the arms on the hips when standing, or by sitting in a sprawl. Although modern parents no longer speak of the pine tree and the bell, the lesson still remains—contemporary children are still encouraged to be reserved and controlled, especially in public.

It helps to conceptualize two bubbles around the individual when he or she is in a public space. The first, personal bubble fits closely against the body, and serves as a restraint to keep the hands and feet close. The second, interpersonal bubble extends approximately two feet from the body, and is in place whenever one is not dealing with close friends or family. The interpersonal bubble prevents two people from approaching each other too closely.

On rare occasion, however, a Western visitor is surrounded by curious (especially rural) onlookers who may even reach out to touch a hairy arm or a strand of light-colored hair, although in general children especially will avoid close contact with alarming-looking strangers. In such instances, the perpetrators are likely folk unaware of etiquette, who therefore do not care what it dictates.

Although the handshake is gaining popularity in Chinese communitites through Western influence, it is still more common to greet, to part, or to acknowledge an exchange of information with a simple nod.

SEGMENT A

Skill: To state own name; handle common personal names

wǒ	*I*		wǒmen	*we (plural)*
nǐ	*you*		nǐmen	*you (plural)*
tā	*he, she, it*		tāmen	*they (plural)*

shì	*to be (am, are, is)*
xìng	*to be surnamed, a surname*
jiào	*to be called (by given name)*
míngzi	*a given name*

Zhāng	*Chang, Cheung (a surname)*
Wáng	*Wang, Wong (a surname)*
Lǐ	*Li, Lee (a surname)*
Chén	*Chen, Chan (a surname)*
Mǎ	*Ma (a surname)*

Wǒ shì Wáng Dàwèi.	*I am David Wang.*
Wǒ xìng Wáng, jiào Dàwèi.	*My last name is Wang, my given name David.*
Shéi?	*Who?*
Tā shì shéi?	*Who is he/she?*
Nǐ xìng shénme?	*What is your family name?*
Nǐ jiào shénme míngzi?	*What is your first name?*
Qǐngwèn, nín guìxìng?	*May I ask your name? (polite)*
Nǐ bú shì Wáng Dàwèi ma?	*Aren't you David Wang?*

Qǐng zài shuō yí cì.	*Please say it again.*

Duì.	*That's right.*
Bú duì.	*That's not right.*
Duì bu duì?	*Is that right?*

Dialogue Practice

The following sets of dialogues presume normal behavior, no unusual circumstances, and no misunderstandings in the contexts indicated. "A" begins the dialogue, "B" responds, "A" responds to "B," etc. Where there is a choice of responses available, please circle the one which is more appropriate.

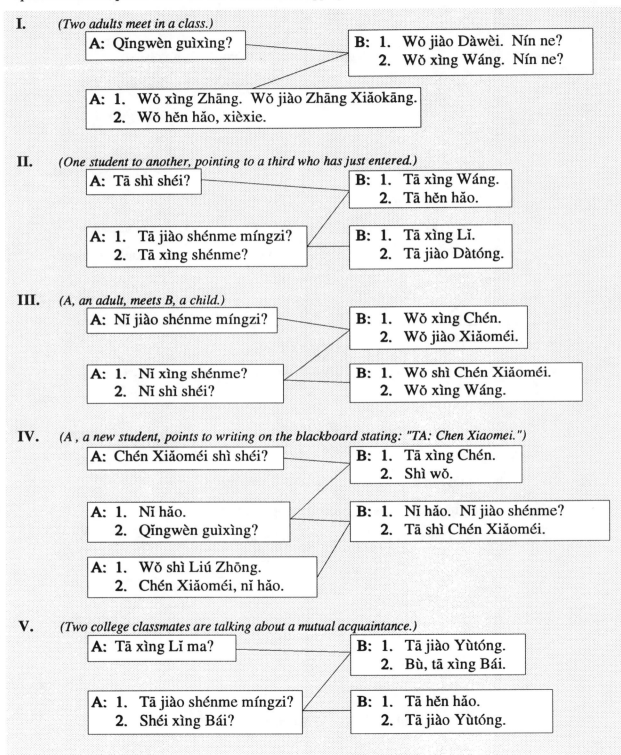

I.   *(Two adults meet in a class.)*

　　A: Qǐngwèn guìxìng?

　　B: 1. Wǒ jiào Dàwèi. Nín ne?
　　　　 2. Wǒ xìng Wáng. Nín ne?

　　A: 1. Wǒ xìng Zhāng. Wǒ jiào Zhāng Xiǎokāng.
　　　　 2. Wǒ hěn hǎo, xièxie.

II. *(One student to another, pointing to a third who has just entered.)*

　　A: Tā shì shéi?

　　B: 1. Tā xìng Wáng.
　　　　 2. Tā hěn hǎo.

　　A: 1. Tā jiào shénme míngzi?
　　　　 2. Tā xìng shénme?

　　B: 1. Tā xìng Lǐ.
　　　　 2. Tā jiào Dàtóng.

III. *(A, an adult, meets B, a child.)*

　　A: Nǐ jiào shénme míngzi?

　　B: 1. Wǒ xìng Chén.
　　　　 2. Wǒ jiào Xiǎoméi.

　　A: 1. Nǐ xìng shénme?
　　　　 2. Nǐ shì shéi?

　　B: 1. Wǒ shì Chén Xiǎoméi.
　　　　 2. Wǒ xìng Wáng.

IV. *(A , a new student, points to writing on the blackboard stating: "TA: Chen Xiaomei.")*

　　A: Chén Xiǎoméi shì shéi?

　　B: 1. Tā xìng Chén.
　　　　 2. Shì wǒ.

　　A: 1. Nǐ hǎo.
　　　　 2. Qǐngwèn guìxìng?

　　B: 1. Nǐ hǎo. Nǐ jiào shénme?
　　　　 2. Tā shì Chén Xiǎoméi.

　　A: 1. Wǒ shì Liú Zhōng.
　　　　 2. Chén Xiǎoméi, nǐ hǎo.

V.   *(Two college classmates are talking about a mutual acquaintance.)*

　　A: Tā xìng Lǐ ma?

　　B: 1. Tā jiào Yùtóng.
　　　　 2. Bù, tā xìng Bái.

　　A: 1. Tā jiào shénme míngzi?
　　　　 2. Shéi xìng Bái?

　　B: 1. Tā hěn hǎo.
　　　　 2. Tā jiào Yùtóng.

Recognition

David Wang and Li Zhongying are chatting outside of a classroom from which they have just emerged. The student with whom Li Zhongying recently collided approaches; David recognizes him.

David: Ei, Xiǎo Zhāng.   *Hey, Zhang.*

Zhāng: Wáng Dàwèi, nǐ hǎo.   *Hello, David Wang.*

David: *(to Zhang)*

           Zhè shì Lǐ Zhōngyīng.   *This is Li Zhongying.*

(The student, whose last name is Zhang, recognizes Li Zhongying. He smiles and nods at her.)

Lǐ: Qǐngwèn guìxìng?   *May I ask your last name?*

Zhāng: Wǒ xìng Zhāng.   *It's Zhang.*

           Wǒ jiào Déshēng.   *My first name is Desheng.*

David: *(to Li)*

           Xiǎo Zhāng gēn wǒ   *Zhang and I are old friends.*

           shì lǎo péngyou.

Lǐ: *(smiling)*

           O, shì ma.   *Oh, I see. (Lit: is that so?)*

Culture notes

Much in China is accomplished through an intermediary. David Wang and Li Zhongying came to know each other because they were in the same class, and David introduced Li Zhongying to Zhang Desheng. It is somewhat unlikely that two people who were not linked somehow, as classmates, coworkers, or through a common friend, would simply introduce themselves to each other. Boldness and directness are often considered rude, uncultured behavior, and therefore to be avoided outside the circle of family and close friends. Change however, is coming quickly to Taiwan and the PRC. Young people may be more direct and self-assertive, especially in dealing with foreigners.

There are between 400 and 500 common Chinese last names. Most consist of a single character, although a handful of "double surnames" such as Ouyang or Zhuge contain two characters each. The family name goes first in a person's full name, followed by the given name.

The majority of Chinese given names were traditionally made up of two characters, although some contained only one. The generation of Chinese in the PRC that roughly coincides with the "baby boom" generation in the U.S. (born between 1940 and 1960) however, largely received single-character first names. Since many cases of mistaken identities ensued as a result, the double-character given name seems to be returning to favor. Chinese families do not select given names for children from a list; they make them up, using sound and meaning as a guide.

Whereas Americans generally prefer the informality of using first names with each other, even very close Chinese friends will often call each other by their last names. Another common practice is to include both family and given names, even in informal contexts. Full names do not usually exceed three syllables anyway, and are therefore not difficult to say. Calling a friend by a given name alone is acceptable, but this is not nearly as common a practice as in America.

Structure notes

The following is a basic sentence pattern in Chinese.

1.   Subject + Equative Verb + Noun

Nǐ shì shéi?	*you + to be + who*	*Who are you?*
Wǒ xìng Wáng.	*I + to be surnamed + Wang*	*My last name is Wang.*
Wǒ de míngzi jiào Dàwèi.	*my + first name + to be called + Dawei*	*My first name is Dawei.*

Nǐ, wǒ, and *wǒde míngzi* are the **subjects** of the example sentences.

The verbs *shì, xìng,* and *jiào* are examples of **equative verbs**—verbs that in one sense or another equate the subject with the noun that follows.

Equative verbs are always followed by a **noun** or **noun-phrase**, or a question word (such as *shéi*) denoting a noun or noun-phrase.

Structure exercise

Fill in each blank in the passage below with one word that fits the context. It is a monologue by a very repetitive young man named Zhang Datong. He has heard of a person named Li Taibai; he introduces himself, and then asks about who Li Taibai is.

> Nǐ hǎo. Wǒ _____ Zhāng Dàtóng. Wǒ _____ Zhāng, jiào
>
> _____. Zhāng shì wǒ de xìng, Dàtóng _____ wǒ de míngzi. Qǐng
>
> wèn, Lǐ Tàibái shì _____? Tā _____ Lǐ, jiào _____. Tàibái shì
>
> tā de _____. _____ shì tā de xìng. Tā _____ shéi? Shéi
>
> _____ Lǐ Tàibái? _____ shì Zhāng Dàtóng. _____ shì Lǐ
>
> Tàibái?

SEGMENT B

Skill: To use & understand titles in addressing others

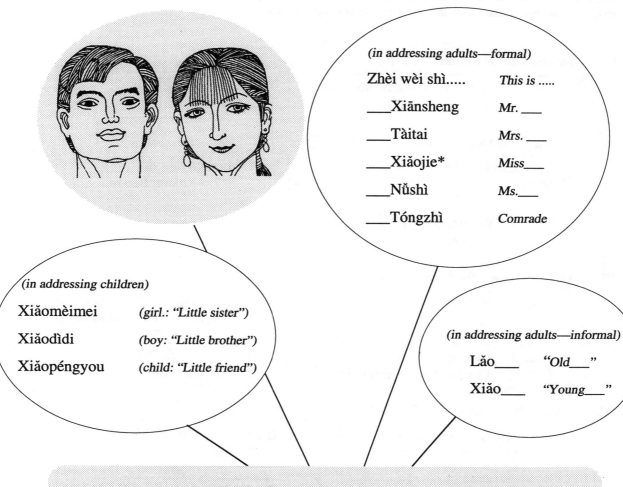

(in addressing adults—formal)

Zhèi wèi shì.....	This is .....
___Xiānsheng	Mr. ___
___Tàitai	Mrs. ___
___Xiǎojie*	Miss___
___Nǚshì	Ms.___
___Tóngzhì	Comrade

(in addressing children)

Xiǎomèimei	*(girl.: "Little sister")*
Xiǎodìdi	*(boy: "Little brother")*
Xiǎopéngyou	*(child: "Little friend")*

(in addressing adults—informal)

| Lǎo___ | *"Old___"* |
| Xiǎo___ | *"Young___"* |

Zhāng Xiānsheng, nǐ hǎo ma?	*How do you do, Mr. Zhang?*
Lǎo Lǐ, hǎo ma?	*How are you, Old Li?*
Wáng Tàitai, Wáng Xiǎojie, nǐmen hǎo ma?	*Mrs. Wang, Miss Wang, how are you?*
Xiǎopéngyoumen dōu hǎo ma?	*How are you all, children?*
Xuéshēngmen yě dōu hǎo ma?	*And how are you all, students?*

*Although jie in xiǎojie is neutral tone, its basic value is jiě; therefore since two third tones appear in succession (even though one of them is neutral), "Miss" is actually said as xiáojie.

Dialogue Practice

The following sets of dialogues presume normal behavior, no unusual circumstances, and no misunderstandings in the contexts indicated. "A" begins the dialogue, "B" responds, "A" responds to "B," etc. Where there is a choice of responses available, please circle the one which is more appropriate.

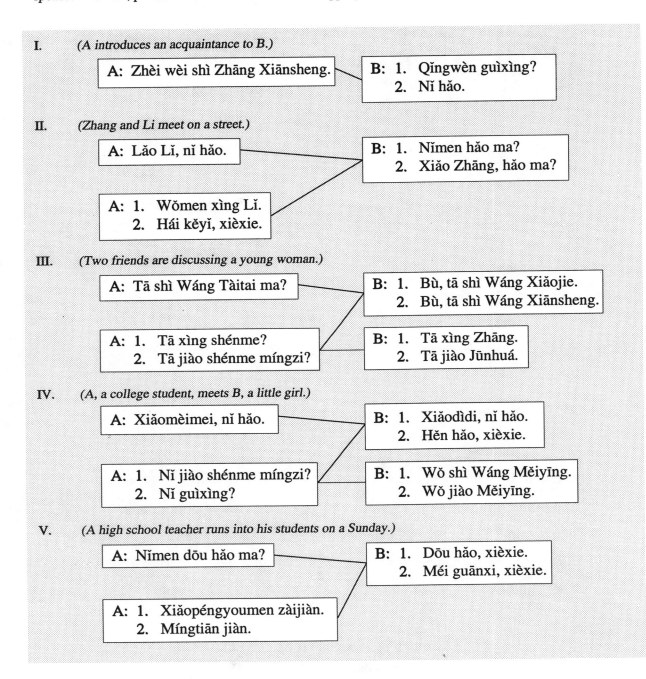

I. *(A introduces an acquaintance to B.)*

A: Zhèi wèi shì Zhāng Xiānsheng.

B: 1. Qǐngwèn guìxìng?
   2. Nǐ hǎo.

II. *(Zhang and Li meet on a street.)*

A: Lǎo Lǐ, nǐ hǎo.

B: 1. Nǐmen hǎo ma?
   2. Xiǎo Zhāng, hǎo ma?

A: 1. Wǒmen xìng Lǐ.
   2. Hái kěyǐ, xièxie.

III. *(Two friends are discussing a young woman.)*

A: Tā shì Wáng Tàitai ma?

B: 1. Bù, tā shì Wáng Xiǎojie.
   2. Bù, tā shì Wáng Xiānsheng.

A: 1. Tā xìng shénme?
   2. Tā jiào shénme míngzi?

B: 1. Tā xìng Zhāng.
   2. Tā jiào Jūnhuá.

IV. *(A, a college student, meets B, a little girl.)*

A: Xiǎomèimei, nǐ hǎo.

B: 1. Xiǎodìdi, nǐ hǎo.
   2. Hěn hǎo, xièxie.

A: 1. Nǐ jiào shénme míngzi?
   2. Nǐ guìxìng?

B: 1. Wǒ shì Wáng Měiyīng.
   2. Wǒ jiào Měiyīng.

V. *(A high school teacher runs into his students on a Sunday.)*

A: Nǐmen dōu hǎo ma?

B: 1. Dōu hǎo, xièxie.
   2. Méi guānxi, xièxie.

A: 1. Xiǎopéngyoumen zàijiàn.
   2. Míngtiān jiàn.

The Following Day

Li Zhongying is studying under a tree when David Wang, Zhang Desheng,
and an American student named Ai Dehua see her and stop to say hello.

David:	Xiǎo Lǐ.	*Hi.*
Lǐ:	David, nǐ hǎo.	*Hello, David.*
David:	Zhè shì Zhāng Déshēng	*This is Zhang Desheng*
	gēn Ài Déhuá.	*and Ai Dehua.*
Lǐ:	Zhāng Xiānsheng, Ài	*Hello, Mr. Zhang,*
	Xiānsheng, nǐmen hǎo.	*Mr. Ai.*
Ài:	Lǐ Xiǎojie hǎo ma?	*How are you, Miss Li?*
Zhāng:	Lǐ Xiǎojie.	*Hello.*

(Li Zhongying nods at them.)

Culture notes

In Taiwan and overseas Chinese communities, the titles Xiānsheng, Tàitai, Xiǎojie and Nǔshì are more or less the equivalents of Mr., Mrs., Miss and Ms. They fell out of favor with the "New Society" of the PRC, which substituted the uniform and egalitarian Tóngzhì, meaning "Comrade," for everyone. An exception was often made, however, in dealing with foreigners, who were not "Comrades" but generally Xiānsheng and Fūren (Madame).

With the advent of liberalization and internationalization in the PRC, Xiānsheng, Tàitai, Xiǎojie and Nǔshi are reappearing, more commonly in large metropolises (such as Canton in the south) that have a great deal of commercial contact with foreign countries, and almost always with foreigners. Tóngzhì on the other hand, while used, is growing less popular.

Lǎo and Xiǎo are popular, informal terms used between friends, Lǎo generally with older people and Xiǎo with younger people. Males are more likely than females to be called Lǎo.

Structure notes

1. Social titles in Chinese **follow** the last name—thus <u>Wáng Xiānsheng</u>, <u>Lǐ Tóngzhì</u>. The only exceptions are <u>Lǎo</u> and <u>Xiǎo</u>, which **precede** the last name. Technically, <u>Lǎo</u> and <u>Xiǎo</u> are not social titles, but rather informal, familiar forms of address for one's friends.

2. The following is a basic sentence pattern in Chinese:

2.   Subject + (hěn) + Adjective

Hǎo, xièxie.	*to be well + thank you*	*I'm fine, thank you.*
Tāmen hěn hǎo.	*they + very + to be well*	*They are very well.*

It is important to note that **adjectives** (that describe a state or condition) do not need to be modified by the equivalent of the English verb "to be." <u>Hǎo</u> means "to be well". Translating "I am well" into Chinese as *<u>Wǒ shì hǎo</u> would be wrong.

<u>Hěn</u> expresses degree ("very"), but when it precedes an adjective, it carries almost no meaning. <u>Wǒ hěn hǎo</u>, for instance, means nothing more than "I'm fine." Its use is considered optional, as indicated by the parentheses around it. However, when the subject is used, <u>hěn</u> is also usually used.

3. Words such as <u>dōu</u> (both, all) and <u>yě</u> (also) modify verbs or adjectives, **NOT** nouns. A common mistake is *<u>Dōu rén hěn hǎo</u> for "Everyone is fine" —do try to avoid it. (Say <u>Dàjiā</u> [everyone] <u>dōu hěn hǎo</u> instead.)

1a.   Subject + <u>yě/dōu</u> + Equative verb + Noun

Wǒ xìng Táo. Tā yě xìng Táo.	*I + to be surnamed + Tao. he/she + also + to be surnamed + Tao*	*My last name is Tao. His/her last name is also Tao.*
Wǒmen dōu xìng Táo.	*I + both + to be surnamed + Tao*	*We both have the last name Tao.*
Nǐ yě xìng Táo ma?	*you + also + to be surnamed + Tao + <u>ma</u>*	*Is your last name Tao too?*
Mǎlì, Yuēhàn yě dōu xìng Táo ma?	*Mary + John + also + both + to be surnamed + Tao + <u>ma</u>*	*Do Mary and John both have the last name Tao, too?*

2a. Subject + yě/dōu + (hěn) + Adjective

Mǎlì hěn hǎo. Yuēhàn yě hěn hǎo.	*Mary + very + to be well . John + also + very + to be well*	*Mary is fine. So is John.*
Mǎlì, Yuēhàn dōu hěn hǎo.	*Mary + John + both + very + to be well*	*Mary and John are both fine.*

Please note that if yě and dōu are used together, then yě precedes dōu.

4. In Chinese, the **subject** of the sentence is often not expressed. If the subject is left out of a declarative sentence (a statement), the subject is generally understood to be "I." If the subject is left off of an interrogative sentence (a question), then the subject is generally understood to be "you."

(Zhang and Wang see each other on the street.)

Zhāng:	Ei! Hǎo ma?	*hey + to be well + ma*	*Hi! How are you?*
Wáng:	Hǎo.	*to be well.*	*I'm fine.*

If the conversation shifts to a third person, then that person will need to be identified as the subject of the sentence. Once identified, further conversation can continue with the subject of the sentence left off again, to be understood as the person identified.

Zhāng:	Xiǎo Lǐ ne? Yě hǎo ma?	*Xiao Li + ne? also + to be well + ma*	*How about Li? Is he doing all right too?*
Wáng:	Yě hěn hǎo.	*also + very + to be well*	*He's fine too.*

5. **Ma** is a question particle. It attaches to the end of a statement to turn that statement into a question.

| Tā xìng Dèng, jiào Dàipíng. | he + to be surnamed + Deng + to be called + Daiping | His last name is Deng, his given name Daiping. |
| Tā xìng Dèng, jiào Dàipíng ma? | He + to be surnamed + Deng + to be called + Daiping + *ma* | Is his last name Deng, his given name Daiping? |

6. **Ne** is another question particle. It attaches to a noun or noun phrase to mean "And what about (the noun/noun phrase)?" The precise meaning of a question formed with **ne** depends on context.

| Wǒ xìng Bái. Nǐ ne? | I + to be surnamed + Bai. you + *ne* | My last name is Bai. What's yours? |
| Tā hěn hǎo. Xiǎo Wáng ne? | she + very + to be well. Xiao Wang + *ne* | She's (very) well. How about Wang? |

Structure exercise

> *Fill in each blank in the dialogue below, between two people who know each other only by sight, who catch a glimpse of a third person.*
>
> A: Tā _____ shéi? Shì Lǎo Lǐ _____?
>
> B: Shì. Shì Lǎo Lǐ. Tā de míngzi _____ Bái.
>
> A: Nǐ _____? Nǐ de míngzi jiào _____?
>
> B: Wǒ _____ Yùqīng. Wǒ _____ Lán Yùqīng.
>
> _____ ne? Nǐ guì _____?
>
> A: Wǒ xìng Zhāng. Wǒ _____ Zhāng Yànyín.

SEGMENT C

Skill: To provide & obtain personal descriptions.

> Tā hěn ___.   *S/he is (very) ___.*

gāo	*(to be) tall*	———————	ǎi	*(to be) short*
pàng	*(to be) fat*	———————	shòu	*(to be) thin*
hēi	*(to be) dark*	———————	bái	*(to be) fair*
zhuàng	*(to be) strong*	———————	ruò	*(to be) weak*
hǎokàn	*(to be) goodlooking*	———————	nánkàn	*(to be) unattractive*
piàoliang	*(to be) pretty, handsome*	———————	chǒu	*(to be) ugly*
měi	*(to be) beautiful*	———————	yīngjùn	*(to be) handsome*

Shénme yìsi?   *What does it (this) mean?*

Wǒ bù dǒng.   *I don't understand.*

Nǐ dǒng bù dǒng?   *Do you understand?*

Tā gāo bù gāo?
Is s/he tall (or not)?

Tā yīngjùn ma?
Is he handsome?

Nǐ juéde wǒ hǎokàn ma?
Do you think (feel) I am goodlooking?

Nǐ juéde wǒ tài pàng le ma?
Do you think (feel) I'm too fat?

Dialogue Practice

The following sets of dialogues presume normal behavior, no unusual circumstances, and no misunderstandings in the contexts indicated. "A" begins the dialogue, "B" responds, "A" responds to "B," etc. Where there is a choice of responses available, please circle the one which is more appropriate.

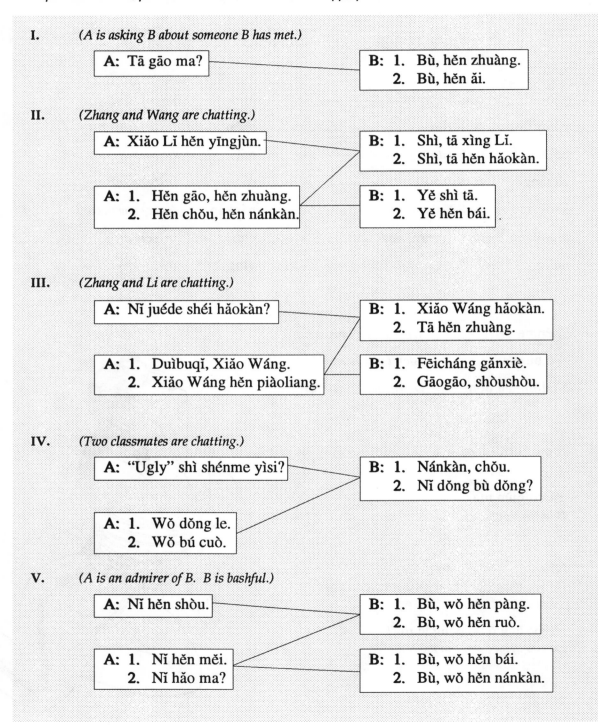

I.   *(A is asking B about someone B has met.)*

   A: Tā gāo ma?

   B: 1. Bù, hěn zhuàng.
       2. Bù, hěn ǎi.

II.   *(Zhang and Wang are chatting.)*

   A: Xiǎo Lǐ hěn yīngjùn.

   B: 1. Shì, tā xìng Lǐ.
       2. Shì, tā hěn hǎokàn.

   A: 1. Hěn gāo, hěn zhuàng.
       2. Hěn chǒu, hěn nánkàn.

   B: 1. Yě shì tā.
       2. Yě hěn bái.

III.   *(Zhang and Li are chatting.)*

   A: Nǐ juéde shéi hǎokàn?

   B: 1. Xiǎo Wáng hǎokàn.
       2. Tā hěn zhuàng.

   A: 1. Duìbuqǐ, Xiǎo Wáng.
       2. Xiǎo Wáng hěn piàoliang.

   B: 1. Fēicháng gǎnxiè.
       2. Gāogāo, shòushòu.

IV.   *(Two classmates are chatting.)*

   A: "Ugly" shì shénme yìsi?

   B: 1. Nánkàn, chǒu.
       2. Nǐ dǒng bù dǒng?

   A: 1. Wǒ dǒng le.
       2. Wǒ bú cuò.

V.   *(A is an admirer of B. B is bashful.)*

   A: Nǐ hěn shòu.

   B: 1. Bù, wǒ hěn pàng.
       2. Bù, wǒ hěn ruò.

   A: 1. Nǐ hěn měi.
       2. Nǐ hǎo ma?

   B: 1. Bù, wǒ hěn bái.
       2. Bù, wǒ hěn nánkàn.

Among friends

Li Zhongying is talking with two close female friends at the cafeteria. After a while she mentions that she has met someone new.

Lǐ:	Tā jiào Zhāng Déshēng. Shì zhèr de xuésheng.	*His name is Zhang Desheng. He's a student here.*
Friend 1:	*(smiling)*	
	Hǎokàn ma?	*Is he goodlooking?*
Lǐ:	*(laughing)*	
	Tā tǐng gāo, shòushòu de.	*He's quite tall, and rather thin.*
	Hěn bái hěn bái.	*He's very fair.*
Friend 2:	Gēn nǐ yíyàng!	*Just like you!*
Lǐ:	Bù. Wǒ bù gāo.	*No, I'm not tall.*
	(They all laugh.)	

Culture notes

Standards of physical beauty in China, as elsewhere, derive from images of the privileged or successful in society. For men in traditional China, one avenue to success and status lay in becoming an accomplished scholar and succeeding in successive levels of civil service examinations. The final successful graduates were eligible for official positions in China's administrative bureaucracy. The women of the scholar-gentry class lived secluded lives at home, tending to embroidery and the general management of a large household. Thus the scholar-elite's fairness of skin is admired in both men and women, likely because it contrasts with the sun-darkened complexion of commoners who labor in the fields or on the streets. Slimness or fragility is attractive, particularly in women. The scholar-model of male beauty also stresses slimness and refinement, but a second model, that of the warrior, emphasizes strength, virility (and bushy eyebrows) .

Traditional ideals of an elegant, refined, scholarly appearance still influence modern Chinese conceptions. However, the desire for good health and physical, athletic ability have also affected modern standards: "good looking" today often means men and women who are tall, slim, fair, with regular features, who are also reasonably active, although a degree of fragility is still tolerated (even admired) in women. For men, "masculine" resolve and vigor combined with scholarly refinement and decorum define the ideal.

Structure notes

1. This lesson provides further examples of basic sentence pattern #2, restated below.

2. Subject + *[bù]* + (hěn) + *[bù]* + Adjective

Wǒ hěn gāo.	*I + very + to be tall*	*I am tall.*
Nǐ hěn ǎi.	*you + very + to be short*	*You are short.*
Wǒ hěn shòu.	*I + very + to be thin*	*I am thin.*
Nǐ hěn pàng.	*you + very + to be fat*	*You are fat.*
Wǒ hěn zhuàng.	*I + very + to be strong*	*I am strong.*
Nǐ hěn ruò.	*you + very + to be weak*	*You are weak.*
Nǐ hěn hǎo.	*you + very + to be good*	*You are good.*
Wǒ bù hǎo.	*I + not + to be good*	*I am not good.*

2. One forms negative statements in Chinese by placing the particle <u>bù</u> before the verb, adjective or adverb (NEVER DIRECTLY BEFORE THE NOUN).

Tā bú xìng Bái.	*he + not + to be surnamed + Bai*	*His last name is not Bai.*
Tā bú shì Bái Xiānsheng.	*he + not + to be + White + Mr.*	*He isn't Mr. White.*
Tā bú zhuàng.	*he + not + to be strong*	*He isn't strong.*
Tā bù hěn pàng.	*he + not + very + to be fat*	*He isn't very fat.*
Tā hěn bù hǎokàn.	*he + very + not + to be good-looking*	*He is very unattractive.*

Note the difference between <u>bù + hěn + Adjective</u> and <u>hěn + bù + Adjective</u>. In the first case, <u>hěn</u> is being negated; in the second, the adjective is first negated, and then intensified in its negative form by <u>hěn</u>. Thus while <u>bù hěn hǎo</u> means "not very good," <u>hěn bù hǎo</u> means "very bad."

3. In addition to using the question particle <u>ma</u>, questions in Chinese can also be formed by using the phrase **Verb + <u>bù</u> + Verb** or **Adjective + <u>bù</u> + Adjective**. Thus:

Tā xìng Bái.

Tā xìng bú xìng Bái? *she + to be surnamed + not + to be surnamed + Bai*
Is she (or isn't she) (sur)named Bai?

Tā shì Bái Xiǎobō.

Tā shì bú shì Bái Xiǎobō? *she + to be + not + to be + Bai Xiaobo*
Is she (or isn't she) Bai Xiaobo?

Tā hěn gāo.

Tā gāo bù gāo? *she + to be tall + not + to be tall*
Is she (or isn't she) tall?

Structure exercises

1. *The following is a brief monologue by a young woman looking at a photograph of a rather good-looking young man named Bai Xiaobo. (Li Mali is her best friend.) Read what she has to say about Bai Xiaobo. Then imagine that this young woman is handed a second photograph, of a young man she does NOT admire. Negate each of her previous utterances by drawing a carat (˄) where the negative particle <u>bù</u> could go. Note that in some of the sentences, <u>bù</u> can be inserted in more than one position.*

Zhèi wèi shì Xiǎobō.

Tā xìng Bái.

Tā hěn gāo.

Tā hěn zhuàng.

Wǒ juéde tā hěn hǎokàn.

Lǐ Mǎlì yě juéde tā hěn hǎokàn.

Wǒmen dōu juéde tā hěn yīngjùn.

2. *After you've negated the remarks above, they will describe a young man who is not named Bai Xiaopo, who is not tall, not strong, and not considered particularly attractive by the two young women named above. You have reason to want a third opinion. Write FIVE QUESTIONS to ask of an unbiased person. Find out the following pieces of information.*

Name? _____

Height? _____

Weight? _____

Complexion? _____

Goodlooking? _____

3. *Write a brief description of someone you know by filling in the blanks below.*

Wǒ yǒu yí ge hǎo péngyou (*I have a good friend*). Tā xìng _____. Tā de

míngzi jiào _____. Tā hěn _____, hěn _____, hěn

_____. Wǒ juéde tā hěn _____. Biérén (*other people*) yě dōu

juéde tā hěn _____.

Nǐ cāi wǒ jǐ suì le?

Nǐ cāi wǒmen duō

dà suìshu le?

SEGMENT D

Skill: To provide & obtain information on age, year/grade, address, tel. #.

Fill in the blanks in the English column on the right with your personal information. Then follow the instructions in the Chinese column on the left.

Wǒ _____ suì le.   I am _____ years old.
    (fill in your own age in Pinyin)

Wǒ niàn _____ níanjí.   I am in the _____ grade/year.
    (fill in your grade level /year in Pinyin)

Wǒ de dìzhǐ shì/ Wǒ zhù zài   *My address is/ I live in (at)*

_____shì,   _____city
    (fill in the name of your city, using Pinyin)

_____ jiē,   _____street, (road, etc.)
    (fill in your street name, using English)

_____hào,   number _____,
    (fill in your street # in Pinyin)

_____shì.   apartment_____.
    (fill in your apartment # in Pinyin)

Wǒ de diànhuà hàomǎ shì_____.   *My telephone number is_____.*
    (fill in your tel. # in Pinyin)

Nǐ jǐ suì le?	*How old are you? (asked of children)*
Nǐ duó dà le?*	*How old are you? (asked of young adults)*
Nín duó dà suìshu le?*	*How old are you? (asked of older adults)*
Nǐ niàn jǐ níanjí?	*What grade/year are you?*
Nǐ jiā zài nǎr?	*Where is your house?*
Nǐ zhù zài nǎr?	*Where do you live?*
Nǐ de diànhuà duóshǎo hào?*	*What is your tel. number?*

Wǒ bù zhīdào.   *I don't know.*

Wǒ wàng le.   *I forgot.*

*The word <u>duō</u> by itself means "much" or "a lot." It combines with the word <u>shǎo</u> meaning "few" or "a little" to mean "how much." However, when <u>duō</u> is used as a question word, it is generally said in the second tone: <u>duó</u>. Thus what is normally pronounced as <u>duóshǎo, duó dà le, duó dà suìshu le,</u> and <u>duóshǎo hào</u> would in proper *pinyin* orthography be written <u>duōshǎo, duō dà le</u>, etc.

Nǐ cāi wǒ niàn jǐ niánjí?

Dialogue Practice

The following sets of dialogues presume normal behavior, no unusual circumstances, and no misunderstandings in the contexts indicated. "A" begins the dialogue, "B" responds, "A" responds to "B," etc. Where there is a choice of responses available, please circle the one which is more appropriate.

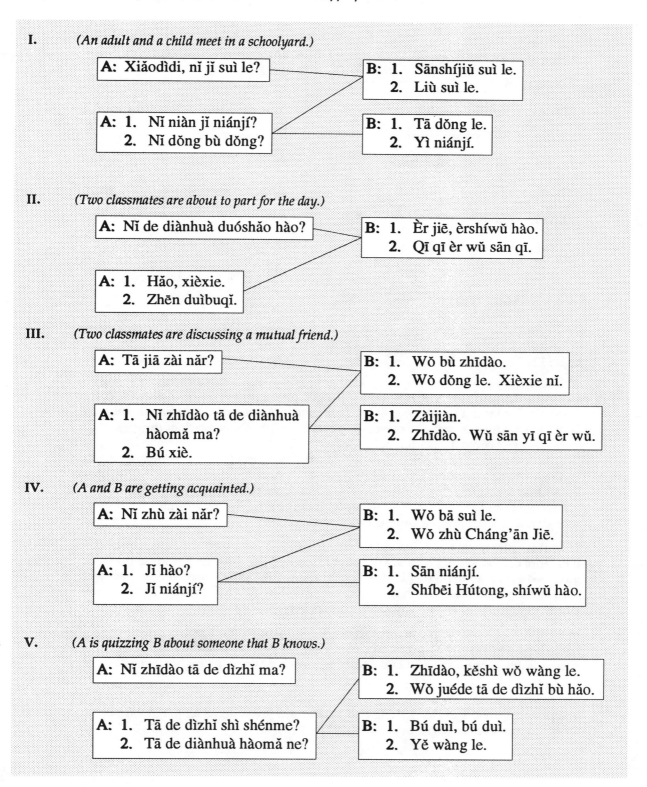

I. *(An adult and a child meet in a schoolyard.)*

A: Xiǎodìdi, nǐ jǐ suì le?

B: 1. Sānshíjiǔ suì le.
　　2. Liù suì le.

A: 1. Nǐ niàn jǐ niánjí?
　　2. Nǐ dǒng bù dǒng?

B: 1. Tā dǒng le.
　　2. Yì niánjí.

II. *(Two classmates are about to part for the day.)*

A: Nǐ de diànhuà duóshǎo hào?

B: 1. Èr jiē, èrshíwǔ hào.
　　2. Qī qī èr wǔ sān qī.

A: 1. Hǎo, xièxie.
　　2. Zhēn duìbuqǐ.

III. *(Two classmates are discussing a mutual friend.)*

A: Tā jiā zài nǎr?

B: 1. Wǒ bù zhīdào.
　　2. Wǒ dǒng le. Xièxie nǐ.

A: 1. Nǐ zhīdào tā de diànhuà hàomǎ ma?
　　2. Bú xiè.

B: 1. Zàijiàn.
　　2. Zhīdào. Wǔ sān yī qī èr wǔ.

IV. *(A and B are getting acquainted.)*

A: Nǐ zhù zài nǎr?

B: 1. Wǒ bā suì le.
　　2. Wǒ zhù Cháng'ān Jiē.

A: 1. Jǐ hào?
　　2. Jǐ niánjí?

B: 1. Sān niánjí.
　　2. Shíbēi Hútong, shíwǔ hào.

V. *(A is quizzing B about someone that B knows.)*

A: Nǐ zhīdào tā de dìzhǐ ma?

B: 1. Zhīdào, kěshì wǒ wàng le.
　　2. Wǒ juéde tā de dìzhǐ bù hǎo.

A: 1. Tā de dìzhǐ shì shénme?
　　2. Tā de diànhuà hàomǎ ne?

B: 1. Bú duì, bú duì.
　　2. Yě wàng le.

More information

Zhang Desheng is visiting David Wang in his room. After a while, Zhang asks about Li Zhongying.

Zhāng:	Lǐ Zhōngyīng duó dà le,	*How old is Li Zhongying;*
	nǐ zhīdào ma?	*do you know?*
David:	Tā shíjiǔ suì le.	*She's nineteen.*
Zhāng:	O.	*Oh.*
David:	Nǐ ne? Nǐ duó dà le?	*How about you? How old are you?*
Zhāng:	Wǒ yě shì shíjiǔ suì.	*I'm nineteen too.*
David:	Wǒ cái shíbā suì.	*I'm only eighteen.*
Zhāng:	Tā niàn jǐ niánjí?	*What year is he(she) in?*
David:	Shéi?	*Who?*
Zhāng:	Lǐ Zhōngyīng.	*Li Zhongying.*
David:	Dà'èr.	*She's a sophomore (in college).*

David grins at Zhang. Zhang looks away.

Culture notes

Although Western influence may be changing traditional behavior in some Hong Kong and Taiwan circles, asking how old a person is (or how much money his or her family makes) is not usually considered too personal, even when asking directly. In fact, NOT asking a so-called "personal question" might show a lack of caring in the Chinese social context. Traditional society generally encourages people to be their "brothers' keepers," to concern themselves with the lives of family members, friends, and neighbors; to lend a hand when things go wrong; to put in words of advice about individual actions; to share in the celebration of successes and good fortune. Individuals who do not concern themselves with the affairs of others around them may be considered self-centered or callous.

Thus it is quite normal for Zhang Desheng to ask about the age of a new acquaintance. It is more convenient for him to ask about Li Zhongying through David, as the intermediary, than to do it of Li directly. Traditionally, young men and women were kept strictly segregated. Such segregation has broken down in modern society, but young people are often still shy about contact between the sexes.

In traditional China people of advanced age commanded more power within the household and greater respect in society. Thus the questions asked to elicit age grow succeedingly more respectful and decorous, as one deals with "higher levels" of age.

Telephone numbers in Hong Kong and Taiwan are seven digits long, but vary between five and seven digits in the PRC.

Table 1: *Grades or class levels in the Chinese educational system are ennumerated as follows.*

Preschool*	Tuō'érsuǒ			
Kindergarten*	Yòuzhìyuán/yòu'éryuán			
Grade 1 Grade 2 Grade 3	Xiǎoxué	Chūxiǎo	Xiǎoxué yī niánjí Xiǎoxué èr niánjí Xiǎoxué sān niánjí	
Grade 4 Grade 5 Grade 6		Gāoxiǎo	Xiǎoxué sì niánjí Xiǎoxué wǔ niánjí Xiǎoxué liù niánjí	
Grade 7 Grade 8 Grade 9	Zhōngxué	Chūzhōng	Chūzhōng yī niánjí Chūzhōng èr niánjí Chūzhōng sān niánjí	(Chūyī) (Chūèr) (Chūsān)
Grade 10 Grade 11 Grade 12		Gāozhōng	Gāozhōng yī niánjí Gāozhōng èr niánjí Gāozhōng sān niánjí	(Gāoyī) (Gāoèr) (Gāosān)
1st year college 2nd year college 3rd year college 4th year college	Dàxué		Dàxué yī niánjí Dàxué èr niánjí Dàxué sān niánjí Dàxué sì niánjí	(Dàyī) (Dà'èr) (Dàsān) (Dàsì)
Graduate school	Yánjiùyuàn (Taiwan) / Yánjiūshēngyuàn (PRC)			

*Preschool children in the PRC are generally 2 years old. By age 3, children enter kindergarten, where they remain for three years. Grade 1 children are usually 6 years old.

Structure notes

1. **De** can be similar to the apostrophe-S in English, to mark a possessive. Thus, <u>Xiǎo Píng de shēngri</u> means "Xiao Ping's birthday," and <u>wǒ de shēngri</u> is "my birthday."

2. **Le** is a complex and hardworking particle in Chinese that serves a variety of functions. The following are two of these functions:

2b. Subject + Verb/Adjective + <u>le</u>

a) To mark a **change** in status or condition.

Tā hěn gāo.	*She's tall.* ---------------------------->	Tā gāo le.	*She's become tall.*
Tā hěn hǎo.	*She's fine.* ---------------------------->	Tā hǎo le.	*She's gotten well.*
Tā hěn pàng.	*She's fat.* ---------------------------->	Tā pàng le.	*She's gotten fat.*
Tā bā suì.	*She's eight.* -------------------------->	Tā bā suì le.	*She's turned eight.*

b) **Le** is used with some verbs having to do with thought and thinking, to mean that a thought process is complete. A change of state is implied.

Wǒ dǒng le.	*I understand. I understood. I have come to understand. I came to understand.*
Wǒ zhīdào le.	*I know (now). I already know. I understand.*
Wǒ wàng le.	*I forgot. I have fogotten.*

Structure exercise

1. *The particles <u>le</u> and <u>de</u> are missing in the brief monologue below, which is spoken by an admirer of a young woman named Mary Jones. Please write them in in the appropriate positions.*

> Mǎlì hěn hǎo. Tā jīnnián *(this year)* èrshí suì. Tā yǐqián *(in the past)* yǒu
>
> yìdiǎnr *(was a little)* pàng, xiànzài *(now)* shòu. Wǒ juéde tā hěn piàoliang.
>
> Kěxī *(too bad)* wǒ wàng tā diànhuà hàomǎ hé dìzhǐ.

SEGMENT E

Skill: **To provide & obtain information on height, weight, & birthday.**

Fill in the blanks in the English columns on the right with your personal information, using Arabic numerals. Then follow the instructions in the Chinese columns on the left. Refer to Tables 2 and 3 to convert between the English, metric, and Chinese systems.

Wǒ _____chǐ_____cùn gāo.   *I am _____'_____" tall.*
(Fill in your height using Pinyin & the English system.)

Wǒ _____ mǐ _____.   *I am _____._____metres tall.*
(Fill in your height, using Pinyin & the metric system.)

Wǒ _____bàng.   *I (weigh) _____ lbs.*
(Fill in your weight, using Pinyin & the English system.)

Wǒ _____gōng jīn.   *I (weigh) _____kilograms.*
(Fill in your weight, using Pinyin & the metric system.)

Wǒ _____jīn.   *I (weigh) _____jīn.*
(Fill in your weight, using Pinyin & the Chinese system.)

shēngāo	*height*
tǐzhòng	*weight*
shēngri	*birthday*

Wǒ shēngri shì   *My birthday is*

____ ____ ____ ____nián,   _____(year)
(Fill in the year of your birth, using Pinyin)

_____yuè,   _____(month)
(Fill in the month of your birth, using Pinyin)

_____hào.   _____(day)
(Fill in the day of your birth, using Pinyin)

Nǐ yǒu duó gāo?	*How tall are you?*
Nǐ yǒu duó zhòng?	*How much do you weigh?*
Nǐ de shēngri shì jǐ yuè jǐ hào?	*When is your birthday?*
Nǐ de shēngri shì shénme shíhou?	*When is your birthday?*
Nǐ shì něi nián shēng de?	*In which year were you born?*

Dialogue Practice

The following sets of dialogues presume normal behavior, no unusual circumstances, and no misunderstandings in the contexts indicated. "A" begins the dialogue, "B" responds, "A" responds to "B," etc. Where there is a choice of responses available, please circle the one which is more appropriate.

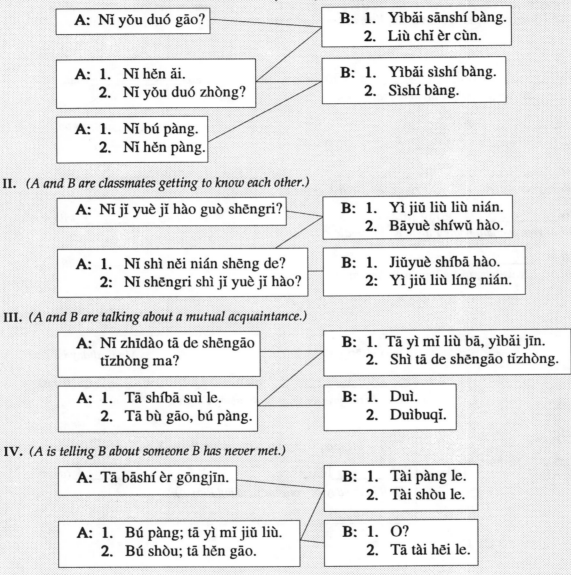

I.   (*Two Chinese-Americans who have never met face-to-face are getting acquainted by telephone.*)

    A: Nǐ yǒu duó gāo?

    B: 1. Yìbǎi sānshí bàng.
       2. Liù chǐ èr cùn.

    A: 1. Nǐ hěn ǎi.
       2. Nǐ yǒu duó zhòng?

    B: 1. Yìbǎi sìshí bàng.
       2. Sìshí bàng.

    A: 1. Nǐ bú pàng.
       2. Nǐ hěn pàng.

II. (*A and B are classmates getting to know each other.*)

    A: Nǐ jǐ yuè jǐ hào guò shēngri?

    B: 1. Yì jiǔ liù liù nián.
       2. Bāyuè shíwǔ hào.

    A: 1. Nǐ shì něi nián shēng de?
       2: Nǐ shēngri shì jǐ yuè jǐ hào?

    B: 1. Jiǔyuè shíbā hào.
       2: Yì jiǔ liù líng nián.

III. (*A and B are talking about a mutual acquaintance.*)

    A: Nǐ zhīdào tā de shēngāo tǐzhòng ma?

    B: 1. Tā yì mǐ liù bā, yìbǎi jīn.
       2. Shì tā de shēngāo tǐzhòng.

    A: 1. Tā shíbā suì le.
       2. Tā bù gāo, bú pàng.

    B: 1. Duì.
       2. Duìbuqǐ.

IV. (*A is telling B about someone B has never met.*)

    A: Tā bāshí èr gōngjīn.

    B: 1. Tài pàng le.
       2. Tài shòu le.

    A: 1. Bú pàng; tā yì mǐ jiǔ liù.
       2. Bú shòu; tā hěn gāo.

    B: 1. O?
       2. Tā tài hēi le.

V.   (*A is quizzing B about B's friend, but B is unable to provide any information.*)

    A: Nǐ zhīdào tā de shēngri shì jǐ yuè jǐ hào ma?

    B: 1. Bù zhīdào.
       2. Duìbuqǐ.

    A: 1. Tā shì něi nián shēng de?
       2. Nǐ bù zhīdào shénme?

    B: 1. Wǒ yě bù dǒng.
       2. Duìbuqǐ, yě bù zhīdào.

Further information

David Wang and Li Zhongying leave class together. David looks at Li curiously.

David: Zhōngyīng, nǐ yǒu duó gāo?   *Zhongying, how tall are you?*

Lǐ: Wǒ yì mǐ liù. Nǐ ne?   *I am 1.6 metres (5' 3").*

David: Wǒ wǔ chǐ bā cùn..   *I am 5 feet 8...*

         nà jiù shì yì mǐ qīsān, duì bu duì?   *that's 1.73 metres, right?*

Lǐ: Nnn, bù zhīdào. Nǐ dàgài yǒu yì mǐ qī.   *Mmm, I don't know. You are probably 1.7 metres.*

David: Nǐ yǒu duó zhòng?   *How heavy are you?*

Lǐ: *(laughing)*

         Wǒ bú gàosu nǐ!   *I'm not telling you!*

David: Nà yǒu shénme guānxi.   *What does (telling me) matter..*

         Wǒ yìbǎi sìshí bàng...liùshísān gōngjīn.   *I'm 140 lbs...63 kg.*

Lǐ: Nǐ shēngri shì jǐ yuè jǐ hào?   *When is your birthday?*

David: *(smiling)*

         Wǒ yě bú gàosu nǐ le.   *Then I'm not telling you either.*

Lǐ: *(laughing and pushing him)*

         Qù nǐ de!*   *Get away!*

(*Caution: This expression can be inflammatory if used with someone other than a friend.)

Culture notes

Chinese people are generally not hesitant about sharing personal information such as height, weight, and birthday, especially with members of the same sex. Shyness may come into play in dealing with members of the opposite sex. In Li Zhongying's case, the ambiguity of the situation is compounded by the confusion of her having to deal with a foreigner, even a pseudo-foreigner (David is Chinese-American).

Young people of the same sex in China and Taiwan (and many non-Western societies) are often very intimate and affectionate with each other. Young women often walk holding hands or linking arms, or sit cheek-to-cheek with their arms around each other. One young man will often put his arm around the shoulder of another while sitting or walking. Young men sometimes rest leaning against each other, with head to shoulder or back to back. This behavior generally does not indicate sexual interest.

Young people of opposite sexes, on the other hand, tend to keep some distance between themselves, unless an overt boyfriend-girlfriend relationship has been established. Even then, public displays of emotion are generally restricted to hand-holding. Kissing and hugging in public does occur in contemporary China, but is viewed with varying degrees of distaste by passersby.

Weight in China is generally given in terms of jīn (a catty), which is conveniently twice the value of a kilogram (i.e. 50 kg = 100 jīn).

Table 2
Conversion Chart for Height

1" = 2.54 cm
1 cm = .394"
1' = .305 m
1 m = 3.28'

6' 5"	1.96 m
6' 4"	1.93 m
6' 3"	1.91 m
6' 2"	1.88 m
6' 1"	1.85 m
6' 0"	1.83 m
5' 11"	1.80 m
5' 10"	1.78 m
5' 9"	1.75 m
5' 8"	1.73 m
5' 7"	1.70 m
5' 6"	1.68 m
5' 5"	1.65 m
5' 4"	1.63 m
5' 3"	1.60 m
5' 2"	1.58 m
5' 1"	1.55 m
5' 0"	1.53 m
4' 11"	1.50 m
4' 10"	1.48 m
4' 9"	1.45 m
4' 8"	1.43 m
4' 7"	1.40 m
4' 6"	1.38 m

Table 3
Conversion Chart for Weight

1 lb = .454 kg = .907 jīn (catties)
1 kg = 2.205 lbs = 2 jīn
1 jīn = .5 kg = 1.103 lbs

250 lbs	113.50 kg	226.75 jīn
240 lbs	108.96 kg	217.68 jīn
230 lbs	104.42 kg	208.61 jīn
220 lbs	99.88 kg	199.54 jīn
210 lbs	95.34 kg	190.47 jīn
200 lbs	90.80 kg	181.40 jīn
190 lbs	86.26 kg	172.33 jīn
180 lbs	81.72 kg	163.26 jīn
170 lbs	77.18 kg	154.19 jīn
160 lbs	72.64 kg	145.12 jīn
150 lbs	68.10 kg	136.05 jīn
140 lbs	63.56 kg	126.98 jīn
130 lbs	59.02 kg	117.91 jīn
120 lbs	54.48 kg	108.84 jīn
110 lbs	49.94 kg	99.77 jīn
100 lbs	45.50 kg	90.70 jīn
90 lbs	40.86 kg	81.63 jīn
80 lbs	36.32 kg	72.56 jīn
70 lbs	31.78 kg	63.49 jīn
9 lbs	4.09 kg	8.16 jīn
8 lbs	3.63 kg	7.26 jīn
7 lbs	3.18 kg	6.35 jīn
6 lbs	2.72 kg	5.44 jīn
5 lbs	2.27 kg	4.54 jīn
4 lbs	1.82 kg	3.63 jīn
3 lbs	1.36 kg	2.72 jīn
2 lbs	.91 kg	1.81 jīn
1 lb	.45 kg	.91 jīn

Zhèr yǒu sān ge rén.

Liǎng ge shì gùkè,

yí ge shì shòuhuòyuán.

Zhèr yǒu nóngmín, yǒu gōngrén.

Nóngmín zài gōngzuò.

Nǐ cāi gōngrén zài zuò shénme?

                           Answer:

                  Tāmen zài dǎ pái.

SEGMENT F

Skill: To provide and obtain information on professions.

Wǒ shì _____.   *I am a _____.*
(Fill in your occupation using Pinyin; see below.)

Wǒ xiǎng zuò ge_____.   *I would like to be a _____.*
(Fill in what you would like to be.)

Wǒ yěxǔ zuò ge_____.   *Perhaps I'll be a _____.*

Zhèige xiǎohár zài kàn shéi?

xuésheng	*student*
lǎoshī	*teacher*
hùshi	*nurse*
yīshēng	*doctor*
mìshū	*secretary*
lùshī	*lawyer*
jǐngchá	*police officer*
shòuhuòyuán	*salesclerk*
fúwùyuán	*attendant, clerk, waitperson*
gōngrén	*worker, laborer*
nóngmín	*farmer, peasant*

zuò	*to do*
gàn	*to do, to engage in*

Wǒ bù dǒng.	*I don't understand.*
Qǐng zài shuō yí cì.	*Please repeat ...*
Qǐng shuō màn yìdiǎr.	*Please speak more slowly.*

Nǐ zuò shénme gōngzuò?	*What (work) do you do?*
Nǐ de gōngzuò shì shénme?	*What is your occupation?*
Nǐ jiānglái xiǎng zuò shénme?	*What would you like to do in the future?*
Nǐ xiǎng gàn shénme?	*What would you like to do?*

Dialogue Practice

The following sets of dialogues presume normal behavior, no unusual circumstances, and no misunderstandings in the contexts indicated. "A" begins the dialogue, "B" responds, "A" responds to "B," etc. Where there is a choice of responses available, please circle the one which is more appropriate.

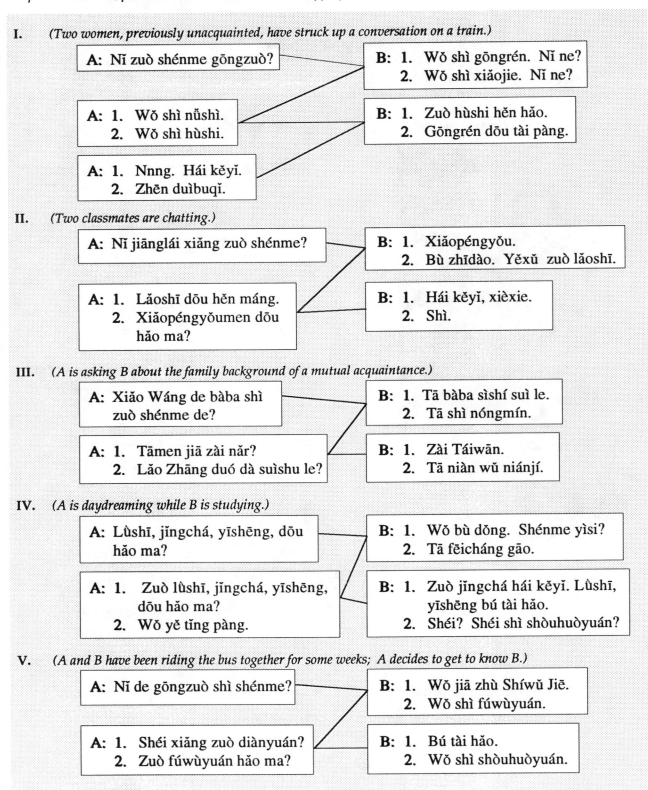

I.   (Two women, previously unacquainted, have struck up a conversation on a train.)

A: Nǐ zuò shénme gōngzuò?

B: 1. Wǒ shì gōngrén. Nǐ ne?
   2. Wǒ shì xiǎojie. Nǐ ne?

A: 1. Wǒ shì nǔshì.
   2. Wǒ shì hùshi.

B: 1. Zuò hùshi hěn hǎo.
   2. Gōngrén dōu tài pàng.

A: 1. Nnng. Hái kěyǐ.
   2. Zhēn duìbuqǐ.

II. (Two classmates are chatting.)

A: Nǐ jiānglái xiǎng zuò shénme?

B: 1. Xiǎopéngyǒu.
   2. Bù zhīdào. Yěxǔ zuò lǎoshī.

A: 1. Lǎoshī dōu hěn máng.
   2. Xiǎopéngyǒumen dōu hǎo ma?

B: 1. Hái kěyǐ, xièxie.
   2. Shì.

III. (A is asking B about the family background of a mutual acquaintance.)

A: Xiǎo Wáng de bàba shì zuò shénme de?

B: 1. Tā bàba sìshí suì le.
   2. Tā shì nóngmín.

A: 1. Tāmen jiā zài nǎr?
   2. Lǎo Zhāng duó dà suìshu le?

B: 1. Zài Táiwān.
   2. Tā niàn wǔ niánjí.

IV. (A is daydreaming while B is studying.)

A: Lùshī, jǐngchá, yīshēng, dōu hǎo ma?

B: 1. Wǒ bù dǒng. Shénme yìsi?
   2. Tā fēicháng gāo.

A: 1. Zuò lùshī, jǐngchá, yīshēng, dōu hǎo ma?
   2. Wǒ yě tǐng pàng.

B: 1. Zuò jǐngchá hái kěyǐ. Lùshī, yīshēng bú tài hǎo.
   2. Shéi? Shéi shì shòuhuòyuán?

V.   (A and B have been riding the bus together for some weeks; A decides to get to know B.)

A: Nǐ de gōngzuò shì shénme?

B: 1. Wǒ jiā zhù Shíwǔ Jiē.
   2. Wǒ shì fúwùyuán.

A: 1. Shéi xiǎng zuò diànyuán?
   2. Zuò fúwùyuán hǎo ma?

B: 1. Bú tài hǎo.
   2. Wǒ shì shòuhuòyuán.

Aspirations

David and Li are walking together to the cafeteria for lunch.

Lǐ:	David, nǐ fùmǔ shì zuò shénme de?	*David, what do your parents do?*
David:	Wǒ bàba shì zhōngxué lǎoshī,	*My father is a high-school teacher,*
	wǒ māma shì hùshi. Nǐ fùmǔ ne?	*my mother is a nurse. How about your parents?*
Lǐ:	Tāmen dōu shì yīshēng. Nǐ jiānglái	*They are both doctors. What would you like*
	xiǎng gàn shénme?	*to do, in the future?*
David:	Bù zhīdào. Yěxǔ dāng gōngrén ba.	*I don't know. Maybe I'll become a factory worker.*
Lǐ:	*(laughing)*	
	Hǎojí le.	*That's great.*
David:	Nǐ ne? Nǐ xiǎng zuò shénme?	*How about you? What do you want to be?*
Lǐ:	Wǒ yě xiǎng zuò yīshēng.	*I want to be a doctor too.*

Culture notes

A professional title is often used as a form of address in social intercourse. Thus, Wang the teacher would be called "Wáng Lǎoshī," Wang the doctor "Wáng Yīshēng," Wang the lawyer "Wáng Lùshī," etc.

Professionals in Chinese societies enjoy the same prestige as in the West, with the exception of lawyers. Since the American adversarial legal system does not exist in the PRC or Taiwan, the Chinese have far less need for lawyers than Americans. As a result, lawyers are not really recognized as a professional group. Scientists and engineers, on the other hand, are well respected as a group, and enjoy perhaps more visibility than in the U.S.

In traditional China, traders and merchants were regarded as money-mongers without a great deal of education. Business-people today still suffer some lingering disdain, but this is rapidly changing as international trade and finance begin to require greater amounts of skill, training, and general education, and earn sizable incomes.

Another occupation that is undergoing change is entertaining. In imperial China, entertainers were near the bottom of the social scale. They were seen as immoral pariahs on the fringes of society, who lived off the largesse of citizens. In contemporary society on the other hand, successful entertainers have become media stars. Their fabulous wealth and lifestyles have made them the role models of many young people.

Teachers in both China and the west are accorded a certain amount of respect by society, but since this is not matched with high salaries, they are not seen to have any real clout. Thus teaching is not a prestigious occupation, although university professors everywhere enjoy some esteem for their erudition.

Structure notes

1. <u>Wǒ shì xuésheng, tā shì lǎoshī</u> etc. are examples of sentence pattern #1: **Subject + Equative Verb + Noun**, where the nouns are names of professions.

2. Another basic sentence pattern is as follows.

> ### 3a. Subject + *[bù]* + Modal verb + Verb + Object

Wǒ xiǎng zuò jǐngchá.	*I + think/plan/intend to + to become + police officer.*
	I would like to become a police officer.
Nǐ xiǎng gàn shénme?	*You + think/plan/intend to + to do + what?*
	What are you thinking of doing?

<u>Xiǎng</u> is an example of a class of words called modal verbs, which precede verbs and adjectives and say something about the subject's willingness, ability, need etc. to perform an action or enter into a state (<u>xiǎng xièxie tā</u> = to intend to thank him/her; <u>xiǎng shòu yìdiǎr</u> = to want to become thinner). <u>Xiǎng</u> indicates that the subject intends, plans, or is considering carrying out an action. Modal verbs meaning "to want/wish to," "to hope to," "to be willing to" etc. will appear later.

3. <u>Shénme</u> is a question-word meaning "what." Other question-words or phrases include <u>shéi</u> (who), <u>shénme shíhou</u> (when), <u>nǎr</u> (where), <u>wèishénme</u> (why), and <u>zěnme</u> (how).

Structure exercise

Please fill in the blanks in the narrative below, based on the English equivalent, about a middle-aged malcontent named Zhang.

Lǎo Zhāng, tā shì ge _____. Jīnnián _____. Tā

shēngāo _____, tǐzhòng yǒu _____. Tā hěn

_____, yě hěn _____. Tā jīnnián niàn dàxué _____. Tā

bù xiǎng zuò _____ le; tā jiānglái _____ hùshi.

Old Zhang, he's a policeman. He's forty-two (years old) this year. He's 6 feet tall, 170 lbs. in weight. He's dark, and he's strong. He's (studying) in the third year of college this year. He doesn't want to be a policeman anymore; he's planning to become a nurse in the future.

SEGMENT G
Skill: To provide and obtain information on nationality.

Wǒ shì _____rén.   *I am a native of_____.*
(Fill in your nationality using Pinyin)

(Wǒ huì shuō _____. *I can speak* _____.)

Měiguó	*America, the U.S.*	
Jiānádà	*Canada*	(Yīngwén, Yīngyǔ)
Àodàlìyà	*Australia*	

Yàzhōu   *Asia*

Zhōngguó	*China*	(Zhōngwén, Zhōngguóhuà)
Rìběn	*Japan*	(Rìwén, Rìběnhuà, Rìyǔ)
Hánguó, Cháoxiǎn	*Korea*	(Hánwén, Hánguóhuà, Hányǔ)
Yìndù	*India*	(Yìndùwén, Yìndùhuà, Yìndùyǔ)
Dōngnányà	*Southeast Asia*	
Zhōngdōng	*The Middle East*	

Ōuzhōu   *Europe*

Yīngguó	*England*	(Yīngwén, Yīngyǔ)
Fǎguó	*France*	(Fǎwén, Fǎguóhuà, Fǎyǔ)
Déguó	*Germany*	(Déwén, Déguóhuà, Déyǔ)
Xībānyá	*Spain*	(Xībānyáwén, Xībānyáhuà, Xībānyáyǔ)
Éguó	*Russia*	(Éwén, Éguóhuà, Éyǔ)

guójí   *nationality*

Nǐ shì něi guó rén?	*Of which country are you a native?*
Nǐ cóng nǎr lái de?	*Where do you come from?*
Nǐ jiā zài nǎr?	*Where is your home?*
Nǐ huì shuō něi guó huà?	*What language(s) can you speak?*

Dialogue Practice

The following sets of dialogues presume normal behavior, no unusual circumstances, and no misunderstandings in the contexts indicated. "A" begins the dialogue, "B" responds, "A" responds to "B," etc. Where there is a choice of responses available, please circle the one which is more appropriate.

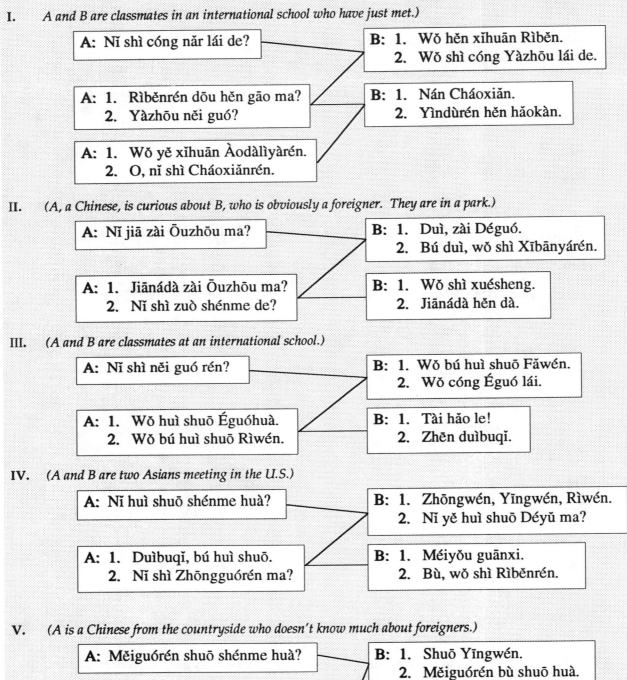

I.   *A and B are classmates in an international school who have just met.)*

> **A:** Nǐ shì cóng nǎr lái de?

> **B: 1.** Wǒ hěn xǐhuān Rìběn.
> **2.** Wǒ shì cóng Yàzhōu lái de.

> **A: 1.** Rìběnrén dōu hěn gāo ma?
> **2.** Yàzhōu něi guó?

> **B: 1.** Nán Cháoxiǎn.
> **2.** Yìndùrén hěn hǎokàn.

> **A: 1.** Wǒ yě xǐhuān Àodàlìyàrén.
> **2.** O, nǐ shì Cháoxiǎnrén.

II.   *(A, a Chinese, is curious about B, who is obviously a foreigner. They are in a park.)*

> **A:** Nǐ jiā zài Ōuzhōu ma?

> **B: 1.** Duì, zài Déguó.
> **2.** Bú duì, wǒ shì Xībānyárén.

> **A: 1.** Jiānádà zài Ōuzhōu ma?
> **2.** Nǐ shì zuò shénme de?

> **B: 1.** Wǒ shì xuésheng.
> **2.** Jiānádà hěn dà.

III.   *(A and B are classmates at an international school.)*

> **A:** Nǐ shì něi guó rén?

> **B: 1.** Wǒ bú huì shuō Fǎwén.
> **2.** Wǒ cóng Éguó lái.

> **A: 1.** Wǒ huì shuō Éguóhuà.
> **2.** Wǒ bú huì shuō Rìwén.

> **B: 1.** Tài hǎo le!
> **2.** Zhēn duìbuqǐ.

IV.   *(A and B are two Asians meeting in the U.S.)*

> **A:** Nǐ huì shuō shénme huà?

> **B: 1.** Zhōngwén, Yīngwén, Rìwén.
> **2.** Nǐ yě huì shuō Déyǔ ma?

> **A: 1.** Duìbuqǐ, bú huì shuō.
> **2.** Nǐ shì Zhōngguórén ma?

> **B: 1.** Méiyǒu guānxi.
> **2.** Bù, wǒ shì Rìběnrén.

V.   *(A is a Chinese from the countryside who doesn't know much about foreigners.)*

> **A:** Měiguórén shuō shénme huà?

> **B: 1.** Shuō Yīngwén.
> **2.** Měiguórén bù shuō huà.

> **A: 1.** Shéi huì shuō Yīngwén?
> **2.** Yīngwén? Bú shì Yīngguórén shuō Yīngwén ma?

> **B: 1.** Duì. Měiguórén yě shuō.
> **2.** Bú duì. Déguórén shuō.

On foreign languages

Zhang, Li, and three other students are practicing speaking English with David. A teacher of Russian stops to observe the group. A conversation ensues.

Lǐ:	Lǎoshī, wǒmen zài liànxí shuō Yīngyǔ.	*Teacher, we are practicing speaking English.*
Teacher:	*(looking at David)*	
	Ei, nǐ Yīngwén shuō de zhēn hǎo.	*Hey, you speak English really well.*
	(Everyone laughs.)	
Zhāng:	Lǎoshī, tā shì Měiguórén a.	*He is an American, teacher.*
Teacher:	Aa?	*Huh?*
David:	Wǒ cóng Měiguó lái de.	*I come from America.*
	Wǒ shì Měiguóguójí de Zhōngguórén.	*I am a Chinese of American nationality.*
Lǐ:	Tā shì Měijí Huárén.	*He is Chinese-American.*
Zhāng:	Tā huì shuō Yīngyǔ, yě huì shuō	*He can speak English, and he can also*
	Zhōngguóhuà. Tā zhēn xíng.	*speak Chinese. He's really something.*
David:	Lǎoshī shì nǎr de rén?	*Where do you come from, teacher?*
Teacher:	Wǒ shì běndìrén, kěshì wǒ huì	*I am from here, but I can speak Russian.*
	shuō Éwén. Hǎo ba. Nǐmen liànxí ba.	*Well then, you go ahead and practice.*
	Zàijiàn.	*Goodbye.*
All:	Lǎoshī zàijiàn.	*Goodbye, teacher.*

Culture notes

In most nations of the world (but not the U.S., yet), the study of foreign languages is treated as a basic required subject in school, and begins early in the elementary grades. English is very popular in Taiwan and the People's Republic of China. American, Canadian, British, and Australian students, tourists, and business-people in China are often approached by local people looking for an opportunity to practice speaking English.

As noted previously, a professional title is often used as a form of address, either alone (<u>Lǎoshī</u>) or preceded by the surname (<u>Lǐ Lǎoshī</u>). In the dialogue above, the students consistently address the teacher by his title, "<u>Lǎoshī</u>." Often, the title even replaces the term "you" in direct address, as in David's question "<u>Lǎoshī shì nǎr de rén?</u>" (rather than "<u>Nín shì nǎr de rén?</u>"). This is a sign of politeness, of deference towards a social superior. The use of the title signifies recognition of the relatively higher social status of the holder of the title, whereas "<u>nǐ</u>" is used widely among social equals or by a superior in reference to an inferior. As an extension of this principle, children sometimes substitute "mom" or "dad" for "you" in direct address, as in "I don't like onions; does Mom like onions?" instead of "Do you like onions, Mom?"

Structure notes

1. <u>Wǒ shì Měiguórén</u> is a further example of Pattern #1: **Subject + Equative Verb + Noun.** The noun here is "an American," which consists of <u>Měiguó</u> (America) modifying <u>rén</u> (person).

2. <u>Wǒ huì shuō Zhōngguóhuà</u> illustrates Pattern #3a: **Subject + Modal verb + Verb + Object.** The modal verb <u>huì</u> means "to know how to (do something)," indicating a learned skill. The verb <u>shuō</u> means "to speak" or "to say."

Structure exercise

Please write answers to the following questions about yourself.

Nǐ shì shénme guójí?

_____

Nǐ jiā zài nǎr?

_____

Nǐ huì shuō Yàzhōu de shénme huà?

_____

Nǐ huì shuō Ōuzhōu de shénme huà?

_____

Nǐ jiānglái xiǎng zuò shénme?

_____

Nǐ shēngri shì jǐ yuè jǐ hào?

_____

Nǐ yǒu duō gāo, duō zhòng?

_____

Nǐ juéde nǐ hǎokàn ma?

_____

SEGMENT H

Skill: To provide and obtain information on family members.

	mǔqīn *mother*	fùqīn *father*
xiǎoháir *child*	māma *mama*	bàba *papa*
nǚ'ér *daughter*	jiějie *older sister*	gēge *older brother*
qīnqì *relatives*		
érzi *son*	mèimei *younger sister*	dìdi *younger brother*

Shéi shì shéi?

bófù *paternal uncle (father's older brother)*	bómǔ *paternal aunt (wife of father's older brother)*
shūshu *paternal uncle (father's younger brother)*	āyí *maternal aunt (mother's sister)*

yéye *paternal grandfather*	nǎinai *paternal grandmother*
wàigōng *maternal grandfather*	wàipó *maternal grandmother*

Nǐ yǒu ___ma?	*Do you have a ____?*
Zhè shì nǐ de ___ma?	*Is this your _____?*
Nǐmen shì jiěmèi ma?	*Are you sisters?*
Nǐmen shì xiōngdì ma?	*Are you brothers?*
Nǐ yǒu xiōngdì jiěmèi ma?	*Do you have brothers & sisters?*
Nǐmen méiyǒu xiǎoháir ma?	*Don't you have any children?*

Dialogue Practice

The following sets of dialogues presume normal behavior, no unusual circumstances, and no misunderstandings in the contexts indicated. "A" begins the dialogue, "B" responds, "A" responds to "B," etc. Where there is a choice of responses available, please circle the one which is more appropriate.

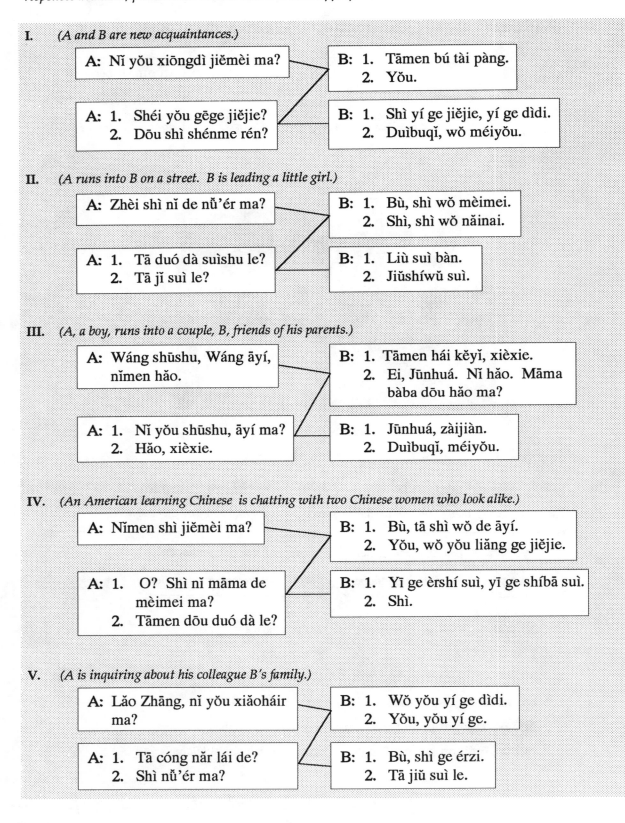

I.   *(A and B are new acquaintances.)*

A: Nǐ yǒu xiōngdì jiěmèi ma?

B: 1. Tāmen bú tài pàng.
    2. Yǒu.

A: 1. Shéi yǒu gēge jiějie?
    2. Dōu shì shénme rén?

B: 1. Shì yí ge jiějie, yí ge dìdi.
    2. Duìbuqǐ, wǒ méiyǒu.

II.   *(A runs into B on a street. B is leading a little girl.)*

A: Zhèi shì nǐ de nǚ'ér ma?

B: 1. Bù, shì wǒ mèimei.
    2. Shì, shì wǒ nǎinai.

A: 1. Tā duó dà suìshu le?
    2. Tā jǐ suì le?

B: 1. Liù suì bàn.
    2. Jiǔshíwǔ suì.

III.   *(A, a boy, runs into a couple, B, friends of his parents.)*

A: Wáng shūshu, Wáng āyí, nǐmen hǎo.

B: 1. Tāmen hái kěyǐ, xièxie.
    2. Ei, Jūnhuá. Nǐ hǎo. Māma bàba dōu hǎo ma?

A: 1. Nǐ yǒu shūshu, āyí ma?
    2. Hǎo, xièxie.

B: 1. Jūnhuá, zàijiàn.
    2. Duìbuqǐ, méiyǒu.

IV.   *(An American learning Chinese is chatting with two Chinese women who look alike.)*

A: Nǐmen shì jiěmèi ma?

B: 1. Bù, tā shì wǒ de āyí.
    2. Yǒu, wǒ yǒu liǎng ge jiějie.

A: 1. O? Shì nǐ māma de mèimei ma?
    2. Tāmen dōu duó dà le?

B: 1. Yī ge èrshí suì, yī ge shíbā suì.
    2. Shì.

V.   *(A is inquiring about his colleague B's family.)*

A: Lǎo Zhāng, nǐ yǒu xiǎoháir ma?

B: 1. Wǒ yǒu yí ge dìdi.
    2. Yǒu, yǒu yí ge.

A: 1. Tā cóng nǎr lái de?
    2. Shì nǚ'ér ma?

B: 1. Bù, shì ge érzi.
    2. Tā jiǔ suì le.

Family

David and Zhang are on their way to a local noodle-shop on a weekend. On the street, they run into Li Zhongying, who is walking with an older woman and a child.

Lǐ:	Hi, David, Xiǎo Zhāng.	*Hi David, Xiao Zhang.*
(to Zhang)	Zhèi shì wǒ māma. Zhèi shì wǒ mèimei.	*This is my mother. This is my younger sister.*
David:	Lǐ bómǔ hǎo.	*Hello, Aunt Li.*
Zhāng:	Lǐ bómǔ hǎo.	*Hello, Aunt Li.*

(The mother smiles and nods at each of them.)

Zhāng:	Xiǎo mèimei jǐ suì le?	*How old are you, little sister?*
Sister:	Wǒ shí suì le.	*I am ten.*
David:	Tā hǎo piàoliang.	*She's very pretty.*
Mother:	Bù zěnme piàoliang. Nǐ jiù shì Zhāng Déshēng ba?	*She's not particularly pretty.* *I take it you are Zhang Desheng?*
Zhāng:	Wǒ jiù shì.	*I am.*
David:	Zhōngyīng, bófù hé nǐ dìdi ne?	*Zhongying, so where are Uncle (your father) and your brother?*
Lǐ:	Tāmen dōu zài jiāli.	*They are both at home.*
Zhāng:	O, nǐ hái yǒu yí ge dìdi.	*Oh, you have a younger brother too.*
Lǐ:	Duì, tā shíwǔ suì le.	*Right, he's fifteen.*

Culture notes

Social acquaintances in Chinese communities like to treat each other as if they were members of an extended family. Children in general are addressed as "little sister" or "little brother," and the parents of one's friends as "uncle" or "aunt." Bófù/bómǔ (uncle, aunt) are commonly used by adults for people of their parent's generation (who are likely to be advanced in age), while shūshu/āyí (uncle, aunt) are used by children in reference to their parent's friends (who are likely to be no more than middle-aged).

Social superiors (by status or age) are acknowledged upon meeting. Zhang and David acknowledge Li's mother by using her "title"—bómǔ—in the greeting. Thus they say Bómǔ hǎo or Bómǔ nín hǎo rather than simply Nǐ hǎo. The response to such a greeting is often wordless—simply a nod (or a series of nods), a grunt, a smile, or some combination of the three, as in Mrs. Li's response to David and Zhang in this conversation.

Compliments paid are often denied by the recipient, to express modesty. Traditionally, a Chinese does not say "Thank you" in response to a personal compliment of any kind. Rather, some sort of demurral is in order. Furthermore, compliments are offered only to a social equal, or by a social superior to a social inferior. A Chinese student would be very unlikely to compliment a teacher on his or her appearance, for instance. In the conversation above, it is natural for Zhang to compliment the little girl (but not her mother), and for her mother to deny the compliment. Current fashion, however, under the influence of the West, permits "acceptance" of personal compliments when given.

Structure notes

1. The following are fundamental sentence structures in Chinese.

3. Subject + *[bù]* + Verb + Object

Tā shuō Yīngwén.	*She speaks English.*
Tā bù shuō Zhōngwén.	*She doesn't speak Chinese.*

4. Subject + Verb + Number + Measure + Noun

Wǒ yǒu yī ge jiějie.	*I have an older sister.*
Wǒ yǒu liǎng ge dìdi.	*I have two little brothers.*

2. One meaning of the verb yǒu is "to have." (Other meanings will be introduced later.) It is unlike other Chinese verbs in that it is negated by the adverb méi—the opposite of yǒu is méiyǒu—whereas other verbs are generally negated by the adverb bù.

3. Measure words are characteristic of Chinese. They exist in English, too, but not as pervasively: one speaks of a *piece* of candy, a *lump* of coal, a *sheet* of paper. In this lesson, the Chinese measure word ge applies to people; English does not have the equivalent measure word for individual people that Chinese utilizes—sān ge rén in Chinese is simply "three people" in English. Measure words will be discussed in greater detail in Unit 5c.

4. De has been used before to indicate possession: wǒ de shēngri means "my birthday." When the possessive refers to a close personal relationship, however, such as in "my mother," "my father," etc., the de is generally omitted. Wǒ māma is more common than wǒ de māma.

Structure exercise

Write the following description in Chinese.

> Xiǎo Chén's first name is Bīngxīn. She has four younger brothers and one younger sister. Her younger sister is a doctor. Two younger brothers are lawyers, one is a salesclerk, and one is a senior in high school. Xiǎo Chén has a daughter who has turned five. She has no son. Her sister has a son but no daughter.
>
> _____
>
> _____
>
> _____
>
> _____
>
> _____

SEGMENT A
Skill: To provide & obtain information on physical condition

Wǒ júede hěn _____.	_I feel very _____._
hǎo	_(to be) well, fine, good_
lèi	_(to) be tired_
máng	_(to be) busy_
kùn	_(to be) sleepy_
lěng	_(to be) cold_
rè	_(to be) hot_
è	_(to be) hungry_
bǎo	_(to be) full, satiated_
kě	_(to be) thirsty_

Wǒ bìng le.	_I'm sick._
Wǒ hǎo le.	_I've recovered._

dōu	_both, all_
yě	_also (used w/verbs only)_
hěn	_very_
bù	_no, not (negative particle)_
ma	_(question particle—used to make a question out of any statement)_
ne	_(question particle—used to make questions meaning "And how/what about X?"—where X is the subject)_

Wǒmen dōu máng.	_We are both busy._
Nǐ ne? Nǐ yě máng ma?	_How about you? Are you busy too?_
Nǐ zěnmeyàng? Hǎo ma?	_How are you? Well?_
Nǐ lèi bú lèi? Kě bù kě?	_Are you tired? Thirsty? (Or not?)_
Yǒu shénme shì ma?	_Is anything the matter?_

Dialogue Practice

The following sets of dialogues presume normal behavior, no unusual circumstances, and no misunderstandings in the contexts indicated. "A" begins the dialogue, "B" responds, "A" responds to "B," etc. Where there is a choice of responses available, please circle the one which is more appropriate.

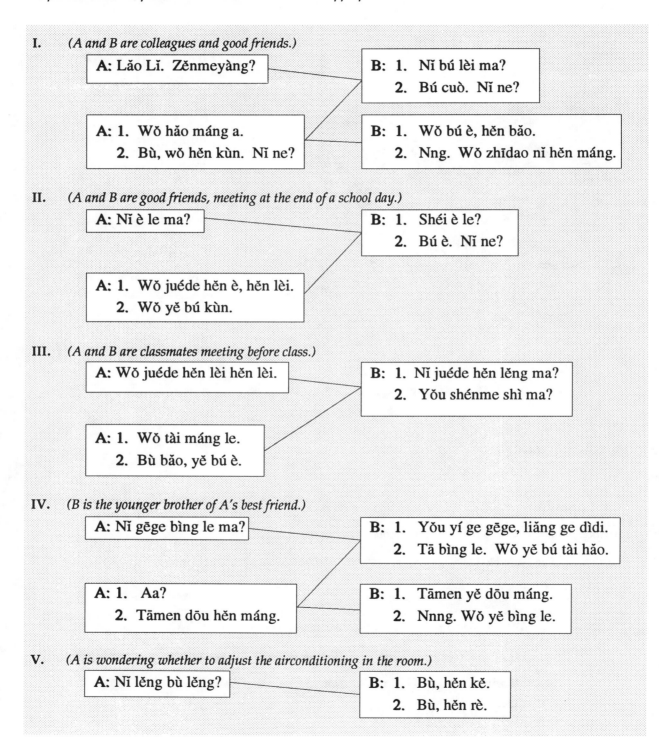

I.   *(A and B are colleagues and good friends.)*

A: Lǎo Lǐ. Zěnmeyàng?

B: 1. Nǐ bú lèi ma?
   2. Bú cuò. Nǐ ne?

A: 1. Wǒ hǎo máng a.
   2. Bù, wǒ hěn kùn. Nǐ ne?

B: 1. Wǒ bú è, hěn bǎo.
   2. Nng. Wǒ zhīdao nǐ hěn máng.

II. *(A and B are good friends, meeting at the end of a school day.)*

A: Nǐ è le ma?

B: 1. Shéi è le?
   2. Bú è. Nǐ ne?

A: 1. Wǒ juéde hěn è, hěn lèi.
   2. Wǒ yě bú kùn.

III. *(A and B are classmates meeting before class.)*

A: Wǒ juéde hěn lèi hěn lèi.

B: 1. Nǐ juéde hěn lěng ma?
   2. Yǒu shénme shì ma?

A: 1. Wǒ tài máng le.
   2. Bù bǎo, yě bú è.

IV. *(B is the younger brother of A's best friend.)*

A: Nǐ gēge bìng le ma?

B: 1. Yǒu yí ge gēge, liǎng ge dìdi.
   2. Tā bìng le. Wǒ yě bú tài hǎo.

A: 1. Aa?
   2. Tāmen dōu hěn máng.

B: 1. Tāmen yě dōu máng.
   2. Nnng. Wǒ yě bìng le.

V.   *(A is wondering whether to adjust the airconditioning in the room.)*

A: Nǐ lěng bù lěng?

B: 1. Bù, hěn kě.
   2. Bù, hěn rè.

Sister

(Li Zhongying and her sister Zhongxiu are sitting together on their living-room sofa, playing cat's cradle.)

Lǐ:	Xiǎomèi, nǐ lěng ma?	*Xiaomei (little sister), are you cold?*
Sister:	Bù lěng.	*I'm not cold.*

(They continue playing in silence.   Some time passes.)

Sister:	Jiějie, wǒ è le.	*Jiejie (big sister), I've gotten hungry.*
Lǐ:	Wǒ yě è le.	*I'm hungry too (now).*
Sister:	*(She puts down the string and runs out of the room. She yells.)*	
	Mā! Jiějie hé wǒ dōu è le ya!	*Mom! Sister and I are both hungry!*
Mother:	*(She enters, wiping her hands on a towel.)*	
	Hǎo le, hǎo le, zhīdao le. Māma zhèng mángzhe; tài lèi le.	*Okay, okay (enough), I know (you're hungry). I'm busy, and I'm really tired.*
	(to Li Zhongying)	
	Zhōngyīng, nǐ qù zuò yìdiǎnr dōngxi chī, hǎo bù hǎo?	*Zhongying, you go make something to eat, alright?*
Lǐ:	Hǎo.	*Alright.*
	(She goes out.)	

Culture notes

String games are just as popular among Chinese children as elsewhere.

Within a family, siblings generally address and refer to each other by their kinship titles—"elder sister," "younger brother," etc. Sometimes the first name or a pet name will be added. Zhongxiu for example might call her elder sister jiějie, or Zhōngyīng jiějie, or perhaps Yīng jiě (Yīng being an abbreviation of Zhōngyīng and jiě an abbreviation of jiějie). If there is more than one of a type of sibling—three elder brothers, for example—a numerator may be added to the title: dàgē (eldest older brother), èrgē (second older brother), and sāngē (third older brother) or xiǎogē (youngest older brother).

Among relatives, the kinship title may be used to refer to oneself as well as to others, as in the following:

Child:	Māma lèi ma?	*Are you tired?*
Mother:	Māma bú lèi.	*No I'm not.*

Siblings often share one character in a two-character given name. The shared character (zhōng in Zhōngyīng and Zhōngxiū) is a generational name, and is sometimes shared not only among siblings but with cousins on the father's side as well.

Structure notes

1. This lesson provides more examples of **adjectives** in Chinese, as used in the pattern **#2 Subject + (hěn) + Adjective.** <u>Hǎo, lèi, máng, kùn</u> etc. are all examples of adjectives describing physical status. <u>Juéde</u> expresses a feeling or opinion, as in <u>Wǒ juéde hěn kùn</u> (*I feel sleepy*) or <u>Wǒ juéde tā hěn yīngjùn</u> (*I feel that he's very handsome*).

2. Adding the particle <u>le</u> to adjectives indicates a change of state (pattern **#2b Subject + Adjective + <u>le</u>,** Unit 2d), which in this lesson refers to a change in the physical condition of the subject. <u>Wǒ è le</u> means essentially "I've become hungry now." Conversely, <u>Wǒ bǎo le</u> means "Now I'm full (because I've eaten)." In both cases, <u>le</u> indicates that a change has taken place—the subject has gone from being not hungry to being hungry in the first example, and from being hungry to being full in the second example.

3. Negating an adjective phrase with <u>le</u> is tricky. <u>Bù</u> attaches to the adjective, negates it, and then <u>le</u> is added to this negative phrase to indicate that the negative condition is a new (changed) state. Thus:

È	*(to be hungry)*
Bú è	*(to not be hungry)*
Bú è le	*(to not be hungry anymore)*
Lèi	*(to be tired)*
Bú lèi	*(to not be tired)*
Bú lèi le	*(to no longer be tired)*

<u>Bù hǎo le</u> is a set expression meaning "Something's gone wrong." If no subject is expressed, it means that something is wrong with the situation in general; if a subject is stated, as in <u>Wǒ bù hǎo le</u>, a rough English equivalent would be "I'm in trouble."

4. To negate the change of state—that is, to deny that conditions have changed, or to say that a change in condition has not yet come about (as in, "I'm not hungry yet", as opposed to "I'm hungry now")—one uses <u>bù</u> "not, do not," <u>méi</u> "did not," <u>hái bù</u> "not yet", or <u>hái méi</u> "did not yet." Since no change has occurred, <u>le</u> is not used. Thus:

Wǒ kùn le	*(I'm sleepy; I've gotten sleepy)*	—	Wǒ bú kùn	*(I'm not sleepy)*
			Wǒ hái bú kùn	*(I'm not sleepy yet)*
			Wǒ hái méi kùn	*(I haven't gotten sleepy yet)*
Wǒ bìng le	*(I'm sick; I've gotten sick)*	—	Wǒ méi bìng	*(I'm not sick; I haven't gotten sick; I didn't get sick)*
Wǒ lèi le	*(I'm tired; I've gotten tired)*	—	Wǒ bú lèi	*(I'm not tired)*
			Wǒ hái bú lèi	*(I'm not tired yet)*

These principles also work with the verbs of cognition discussed previously (p. 38), as in the following examples.

Wǒ dǒng le	*(I understand; now I understand)*	—	Wǒ bù dǒng	*(I don't understand)*
			Wǒ hái bù dǒng	*(I still don't understand)*
Wǒ wàng le	*(I've forgotten)*	—	Wǒ méi wàng	*(I haven't forgotten)*

Structure exercise

Fill in the blanks in the Chinese versions of the following dialogues, based on the English equivalents. They are brief exchanges between two friends in the course of one day.

---

1. *(Shortly before lunchtime)*

A: Nǐ è le ma?   *Are you hungry?*

B: Wǒ _____. Nǐ ne?   *Not yet. How about you?*

A: Wǒ _____.   *I'm hungry (now).*

---

2. *(Near the end of lunch)*

B: Nǐ bǎo le ma?   *Are you full?*

A: Wǒ _____. Nǐ ne?   *Not yet. How about you?*

B: Wǒ yě _____.   *I'm not full yet either.*

---

3. *(In late afternoon)*

A: Jīntiān shì wǒ de shēngri. Nǐ   *Today is my birthday.*

      _____?   *Have you forgotten?*

B: Wǒ _____.   *I didn't forget. (I haven't forgotten.)*

      Zhèi shì nǐ de shēngri lǐwù.   *Here's your birthday present.*

---

4. *(Four hours and thirty-six sneezes later)*

B: Nǐ bìng le ma?   *Are you sick?*

A: Wǒ _____. Xiǎo   *I'm not sick. Xiao Li got sick. How*

      Lǐ, tā _____. Nǐ ne?   *about you?*

B: Wǒ _____.   *I'm not sick either.*

---

5. *(At the end of the day)*

A: Nǐ kùn le ma?   *Are you sleepy?*

B: Wǒ _____. Nǐ ne?   *I haven't gotten sleepy yet. How about you?*

A: Wǒ hěn _____.   *I'm very sleepy.*

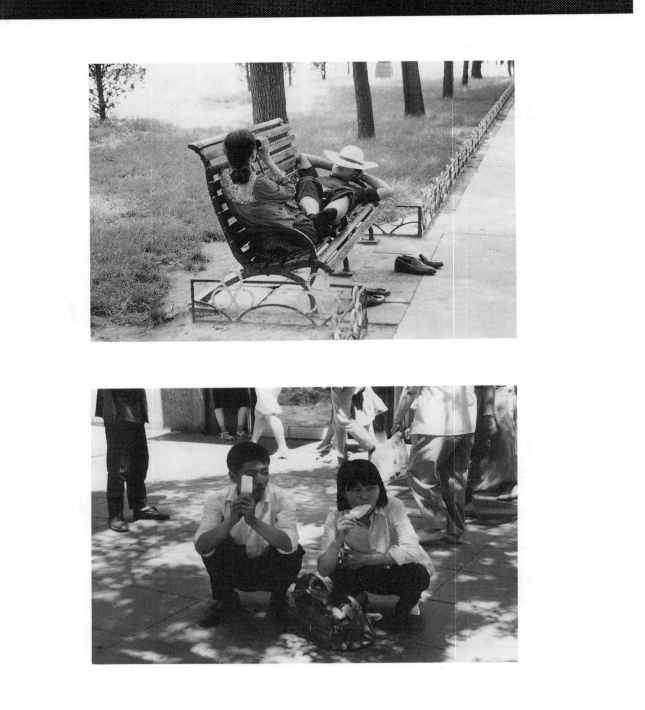

*Nǐmen xiūxi xiūxi, wǒmen chīchī dōngxi, zhè
bú shì hěn hǎo ma?*

SEGMENT B

Skill: To provide and obtain information on personal needs and wants, based on physical condition.

xūyào	*to need to*
yào	*to want to*
děi	*to have to*
xiǎng	*to feel like (doing something)*

chī dōngxi	*to eat something*
chī fàn	*to eat a meal*
hē chá	*to drink tea*
hē shuǐ	*to drink water*

— — — — — — — — — —

shàng cèsuǒ	*to use the toilet*
xiūxi	*to rest*
zuòxià	*to sit down*
tǎngxià	*to lie down*
xǐzǎo	*to take a bath*
shuìjiào	*to sleep*

— — — — — — — — — —

qǐlái	*to get up, to rise up*
sànbù	*to take a walk*
kàn shū	*to read a book*
kàn diànshì	*to watch television*

Lèi le; xiūxi yìhuǐr ba.

Nǐ xiǎng qù chī fàn ma?	*Do you feel like going to eat?*
Nǐ (zài) zuò shénme?	*What are you doing?*
Nǐ (zài) gàn shénme?	*What are you doing?*
Nǐ xiǎng zuò shénme?	*What do you feel like doing?*
Shéi zài xǐzǎo?	*Who is taking a bath?*

Dialogue practice

The following sets of dialogues presume normal behavior, no unusual circumstances, and no misunderstandings in the contexts indicated. "A" begins the dialogue, "B" responds, "A" responds to "B," etc. Where there is a choice of responses available, please circle the one which is more appropriate.

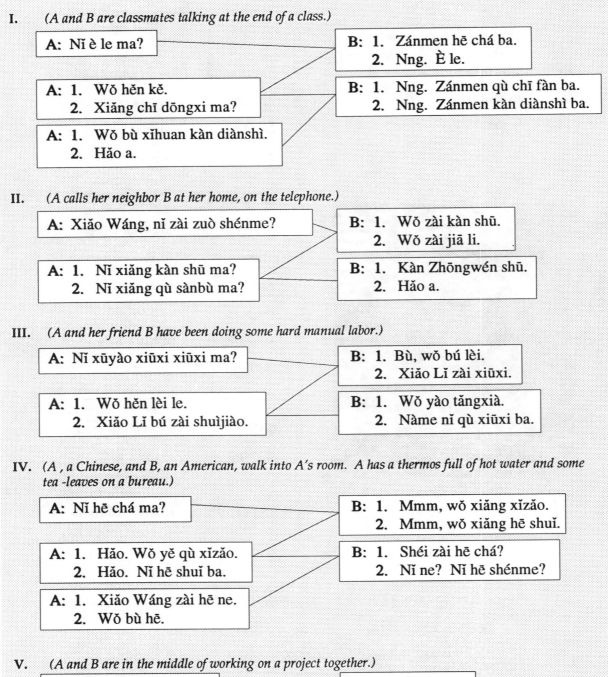

I.   (A and B are classmates talking at the end of a class.)

A: Nǐ è le ma?

B: 1. Zánmen hē chá ba.
    2. Nng. È le.

A: 1. Wǒ hěn kě.
    2. Xiǎng chī dōngxi ma?

B: 1. Nng. Zánmen qù chī fàn ba.
    2. Nng. Zánmen kàn diànshì ba.

A: 1. Wǒ bù xǐhuan kàn diànshì.
    2. Hǎo a.

II.   (A calls her neighbor B at her home, on the telephone.)

A: Xiǎo Wáng, nǐ zài zuò shénme?

B: 1. Wǒ zài kàn shū.
    2. Wǒ zài jiā li.

A: 1. Nǐ xiǎng kàn shū ma?
    2. Nǐ xiǎng qù sànbù ma?

B: 1. Kàn Zhōngwén shū.
    2. Hǎo a.

III.   (A and her friend B have been doing some hard manual labor.)

A: Nǐ xūyào xiūxi xiūxi ma?

B: 1. Bù, wǒ bú lèi.
    2. Xiǎo Lǐ zài xiūxi.

A: 1. Wǒ hěn lèi le.
    2. Xiǎo Lǐ bú zài shuìjiào.

B: 1. Wǒ yào tǎngxià.
    2. Nàme nǐ qù xiūxi ba.

IV.   (A , a Chinese, and B, an American, walk into A's room. A has a thermos full of hot water and some tea -leaves on a bureau.)

A: Nǐ hē chá ma?

B: 1. Mmm, wǒ xiǎng xǐzǎo.
    2. Mmm, wǒ xiǎng hē shuǐ.

A: 1. Hǎo. Wǒ yě qù xǐzǎo.
    2. Hǎo. Nǐ hē shuǐ ba.

B: 1. Shéi zài hē chá?
    2. Nǐ ne? Nǐ hē shénme?

A: 1. Xiǎo Wáng zài hē ne.
    2. Wǒ bù hē.

V.   (A and B are in the middle of working on a project together.)

A: Wǒ děi shàng cèsuǒ.

B: 1. Qǐng zuò.
    2. Nǐ qù ba.

A meal

(Li Zhongying and her younger sister Li Zhongxiu have set bowls of rice, three dishes of meats and vegetables, and chopsticks on the table. They call everyone in to lunch.)

Sister:	Chī fàn la!	*It's time to eat!*
Lǐ:	Māma! Bàba! Dìdi!	*Mom! Dad! (Little) brother!*

(Zhongxiu goes out to look for them, then returns alone.)

Lǐ:	Tāmen zài zuò shénme?	*What are they doing?*
Sister:	Bàba zài shàng cèsuǒ, māma zài	*Father's on the toilet, mother's resting.*
	xiūxi. Wǒ bù zhīdao gēge zài	*I don't know what (Older) brother is doing.*
	zuò shénme.	

(Li 's brother comes in, buttoning up his shirt.)

Lǐ:	Nǐ xǐzǎo le ma?	*Did you take a bath?*
Brother:	Nnng. Bàba māma ne?	*Uh-huh. Where are Dad and Mom?*
Lǐ:	Tāmen jiù lái le. Nǐ zuòxià.	*They'll come soon. Sit down.*

(He goes over to the sideboard.)

Brother:	Wǒ mǎshàng lái.	*I'll be there in a minute.*
	Yǒu shéi yào hē chá hē shuǐ ma?	*Does anyone want tea or water?*
Sister:	Wǒ yào hē shuǐ.	*I want water.*
Lǐ:	Wǒ bú yào.	*I don't want any.*

(As the parents enter, they sit down to eat together.)

Culture notes

Drinking water in China is boiled, and stored in thermos containers. It is usually drunk hot throughout the day, often flavored with tea leaves.

In most Chinese families, it is still the mother or a daughter who prepares the meals. This tendency appeared to be changing in the heyday of the Cultural Revolution, when the equality of the sexes was advocated as a party ideal. Ironically, with the advent of economic liberalization in China, many traditional social mores are making a come-back; there is evidence that women in the PRC are losing ground in terms of economic opportunity.

In professional families everywhere, however, particularly in Hong Kong and Taiwan, it is not uncommon for all adult members of the family, male and female alike, to share household chores equally. In rare cases, the husband of a successful career woman will shoulder much or all of the responsibility for home and children.

Structure notes

1. Many of the verbs in this lesson conform structurally to Sentence pattern #3: **Subject + Verb + Object**. <u>Chīfàn</u>, meaning "to eat" (generally in the sense of "to eat a meal," rather than snacks), is made up of the verb <u>chī</u> "to eat" and its object <u>fàn</u> "rice." <u>Chī dōngxi</u> consists of <u>chī</u> and its object <u>dōngxi</u> "thing, object." Each of the following verbs is a verb-object construction:

chīfàn	*to eat + rice*	*to eat (a meal)*
chī dōngxi	*to eat + a thing/object*	*to eat something*
hē chá	*to drink + tea*	*to drink tea*
hē shuǐ	*to drink + water*	*to drink water*
shàng cèsuǒ	*to ascend + toilet*	*to use the toilet*
xǐzǎo	*to wash + a bath*	*to take a bath*
shuìjiào	*to sleep + a sleep*	*to sleep*
sànbù	*to distribute + footsteps*	*to take a walk*
kàn shū	*to look at + a book*	*to read*
kàn diànshì	*to look at + television*	*to watch television*
Zuò shénme?	*to do + what*	*What are you doing?*

2. Another subset of Chinese verbal expressions consists of two verbs with essentially the same meaning joined together to form a compound. An example of this occurs in this lesson: <u>xiūxi</u> "to rest" is made up of the verb <u>xiū</u> "to cease, to rest" and the verb <u>xī</u> "to cease, to rest," neither of which can be used alone.

3. <u>Yào</u> "to want to," <u>děi</u> "to have to," and <u>xiǎng</u> "to feel like doing (something)" are further examples of **modal verbs** (see p. 52).

4. <u>Zài</u> plus a verb indicates that the subject is in the process of doing the verb.

> **3c. Subject + *[bú]* + <u>zài</u> + Verb + Object**

Tā zài zuò shénme?	*she + at + to do + what*	*What is she doing?*
Tā zài kàn shū.	*she + at + to look at + book*	*She's reading a book.*

Structure exercise

Fill in the blanks in each of the following sentences with a term that fits.

1. *(Said late at night by a tired student who would like to go to sleep but has to study)*

   Wǒ hěn lèi le. Wǒ _____ shuìjiào, kěshì *(but)* wǒ hái _____ niànshū.

2. *(Said by a teenager who is too full of "junk-food" to eat dinner)*

   Wǒ chīle hěn duō dōngxi le. Wǒ bù _____ chīfàn le.

3. *(Said by a bratty younger sibling who is tattling on an older sibling)*

   Nǐ zhīdao *(to know)* tā zài _____ shénme ma? Tā zài _____ diànshì. Māma shuō tā děi kàn shū, kěshì *(but)* tā _____ kàn diànshì.

SEGMENT A
Skill: To state & negotiate time by the clock.

(x) diǎnzhōng	*(x) o'clock*
yì diǎn	*1:00*
liǎng diǎn	*2:00*
(x) diǎn yí kè	*a quarter after (x)*
yì diǎn yí kè	*1:15*
liǎng diǎn yí kè	*2:15*
(x) diǎn bàn	*half past (x)*
yì diǎn bàn	*1:30*
(x) diǎn sān kè	*three-quarters past (x)*
yì diǎn sān kè	*1:45*
(x) diǎn guò (y) fēn	*(y) minutes after (x)*
yì diǎn guò wǔ fēn	*1:05*
liǎng diǎn shí fēn	*2:10*
(x) diǎn chà (y) fēn	*(y) minutes to (x)*
yì diǎn chà wǔ fēn	*12:55*
liǎng diǎn chà shí fēn	*1:50*

gāngcái
just now; a few moments ago

xiànzài
now; at this moment

yìhuǐr
in a little while

Xiànzài jǐ diǎnzhōng?
What time is it now?

Bā diǎn le ma?
Is it eight o'clock (yet)?

Nǐ shénme shíhou shuìjiào?
When do you go to sleep?

Nǐ gāngcái zài zuò shénme?
What were you doing just now?

Dialogue Practice

The following sets of dialogues presume normal behavior, no unusual circumstances, and no misunderstandings in the contexts indicated. "A" begins the dialogue, "B" responds, "A" responds to "B," etc. Where there is a choice of responses available, please circle the more appropriate one.

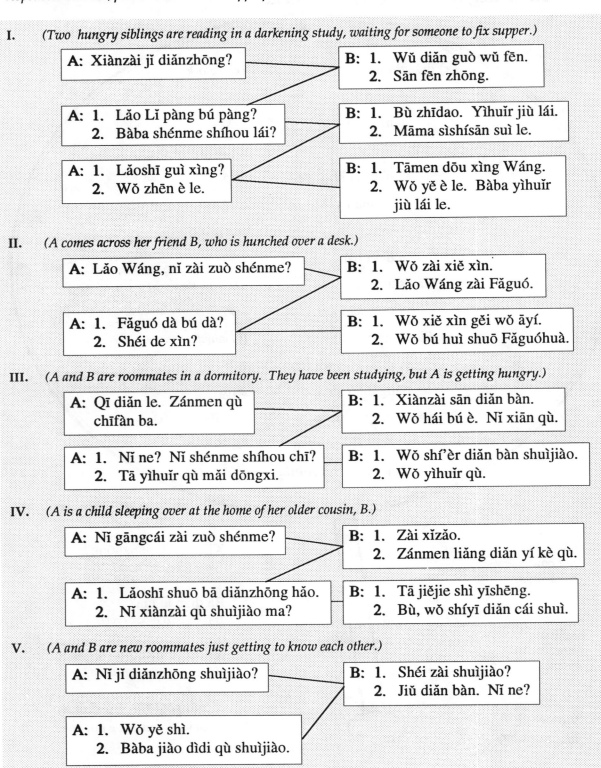

I.   (Two hungry siblings are reading in a darkening study, waiting for someone to fix supper.)

A: Xiànzài jǐ diǎnzhōng?

B: 1. Wǔ diǎn guò wǔ fēn.
   2. Sān fēn zhōng.

A: 1. Lǎo Lǐ pàng bú pàng?
   2. Bàba shénme shíhou lái?

B: 1. Bù zhīdao. Yìhuǐr jiù lái.
   2. Māma sìshísān suì le.

A: 1. Lǎoshī guì xìng?
   2. Wǒ zhēn è le.

B: 1. Tāmen dōu xìng Wáng.
   2. Wǒ yě è le. Bàba yìhuǐr jiù lái le.

II. (A comes across her friend B, who is hunched over a desk.)

A: Lǎo Wáng, nǐ zài zuò shénme?

B: 1. Wǒ zài xiě xìn.
   2. Lǎo Wáng zài Fǎguó.

A: 1. Fǎguó dà bú dà?
   2. Shéi de xìn?

B: 1. Wǒ xiě xìn gěi wǒ āyí.
   2. Wǒ bú huì shuō Fǎguóhuà.

III. (A and B are roommates in a dormitory. They have been studying, but A is getting hungry.)

A: Qī diǎn le. Zánmen qù chīfàn ba.

B: 1. Xiànzài sān diǎn bàn.
   2. Wǒ hái bú è. Nǐ xiān qù.

A: 1. Nǐ ne? Nǐ shénme shíhou chī?
   2. Tā yìhuǐr qù mǎi dōngxi.

B: 1. Wǒ shí'èr diǎn bàn shuìjiào.
   2. Wǒ yìhuǐr qù.

IV. (A is a child sleeping over at the home of her older cousin, B.)

A: Nǐ gāngcái zài zuò shénme?

B: 1. Zài xǐzǎo.
   2. Zánmen liǎng diǎn yí kè qù.

A: 1. Lǎoshī shuō bā diǎnzhōng hǎo.
   2. Nǐ xiànzài qù shuìjiào ma?

B: 1. Tā jiějie shì yīshēng.
   2. Bù, wǒ shíyī diǎn cái shuì.

V.   (A and B are new roommates just getting to know each other.)

A: Nǐ jǐ diǎnzhōng shuìjiào?

B: 1. Shéi zài shuìjiào?
   2. Jiǔ diǎn bàn. Nǐ ne?

A: 1. Wǒ yě shì.
   2. Bàba jiào dìdi qù shuìjiào.

Cramming

(Zhang wakes up late in the night in his dorm room, to find that one of his roommates is still huddled over his books by a dim light.)

Zhāng:	Lǎo Qiū, jǐ diǎn le?	*Qiu, what time is it?*
Qiū:	*(in a whisper)*	
	Liǎng diǎn bàn.	*Two thirty.*
Zhāng:	Nǐ hái bú shuì?	*Aren't you going to sleep yet?*
Qiū:	Yìhuǐr jiù shuì. Nǐ shuì ba.	*I will in a while. Go back to sleep.*
Zhāng:	Nng.	*(grunt)*

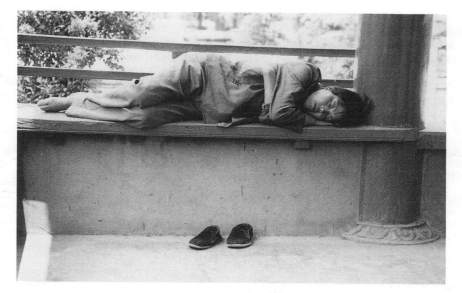

Zài nǎr dōu kěyǐ shuìjiào.

Culture notes

Privacy is not something one expects or can always demand in a Chinese community. (There is no common equivalent of the term "privacy" in the Chinese language.) The majority of the Chinese live under extremely crowded conditions by Western standards—a private room is a luxury that most people have never experienced in any context—at home, school, or work—and therefore do not expect. Communal living requires a certain set of behavioral conventions. People are more restrained and less assertive, so as to disturb others as little as possible. The student Li, for example, may very well have a shirt or some such item placed over his lamp so that it shines only on his books and not into his roommates' eyes. He would probably take great care not to move about the room or make extraneous movements at his desk, and to turn pages as quietly as possible so as not to intrude on the others as they sleep.

Structure notes

1. In the statement Xiànzài sān diǎnzhōng, the verb may be understood to be shì. It is possible, in other words, to say Xiànzài shì sān diǎnzhōng with no appreciable change in meaning, but the shì is almost always omitted.

2. Bàn means literally "half" (yíbàn = "one half"). Thus, yì diǎn bàn means "half-past one" and yí ge bàn means "one and a half (of an unspecified noun marked by the measure ge)."

3. Guò in the statement yì diǎn guò wǔ fēn means "to exceed." Guò wǔ fēn means literally "to exceed by five minutes."

4. Chà in yì diǎn chà wǔ fēn means "to lack, to fall short." Yì diǎn chà wǔ fēn means "To be five minutes short of one o'clock."

5. The le appended to a time expression indicates a change of state, similar to the use of le with adjectives, to indicate a change in condition—Tā hǎo le "He has recovered;" wǒ è le "I'm hungry now." Sān diǎnzhōng le means literally "It has now become three o'clock," (when it wasn't three o'clock a moment ago), indicating a consciousness of the passage of time. The implication is: "It's three o'clock (already, and time to get on with our planned activities)."

6. The use of zài (literally, "at") in Nǐ gāngcái zài zuò shénme "What were you doing just now?" indicates an action in progress. (See Unit 3b, pattern #3c **Subject** + **zài** + **Verb** + **Object**.)

Dìdi zài xǐzǎo.	*younger brother + at + to bathe*	*Younger brother is taking a bath.*
Mèimei zài shuìjiào.	*younger sister + at + to sleep*	*Younger sister is sleeping.*
Jiějie zài niànshū.	*older sister + at + to study*	*Older sister is studying.*

Structure exercise

Write in the Chinese equivalents of the digital times below.

1:00	**1:11**	**1:26**
2:15	**2:22**	**2:30**
3:15	**4:45**	**5:55**
6:45	**7:10**	**7:30**
8:05	**9:23**	**10:15**
11:00	**11:39**	**11:58**

SEGMENT B
Skill: To state & negotiate time in terms of segments of the day.

zǎofàn	*breakfast*
zhōngfàn	*lunch*
wǔfàn	*lunch*
wǎnfàn	*dinner, supper*
yèxiāo	*late-night snack*

zǎochén	*morning*
zǎoshang	*morning*
shàngwǔ	*before noon, a.m.*
zhōngwǔ	*noon*
xiàwǔ	*afternoon, p.m.*
wǎnshang	*evening*
bànyè	*late at night, midnight*

chī wǔfàn yǐqián	*before lunch*
chī wǔfàn de shíhou	*during lunch*
chīle wǔfàn yǐhòu	*after lunch*

zǎo yìdiǎnr	*a little earlier*
wǎn yìdiǎnr	*a little later*

Wǒmen shénme shíhou jiàn?	*When shall we meet?*
Nǐ shénme shíhou yǒu kòng?	*When are you free?*
Xiàwǔ sān diǎnzhōng xíng ma?	*Is three p.m. alright?*
Wǎn yìdiǎnr xíng ma?	*Is a little later okay?*
Yí ge zhōngtóu yǐhòu kěyǐ ma?	*Would an hour from now be alright?*
Nǐ xiàwǔ yǒushì ma?	*Are you busy in the afternoon? (Is there something you have to do?)*
Wǒ méi shì.	*I have nothing planned. (There's nothing I have to do.)*

Wǒ zǒu le.	*I'm going now.*
Qǐng děng yíxià.	*Please wait a moment.*
Qǐng nǐ děng wǒ yíxià.	*Please wait for me a moment.*
Méiguānxi, bù jí.	*It doesn't matter, there's no hurry.*

Dialogue Practice

The following sets of dialogues presume normal behavior, no unusual circumstances, and no misunderstandings in the contexts indicated. "A" begins the dialogue, "B" responds, "A" responds to "B," etc. Where there is a choice of responses available, please circle the one which is more appropriate.

I.   *(A and B are friends. A has called B just after dawn, and they have decided to go hiking.)*

A: Wǒmen shénme shíhou qù?

B: 1. Xiǎo Wáng zài mǎi dōngxi.
    2. Nǐ shénme shíhou yǒu kòng?

A: 1. Wǒ gēge zài chī zhōngfàn.
    2. Chīle zǎofàn yǐhòu zǒu, xíng ma?

B: 1. Hǎo. Jǐ diǎnzhōng?
    2. Hǎo. Yèlǐ chī yèxiāo.

A: 1. Qī diǎnzhōng zěnmeyàng?
    2. Shí'èr diǎn chī wǔfàn xíng ma?

B: 1. Zǎo yìdiǎnr chī wǎnfàn.
    2. Hǎo. Huíjiàn.

II.   *(A and B are classmates. They have just finished breakfast together in the cafeteria.)*

A: Nǐ shàngwǔ zuò shénme?

B: 1. Wǒ liù diǎn sān kè chī wǎnfàn.
    2. Bú zuò shénme.

A: 1. Zánmen qù yóuyǒng hǎo ma?
    2. Wǒmen bù chī wǎnfàn, chī yèxiāo.

B: 1. Wǒ yě xiǎng zǎo yìdiǎnr chī.
    2. Hǎo a. Zǒu ba.

III.   *(A and B have decided to go together to visit a mutual friend. It is almost noon.)*

A: Nǐ shénme shíhou yǒu kòng?

B: 1. Wǒ chīle yèxiāo yǐhòu qù shuìjiào.
    2. Wǒ xiàwǔ méi shì.

A: 1. Xiàwǔ qù xíng ma?
    2. Wǒ xǐhuan wǎn yìdiǎnr shuì.

B: 1. Xíng. Chīle wǔfàn yǐhòu ba.
    2. Nǐ hái è ma? Qù chī wǔfàn ba.

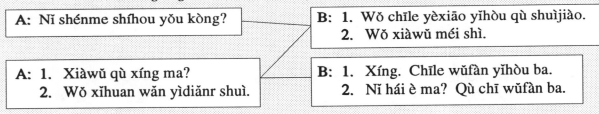

IV.   *(A and B are shopping together. They are about to leave a department store.)*

A: Bié zǒu, qǐng děng wǒ yíxià.

B: 1. Bàba zài zuò wǎnfàn.
    2. Nǐ zuò shénme?

A: 1. Wǒ mǎi yí yàng dōngxi.
    2. Wǒ wǎnshang lái kàn nǐ.

B: 1. Tā bǎo le, bù chī le.
    2. Xíng. Méi shì, bù jí.

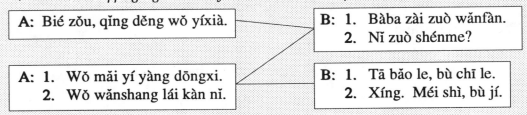

V.   *(A has asked to visit B for some help with homework. B has agreed.)*

A: Chīle wǎnfàn yǐhòu xíng ma?

B: 1. Jǐ diǎnzhōng?
    2. Shàngwǔ hǎo bù hǎo?

A: 1. Bā diǎn bàn zěnmeyàng?
    2. Jǐ diǎn chī zhōngfàn?

B: 1. Wǒ chī zǎofàn, bù chī wǔfàn.
    2. Xíng. Bā diǎn bàn jiàn.

Breakfast

(David has just run into Zhang coming out of the dorms.)

David: Ei, Xiăo Zhāng. Qù chī zăofàn ma? — *Hi, Zhang. Going to breakfast?*

Zhāng: Wŏ bù zĕnme è. Zuótiān shuì de bù hăo. — *I'm not particularly hungry. I didn't get enough sleep last night.*

David: Zĕnme le? — *What happened?*

Zhāng: Lăo Qiū niànshū niàn dào sì diăn cái shuì, găo de wŏ méi shuì hăo. — *Qiu studied until four o'clock before he went to bed, (which made it) so (that) I didn't sleep well.*

David: Nà nĭ jiù bù chī zăofàn le ma? Nà zĕnme xíng? — *So therefore you won't eat breakfast? How will that do?*

Zhāng: Méi guānxi. Nĭ qù chī ba. Wŏ zăo yìdiănr chī zhōngfàn. — *It doesn't matter...you go eat. I'll just get lunch a little early.*

Culture notes

Invitations are sometimes extended rather tentatively, to protect the person making the offer in case of rejection. David, in this case, opens the conversation with a prelude to an invitation to eat breakfast together. The tacit invitation is recognized by Zhang—he explains why he prefers not to go, and encourages David to go without him. Zhang's explanation is an indirect way of rejecting the offer without actually saying no. Characteristic American abruptness, as illustrated in the dialogue following between two acquaintances, is generally unacceptable to the Chinese.

> A: Hi! Want to go to breakfast?
>
> B: No thanks. I'm not hungry.
>
> A: Okay, catch you later then.
>
> B: Yeah.

Chinese casual acquaintances are likely to be more circumspect and solicitous of each other. Growing friendship and greater intimacy, however, usually bring more directness of speech.

Structure notes

1. In Chinese usage, major divisions (of time and place) go before progressively more minor ones. Thus, to state a date, the year goes first, followed by the month, followed by the day.

1776 nián Qīyuè sì hào	*one seven seven six year +* *seven month + four day*	*July 4, 1776*

Similarly, in specifying time of day, the major divisions precede more minor ones.

zǎoshang bā diǎn guò wǔ fēn	*morning + eight o'clock +* *to pass + five minutes*	*8:05 a.m.*

In combining date and time of day, the same principle applies.

1776 nián Qīyuè sì hào zǎoshang bā diǎn guò wǔ fēn	*one seven seven six year +* *seven month + four day +* *morning + eight o'clock +* *to pass + five minutes*	*8:05 a.m. on July 4, 1776*

2. Time phrases may either precede or directly follow the subject; in either case, the time phrase always precedes the verb.

Nǐ jīntiān zǎoshang liù diǎn zhōng zài zuò shénme?	*you + today + morning +* *six o'clock + at +* *to do + what*	*What were you doing this morning at six o'clock?*
Jīntiān zǎoshang liù diǎn zhōng wǒ zài shuìjiào.	*today + morning + six* *o'clock + I + at + to sleep*	*This morning at six o'clock I was asleep.*
Wǒ míngtiān zǎoshang liù diǎnzhōng jiù děi chūmén le.	*I + tomorrow + morning +* *six o'clock + right away +* *must + go out + le*	*I must leave the house at six o'clock tomorrow morning.*

3. The particle le, in addition to indicating a **change of status or condition** when it follows an **adjective**, can also mark the **completion of an action** following **active verbs** such as chī (to eat), zuò (to do), mǎi (to buy), shuō (to speak). Adding le to chī, for instance, indicates that the process of eating is over, and the subject has finished eating. Le added to zuò means that the process of doing something is over, and the job is done.

3b. Subject + Verb + Object + le/ [Subject méi(you) + Verb + Object]

Wǒ chī wǔfàn le.	*I+ to eat + lunch + le*	*I ate lunch.*
Wǒ méi chī zǎofàn.	*I + not + to eat + breakfast*	*I didn't eat breakfast.*

The phrase chīle wǔfàn yǐhòu means, literally, "after the eating of lunch is over." Phrases meaning "during" and "before" an action do not take le after the verb, because, of course, the action in question is not yet complete.

Please note that while le conveys a sense of the completion of a specific action, you should NOT EQUATE THIS WITH THE ENGLISH PAST TENSE. In English, each occurence of a verb must be marked for tense: past, present, or future. This is not the case in Chinese. When actions have been completed, they are marked with le; if "completion of action" does not apply, le is not used, even if reference is being made to a past event.

For example, in the English sentence "I read the book and I liked it," both the verbs "read" and "liked" are in the past, because the event occurred in the past. In Chinese, the action "to read" has been completed and therefore takes le. The act of "liking" the book continues, however; "to like" is not something one completes and then doesn't do anymore. Presumably the speaker still likes the book, having read it once. Thus the Chinese equivalent of the English sentence is Wǒ kànle nèiběn shū; hěn xǐhuān.

Past narrative is sometimes marked by nothing more than a time expression such as "That summer," "Two years ago," etc.

Nèi nián xiàtiān wǒ zhēn lèi.	*that + year + summer + I + really + tired*	*I was really tired that summer.*

Conversely, a completed action that is to take place in the future also requires le.

Nǐ lái le wǒmen jiù chī.	*you + to come + le + we + right away + to eat*	*We'll eat as soon as you get here.*

4. To negate a verb + le sentence—that is, to deny that an action took place—insert méi or méiyou before the verb.

Tā chī le. Nǐ méi chī.	*he+ to eat +le . you + not + to eat.*	*He ate. You didn't eat.*
Wǒ yě méiyou chī.	*I + also + not + to eat*	*I also didn't eat.*

5. Zhōngtóu is a noun meaning "hour" and takes the measure ge. It can be followed by yǐqian or yǐhòu.

Yí ge zhōngtóu yǐqián, wǒ zài kàn shū.	*one + ge + hour + before + I + at to read*	*An hour ago, I was reading a book.*
Zánmen liǎng ge zhōngtóu yǐhòu jiàn, hǎo bù hǎo?	*we + two + ge + hour + after + to meet + fine + not + fine*	*Let's meet two hours from now, okay?*

To convey "during" with zhōngtóu, simply add the specifier zhèige or nèige to zhōngtóu.

Nǐ zài niànshū de nèige zhōngtóu, wǒ zài kàn diànshi.	*you + at + to study + de + that + ge + hour + I + at + to look + television*	*During the hour in which you were studying, I was watching television.*
Nèige zhōngtóu, māma zài kàn shū.	*that + ge + hour + mother + at + to look + book*	*During that hour, Mother was reading a book.*

Structure exercise

The following is a conversation between two cousins who are in the same class at school. Fill in the blanks as appropriate, based on the English equivalent.

A: Zánmen míngtiān _____ qī diǎn _____ jiàn, hǎo ma?

Let's meet at seven a.m. tomorrow, ok?

B: Bù xíng, tài _____ le.

No, that's too early.

A: _____ zhōng ne?

How about eight?

B: Zài wǎn _____, hǎo ma?

Would a little later be alright?

A: Jiǔ _____ ne?

How about nine?

B: Zài wǎn bàn ge _____, hǎo ma?

Another half hour later, okay?

A: Nàme _____ jiàn.

In that case we'll meet at nine thirty.

B: _____ nǐ chīle _____ le ma?

Will you have eaten breakfast by nine thirty?

A: Méi—zánmen chī _____ jiàn.

No—we're meeting before breakfast.

B: Hǎo. Nǐ niànshū le ma?

Okay. Have you studied?

A: Zánmen míngtiān _____ niànshū.

Let's study while we eat breakfast tomorrow.

B: Zánmen _____ zuò shénme?

What will we do after breakfast?

A: Míngtiān zài shuō ba.

Let's decide tomorrow.

SEGMENT C

Skill: To state & negotiate time by the calendar

nián yuè rì — *year and date*

nián	*year*
(yì jiǔ jiǔ sān) nián*	*1993*
(èr qī líng wǔ) nián	*2705*

rì, hào	*day*
yí hào	*1st day (of the month)*
èr hào	*2nd*
sān hào	*3rd*
sānshíyī hào	*31st*

xīngqī, lǐbài	*week*
Xīngqīyī	*Monday*
Xīngqī'èr	*Tuesday*
Xīngqīsān	*Wednesday*
Xīngqīsì	*Thursday*
Xīngqīwǔ	*Friday*
Xīngqīliù	*Saturday*
Xīngqītiān	*Sunday*

yuè	*month*
Yíyuè	*January*
Èryuè	*February*
Sānyuè	*March*
Sìyuè	*April*
Wǔyuè	*May*
Liùyuè	*June*
Qīyuè	*July*
Bāyuè	*August*
Jiǔyuè	*September*
Shíyuè	*October*
Shíyīyuè	*November*
Shíèryuè	*December*

Wèishénme?	*Why?*
Yīnwei...	*Because...*

Něi nián?	*Which year?*
Jǐ yuè jǐ hào?	*What date?*
Xīngqī jǐ?	*Which day of the week?*
Nǐ shì něi nián shēng de?	*What year were you born?*
Nǐ shēngri shì jǐ yuè jǐ hào?	*When is your birthday?*
Bāyuè yí hào lǐbàiyī xíng ma?	*Is Monday August 1st okay?*

*In standard <u>pinyin</u> orthography,
the number of the year is given in
Arabic numerals followed by
<u>nián</u> (1993 nián, 2705 nián).
Here, it has been spelled out for
the student's benefit.

Dialogue Practice

The following sets of dialogues presume normal behavior, no unusual circumstances, and no misunderstandings in the contexts indicated. "A" begins the dialogue, "B" responds, "A" responds to "B," etc. Where there is a choice of responses available, please circle the one which is more appropriate.

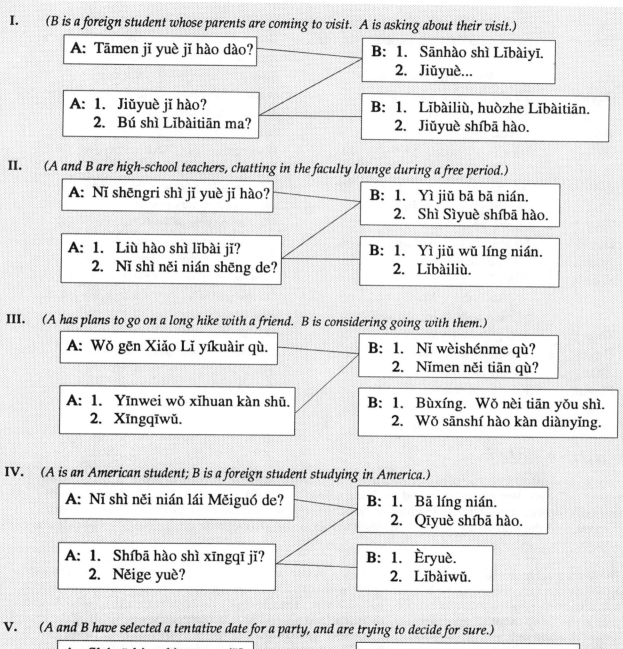

I. *(B is a foreign student whose parents are coming to visit. A is asking about their visit.)*

A: Tāmen jǐ yuè jǐ hào dào?

B: 1. Sānhào shì Lǐbàiyī.
   2. Jiǔyuè...

A: 1. Jiǔyuè jǐ hào?
   2. Bú shì Lǐbàitiān ma?

B: 1. Lǐbàiliù, huòzhe Lǐbàitiān.
   2. Jiǔyuè shíbā hào.

II. *(A and B are high-school teachers, chatting in the faculty lounge during a free period.)*

A: Nǐ shēngri shì jǐ yuè jǐ hào?

B: 1. Yì jiǔ bā bā nián.
   2. Shì Sìyuè shíbā hào.

A: 1. Liù hào shì lǐbài jǐ?
   2. Nǐ shì něi nián shēng de?

B: 1. Yì jiǔ wǔ líng nián.
   2. Lǐbàiliù.

III. *(A has plans to go on a long hike with a friend. B is considering going with them.)*

A: Wǒ gēn Xiǎo Lǐ yíkuàir qù.

B: 1. Nǐ wèishénme qù?
   2. Nǐmen něi tiān qù?

A: 1. Yīnwei wǒ xǐhuan kàn shū.
   2. Xīngqīwǔ.

B: 1. Bùxíng. Wǒ nèi tiān yǒu shì.
   2. Wǒ sānshí hào kàn diànyǐng.

IV. *(A is an American student; B is a foreign student studying in America.)*

A: Nǐ shì něi nián lái Měiguó de?

B: 1. Bā líng nián.
   2. Qīyuè shíbā hào.

A: 1. Shíbā hào shì xīngqī jǐ?
   2. Něige yuè?

B: 1. Èryuè.
   2. Lǐbàiwǔ.

V. *(A and B have selected a tentative date for a party, and are trying to decide for sure.)*

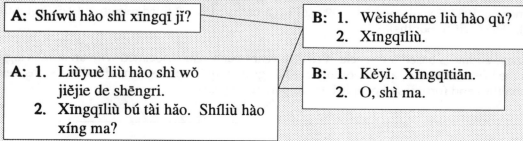

A: Shíwǔ hào shì xīngqī jǐ?

B: 1. Wèishénme liù hào qù?
   2. Xīngqīliù.

A: 1. Liùyuè liù hào shì wǒ jiějie de shēngri.
   2. Xīngqīliù bú tài hǎo. Shíliù hào xíng ma?

B: 1. Kěyǐ. Xīngqītiān.
   2. O, shì ma.

The zodiac

(Zhang, David, Li, and some friends are strolling along a street. They run into Wu Xianling.)

David, Lǐ:	Ei, Xiǎo Wú.	*Hi, Wu.*
Zhāng:	Nǐmen jiā de xiǎo bǎobao hǎo ma?	*How's the baby? (Is the little precious one in your family well?)*
Wú:	Hǎo. Zhǎng de zhēn kuài.	*Fine. (She's) growing really fast.*
David:	Tā shì jǐ yuè jǐ hào shēng de?	*When was she born? (Which month, which day was she born?)*
Wú:	Yīyuè shíqī hào.	*January 17th.*
David:	Nà shǔ shénme? Shǔ yáng ma?	*What sign is that? (What animal does she belong under?) The sheep?*
Wú:	Bù, háishì shǔ mǎ. Jīnnián Èryuè cái shì yīnlì xīnnián.	*No, it's still the horse. Chinese new year isn't until February this year.*
Friend:	O, wǒ yě shǔ mǎ.	*Oh, I'm the year of the horse too.*
David:	Nǐ shì něi nián shēng de?	*In which year were you born?*
Friend:	1966 nián. Mǎ nián.	*1966. The year of the horse.*
Zhāng:	Xiǎo Lǐ, nǐ ne? Nǐ shǔ shénme?	*Li, what about you? What's your sign?*
Li:	Wǒ shǔ zhū. Wǒ shì yì jiǔ qī yī nián shēng de. Nǐ ne?	*I'm the year of the pig. I was born in 1971. How about you?*
Zhāng:	Wǒ gēn nǐ yíyàng.	*I'm the same as you.*
David:	Wǒ bǐ nǐmen xiǎo yí suì.	*I'm a year younger than you (two).*
Zhāng:	Nǐ shì lǎoshǔ!	*You're a rat!*
David:	Kě bú shì ma.	*Isn't that a fact.*

Culture notes

Taiwan and many Chinese communities in the PRC and elsewhere operate under a dual calendar system. The western calendar, called the Yang calendar (yánglì), is used for most business, school and government transactions. Traditional holidays such as Chinese New Year, the Dragon-boat Festival, and the Mid-Autumn (harvest) festival follow the Yin calendar (yīnlì), the Chinese calendar system.

There are twelve months a year and thirty days a month in the Chinese system. The month is based on the cycle of the moon: at the beginning of the month the moon is in crescent, by mid-month it is full, and by the end of the month it has waned again. The Chinese counterpart for the western leap year is the "leap month": an intercalary month added seven times in nineteen years, to bring the lunar schedule in line with the solar. For example, each of the following years had (will have) an added month: 1987 (2 sixth months); 1990 (2 fifth months); 1993 (2 third months); 1995 (2 eighth months); 1998 (2 fifth months).

The Chinese zodiac is based on a cycle of twelve years, each year associated with an animal sign. As with the Western zodiac, a body of folklore has grown up in connection with these signs, relating to personalities and fortunes of people born in particular years.

The Chinese Zodiac

There are twelve animal signs in the Chinese zodiac. Each year is assigned an animal, beginning with the rat and ending with the pig.

Nǐ shǔ shénme?

Rat	1912	1924	1936	1948	1960	1972	1984	1996	2008
Ox	1913	1925	1937	1949	1961	1973	1985	1997	2009
Tiger	1914	1926	1938	1950	1962	1974	1986	1998	2010
Rabbit	1915	1927	1939	1951	1963	1975	1987	1999	2011
Dragon	1916	1928	1940	1952	1964	1976	1988	2000	2012
Snake	1917	1929	1941	1953	1965	1977	1989	2001	2013
Horse	1918	1930	1942	1954	1966	1978	1990	2002	2014
Sheep	1919	1931	1943	1955	1967	1979	1991	2003	2015
Monkey	1920	1932	1944	1956	1968	1980	1992	2004	2016
Chicken	1921	1933	1945	1957	1969	1981	1993	2005	2017
Dog	1922	1934	1946	1958	1970	1982	1994	2006	2018
Pig	1923	1935	1947	1959	1971	1983	1995	2007	2019

Structure notes

1. As mentioned earlier, descriptions of time and place proceed from the largest divisions to the smallest. In addresses on letters, for instance, first the country, then the state/province, city, street, number, and finally the individual receiving the letter are listed. Thus, a letter to the White House would be addressed approximately as follows:

> USA
> District of Columbia, Washington
> Pennsylvania Ave. Number 1
> To Mr./Ms. President

In the same fashion, a statement of date proceeds from the year, to the month, to the day, to the day of the week, to the hour of the day (if warranted). The Chinese term for "year and date" — nián yuè rì — indicates this progression. (A more commonly used term for "date" is rìqī.)

2. Wèishénme is literally "for the sake of what?" Wèi means "for the sake of," as in Wǒ shì wèile nǐ. "I (did it) for your sake."

A: Nǐ wèishénme wǔyuè qù Zhōngguó?	*you + why + May + to go + China*	*Why are you going to China in May?*
B: Yīnwei wǒ xǐhuan wǔyuè.	*because + I + to like + May*	*Because I like May.*
A: Wèishénme?	*why*	*Why?*
B: Yīnwei wǔyuè bú tài rè.	*because + May + not + too + to be hot*	*Because May isn't too hot.*

Note that the time expression in a sentence may also precede or directly follow the subject, so that wèishénme ends up jockeying for position with the time expression. Which goes first depends on the meaning to be expressed. The item being questioned by wèishénme follows wèishénme. Thus in the sentence above, Nǐ wèishénme wǔyuè qù Zhōngguó, since wǔyuè follows wèishénme, it is the item being called into question: "(I know you are going to China, but) why in May? If the time expression wǔyuè were to precede wèishénme, it would no longer be the object of the question. In the sentence Nǐ wǔyuè wèishénme qù Zhōngguó "In May, why are you going to China?", the object of wèishénme is either the verb "to go," or the destination "China." There would be two possible contexts of the question. One would be, approximately, "You know lots of things are happening in the month in question: May. Why are you going to China then? Why don't you stay here instead?" The other would be, "There are lots of places you can go to in May. Why are you going to China, of all places?"

3. The table below differentiates between stating a point in time and a duration of time, in regards to the time divisions covered in this lesson.

	Point in time	*Duration of time*
hour	yì diǎnzhōng *(one o'clock)*	yí ge zhōngtóu *(one hour)*
day	yí hào *(the first day of the month)*	yì tiān *(one day)*
week	Xīngqīyī *(Monday)*	yí ge xīngqī *(one week)*
month	Yíyuè *(January)*	yí ge yuè *(one month)*
year	(yì jiǔ jiǔ qī nián)* *(1997)*	yì nián *(one year)*

　　　　*In standard pīnyīn orthography, the year is written "1997" rather than spelled out .

When asking questions about point in or duration of time, either jǐ or něi is used, as indicated in the following table.

	Point in time	*Duration of time*
hour	jǐ diǎnzhōng *(at what hour)*	jǐ ge zhōngtóu *(how many hours)*
day	jǐ hào *(which day of the month)*	jǐ tiān *(how many days)*
week	Xīngqījǐ *(which day of the week)*	jǐ ge xīngqī *(how many weeks)*
month	jǐ yuè *(which month of the year)*	jǐ ge yuè *(how many months)*
year	něi nián *(which year)*	jǐ nián *(how many years)*

Structure exercise

1. Write the Chinese equivalents of the following dates:

Tuesday, October 10, 1911   Sunday, May 4, 1919

_____   _____

Saturday, October 1, 1949   Sunday, June 4, 1989

_____   _____

(Extra: Match the dates above with the following historical events.
a. The Tian'anmen Incident.   b. The founding of the People's Republic of China.
c. The founding of the Republic of China.   d. The May Fourth Student Movement.)

2. Fill in the blanks in the sentences below, using the internal logic of the sentence as a guide. Each is a statement regarding a length of time. The English equivalent of the first sentence is provided as an example of the structure of the sentences.

1. Bā diǎnzhōng dào *(to)* jiǔ diǎnzhōng shì yī ge zhōngtóu.
   From eight o'clock to nine o'clock is one hour.

2. Wǔ diǎn yī kè dào wǔ diǎn èrshí fēn shì _____fēnzhōng.

3. Zǎoshang liù diǎn dào wǎnshang liù diǎn shì _____ zhōngtóu.

4. Xīngqīsān dào Xīngqīwǔ shì _____.

5. Wǔyuè yī hào dào _____ yī hào shì qī ge yuè.

6. _____ nián dào 1985 nián shì wǔ nián.

3. Write questions to elicit the answers provided.

Q: _____?

A: Wǒ shì 1970 nián lái de.

Q: _____?

A: Wǒ wǔyuè wǔ hào lái de.

Q: _____?

A: Wǒ Xīngqīwǔ lái de.

Q: _____?

A: Wǒ bā diǎn bàn lái de.

88

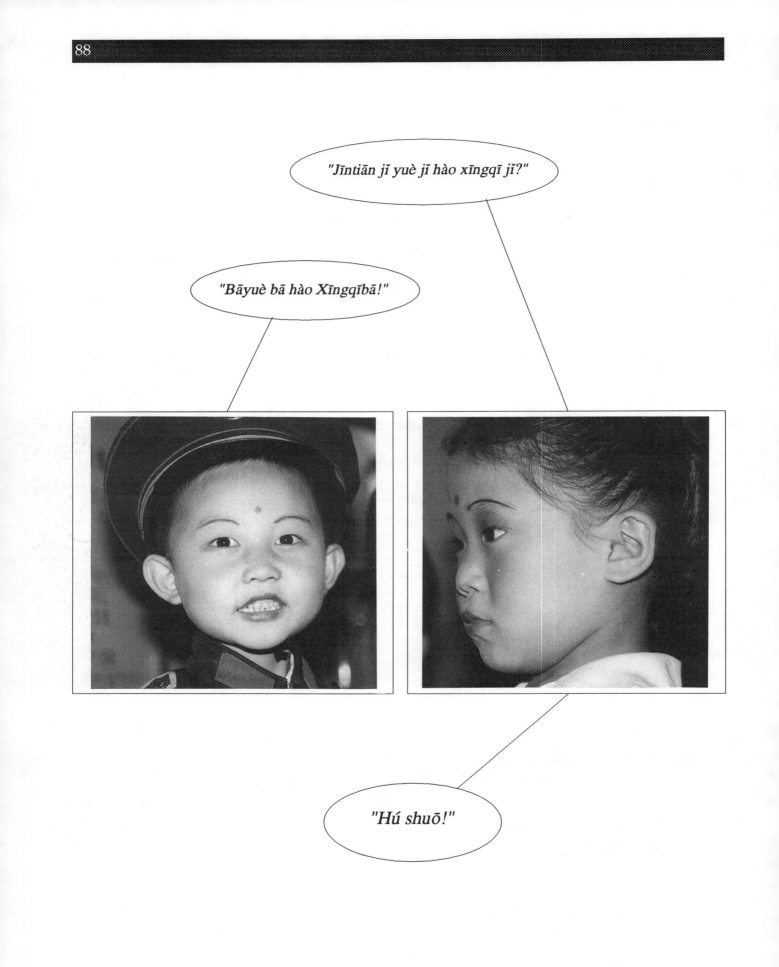

UNIT FOUR: *WHEN CAN WE MEET?*

SEGMENT D

Skill: To state & negotiate relative time by day & week

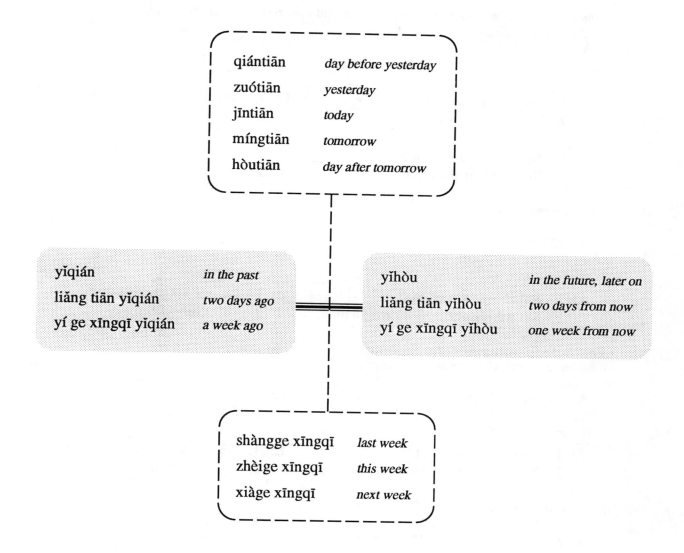

qiántiān	*day before yesterday*
zuótiān	*yesterday*
jīntiān	*today*
míngtiān	*tomorrow*
hòutiān	*day after tomorrow*

yǐqián	*in the past*
liǎng tiān yǐqián	*two days ago*
yí ge xīngqī yǐqián	*a week ago*

yǐhòu	*in the future, later on*
liǎng tiān yǐhòu	*two days from now*
yí ge xīngqī yǐhòu	*one week from now*

shàngge xīngqī	*last week*
zhèige xīngqī	*this week*
xiàge xīngqī	*next week*

Jīntiān jǐ yuè jǐ hào?	*What's the date today?*
Sān tiān yǐqián nǐ zài nǎr?	*Where were you three days ago?*
Yǐqián nǐ láiguo ma?	*Have you been here before?*
Xiàge Xīngqīsān hǎo ma?	*Is next Wednesday okay?*
Nǐ yǐhòu yǒu kòng ma?	*Will you be free later on?*

Dialogue Practice

The following sets of dialogues presume normal behavior, no unusual circumstances, and no misunderstandings in the contexts indicated. "A" begins the dialogue, "B" responds, "A" responds to "B," etc. Where there is a choice of responses available, please circle the one which is more appropriate.

I.   (A and B are classmates working together. They cannot quite remember that day's date.)

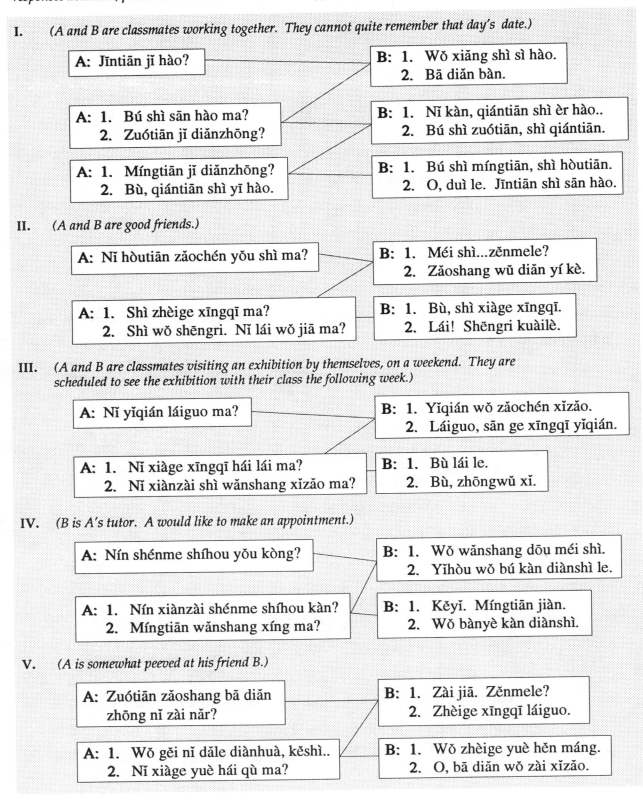

A: Jīntiān jǐ hào?

B: 1. Wǒ xiǎng shì sì hào.
     2. Bā diǎn bàn.

A: 1. Bú shì sān hào ma?
     2. Zuótiān jǐ diǎnzhōng?

B: 1. Nǐ kàn, qiántiān shì èr hào..
     2. Bú shì zuótiān, shì qiántiān.

A: 1. Míngtiān jǐ diǎnzhōng?
     2. Bù, qiántiān shì yī hào.

B: 1. Bú shì míngtiān, shì hòutiān.
     2. O, duì le. Jīntiān shì sān hào.

II. (A and B are good friends.)

A: Nǐ hòutiān zǎochén yǒu shì ma?

B: 1. Méi shì...zěnmele?
     2. Zǎoshang wǔ diǎn yí kè.

A: 1. Shì zhèige xīngqī ma?
     2. Shì wǒ shēngri. Nǐ lái wǒ jiā ma?

B: 1. Bù, shì xiàge xīngqī.
     2. Lái! Shēngri kuàilè.

III. (A and B are classmates visiting an exhibition by themselves, on a weekend. They are scheduled to see the exhibition with their class the following week.)

A: Nǐ yǐqián láiguo ma?

B: 1. Yǐqián wǒ zǎochén xǐzǎo.
     2. Láiguo, sān ge xīngqī yǐqián.

A: 1. Nǐ xiàge xīngqī hái lái ma?
     2. Nǐ xiànzài shì wǎnshang xǐzǎo ma?

B: 1. Bù lái le.
     2. Bù, zhōngwǔ xǐ.

IV. (B is A's tutor. A would like to make an appointment.)

A: Nín shénme shíhou yǒu kòng?

B: 1. Wǒ wǎnshang dōu méi shì.
     2. Yǐhòu wǒ bú kàn diànshì le.

A: 1. Nín xiànzài shénme shíhou kàn?
     2. Míngtiān wǎnshang xíng ma?

B: 1. Kěyǐ. Míngtiān jiàn.
     2. Wǒ bànyè kàn diànshì.

V.   (A is somewhat peeved at his friend B.)

A: Zuótiān zǎoshang bā diǎn zhōng nǐ zài nǎr?

B: 1. Zài jiā. Zěnmele?
     2. Zhèige xīngqī láiguo.

A: 1. Wǒ gěi nǐ dǎle diànhuà, kěshì..
     2. Nǐ xiàge yuè hái qù ma?

B: 1. Wǒ zhèige yuè hěn máng.
     2. O, bā diǎn wǒ zài xǐzǎo.

An appointment

(Zhang, David, Li, and their friends are still talking to Wu Xianling.)

Zhāng:	Wǒmen shénme shíhou qù kànkan nǐ de xiǎo wáwa ba.	*Let's go see your new baby sometime.*
Wú:	Hǎo a...suíshí huānyíng nǐmen lái.	*Sure...you're welcome anytime.*
Zhāng:	*(to the others)*	
	Zěnmeyàng? Nǐmen míngtiān yǒu kòng ma?	*How about it? Are you free tomorrow?*
David:	Aiya, míngtiān bùxíng a. Wǒ míngtiān yǒu shì. Hòutiān hǎo ma?	*(Too bad), tomorrow won't work. I have something to do tomorrow. How about the day after tomorrow?*
Lǐ:	Wǒ hòutiān bùxíng.	*The day after tomorrow won't work either, for me.*
Friend:	Wǒ yě shì; wǒ zhèige xīngqī dōu hěn máng. Xiàge xīngqī hǎo ma?	*Me too. This whole week is very busy for me. How about next week?*
David:	Wǒ xiàge xīngqī kěyǐ.	*Next week is okay for me.*
Friend:	Duì, xiàge xīngqī kěyǐ. Xiǎo Lǐ, nǐ ne?	*Right, next week is fine. Li, how about you?*
Lǐ:	Wǒ xiàge xīngqī yě méi shì. Něi tiān dōu kěyǐ.	*I don't have anything to do next week either. Any day is fine.*
Zhāng:	Xīngqīyī hǎo bù hǎo?	*How about Monday?*
Lǐ:	Hǎo.	*Fine.*
David:	Kěyǐ.	*Okay.*
Friend:	Xíng.	*Can do.*
Zhāng:	*(to Wu Xianling)*	
	Nà wǒmen jiù xiàge Xīngqīyī qù kàn nǐmen ba.	*Then we'll be coming to see you next Monday.*
Wú:	Hǎo jí le.	*That's great.*

Culture notes

David's utterance that begins "Aiya..." (a common expression of regret) is typical of refusals in Chinese society. Since David cannot acquiesce to the date being suggested, he begins with an exclamation of sorrow or regret, to soften the impact of the refusal that follows. The refusal itself, "Tomorrow won't work," is quickly followed by an explanation of his unfortunate situation, and a suggestion of an alternative. The explanation and alternative serve to repair any damage to Zhang's self-esteem done by the refusal.

Often Chinese friends, neighbours, and other acquaintances will pay informal visits to each other, with no purpose other than simply to chat and enjoy each other's company. Such purely social visits occur even in business and academic contexts and during working hours; they serve to maintain useful relationships among individuals. Here, Zhang and the others may have a sincere interest in seeing Wu Xianling's new baby; it may also be simply a convenient reason to pay her a social visit.

Structure notes

1. It may help to think of yourself rappelling on a rope from the top of a mountain towards the bottom, to visualize the Chinese sense of passage through time. As you proceed downwards, you are facing the top of the mountain, where you came from, and must look behind you to see where you are going.

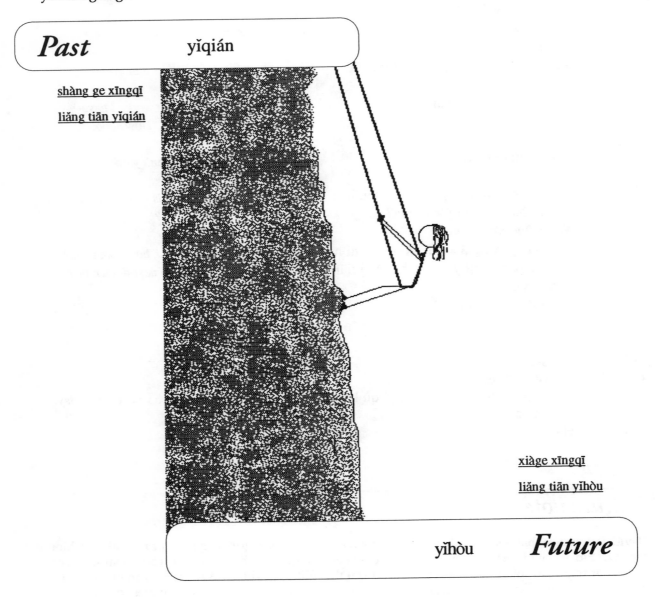

Past   yǐqián

shàng ge xīngqī

liǎng tiān yǐqián

xiàge xīngqī

liǎng tiān yǐhòu

yǐhòu   *Future*

In Chinese, the past is the top of the mountain. You descend, backwards, into the future. Thus, yǐqián (literally, "in front") refers to the past, and yǐhòu (literally, "behind") refers to the space behind you—the future. Liǎng tiān yǐqián ("two days in front of you") is two days in the past; liǎng tiān yǐhòu ("two days behind you") is two days in the future. Shàng ge xīngqī ("the week above") refers to a point closer to the top of the mountain, therefore in the past; xiàge xīngqī ("the week below") indicates a point closer to the bottom, in the future.

2. <u>Sān tiān yǐqián nǐ zài nǎr?</u> utilizes a basic Chinese sentence pattern.

5. Subject + [bú] + zài + place

Nǐ zài nǎr?	you + to be at + where	Where are you?
Wǒ zài jiā.	I + to be at + home	I'm at home.
Nǐ jiā bù zài Sānjiē ma?	your home + not + to be at + third avenue + ma	Isn't your home on Third Avenue?
Bù, wǒ jiā zài Wǔjiē.	not + my home + to be at + fifth avenue	No, my home is on Fifth Avenue.

3. <u>Yǐqián nǐ láiguo ma?</u> utilizes another basic pattern in Chinese. <u>Guo</u> appended to the verb in this pattern indicates that the subject has had the experience of doing the verb, that the subject has done the action indicated by the verb sometime in the past.

6. Subject + [méi] + verb-guo (+ object)

Nǐ láiguo ma?	you + to come + guo + ma	Have you been here (before)?
Wǒ sān nián yǐqián láiguo.	I + three years ago + to come + guo	I was here three years ago.
Nǐ kànguo Rìběn diànyǐng ma?	you + to see + guo + Japan + movie + ma	Have you ever seen a Japanese movie?
Méi kànguo. Kěshì wǒ kànguo Zhōngguó diànyǐng.	not + to see + guo + but + I + to see + guo + China + movie	No. But I've seen a Chinese movie.

Structure exercises

The ovals below represent 9 points in time, beginning with "last week" and ending with "next week." Please make up and write in seven intervening points in chronological order.

shàngge xīngqī

xiàge xīngqī

Answer the questions below based on your own experience.

1. Zuótiān zǎoshang wǔ diǎn zhōng nǐ zài zuò shénme?

_____

2. Jīntiān xiàwǔ sì diǎn bàn nǐ zài nǎr?

_____

3. Xiàge xīngqī de Xīngqītiān nǐ yào zuò shénme?

_____

4. Nǐ qùguo Zhōngguó ma?

_____

SEGMENT E
Skill: To state & negotiate relative time by month, year, season.

liǎng ge yuè yǐqián	*two months ago*
shàngge yuè	*last month*
zhèige yuè	*this month*
xiàge yuè	*next month*
liǎng ge yuè yǐhòu	*two months from now*
liǎng nián yǐqián	*two years ago*
qùnián	*last year*
jīnnián	*this year*
míngnián	*next year*
liǎng nián yǐhòu	*two years from now*

Question:
Zhè shì chūntiān háishi qiūtiān?
Answer:

Shéi zhīdào!

sìjì	*the four seasons*
chūntiān	*spring*
xiàtiān	*summer*
qiūtiān	*fall*
dōngtiān	*winter*

Nǐ xiàge yuè lái ma?	*Are you coming next month?*
Nǐ míngnián xiàtiān zuò shénme?	*What will you do next summer?*
Nǐ jīnnián dào nǎr qù?	*Where are you going this year?*
Liǎng nián yǐhòu nǐ zài nǎr?	*Where will you be two years from now?*

Dialogue Practice

The following sets of dialogues presume normal behavior, no unusual circumstances, and no misunderstandings in the contexts indicated. "A" begins the dialogue, "B" responds, "A" responds to "B," etc. Where there is a choice of responses available, please circle the one which is more appropriate.

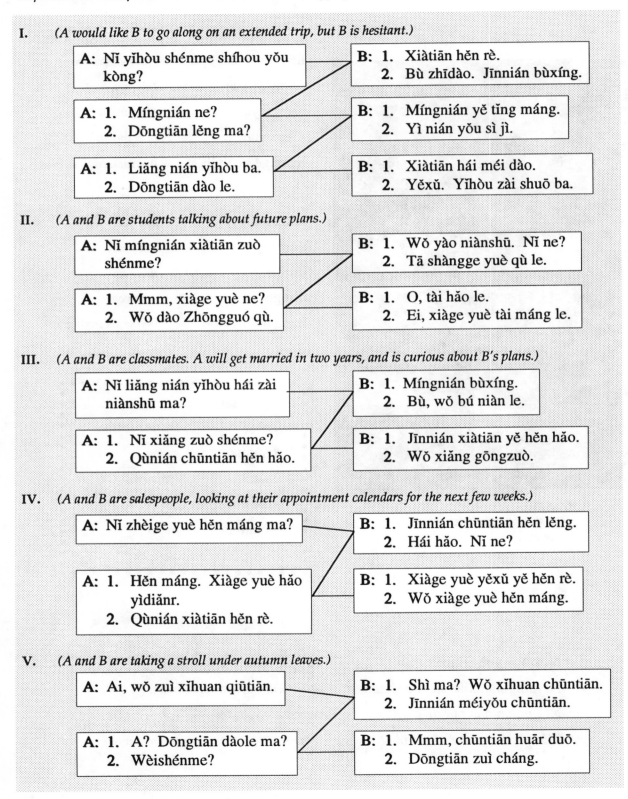

I.   (*A would like B to go along on an extended trip, but B is hesitant.*)

A: Nǐ yǐhòu shénme shíhou yǒu kòng?

B: 1. Xiàtiān hěn rè.
   2. Bù zhīdào. Jīnnián bùxíng.

A: 1. Míngnián ne?
   2. Dōngtiān lěng ma?

B: 1. Míngnián yě tǐng máng.
   2. Yì nián yǒu sì jì.

A: 1. Liǎng nián yǐhòu ba.
   2. Dōngtiān dào le.

B: 1. Xiàtiān hái méi dào.
   2. Yěxǔ. Yǐhòu zài shuō ba.

II.   (*A and B are students talking about future plans.*)

A: Nǐ míngnián xiàtiān zuò shénme?

B: 1. Wǒ yào niànshū. Nǐ ne?
   2. Tā shàngge yuè qù le.

A: 1. Mmm, xiàge yuè ne?
   2. Wǒ dào Zhōngguó qù.

B: 1. O, tài hǎo le.
   2. Ei, xiàge yuè tài máng le.

III.   (*A and B are classmates. A will get married in two years, and is curious about B's plans.*)

A: Nǐ liǎng nián yǐhòu hái zài niànshū ma?

B: 1. Míngnián bùxíng.
   2. Bù, wǒ bú niàn le.

A: 1. Nǐ xiǎng zuò shénme?
   2. Qùnián chūntiān hěn hǎo.

B: 1. Jīnnián xiàtiān yě hěn hǎo.
   2. Wǒ xiǎng gōngzuò.

IV.   (*A and B are salespeople, looking at their appointment calendars for the next few weeks.*)

A: Nǐ zhèige yuè hěn máng ma?

B: 1. Jīnnián chūntiān hěn lěng.
   2. Hái hǎo. Nǐ ne?

A: 1. Hěn máng. Xiàge yuè hǎo yìdiǎnr.
   2. Qùnián xiàtiān hěn rè.

B: 1. Xiàge yuè yěxǔ yě hěn rè.
   2. Wǒ xiàge yuè hěn máng.

V.   (*A and B are taking a stroll under autumn leaves.*)

A: Ai, wǒ zuì xǐhuan qiūtiān.

B: 1. Shì ma? Wǒ xǐhuan chūntiān.
   2. Jīnnián méiyǒu chūntiān.

A: 1. A? Dōngtiān dàole ma?
   2. Wèishénme?

B: 1. Mmm, chūntiān huār duō.
   2. Dōngtiān zuì cháng.

At Wu's house

(Li, David, Zhang, and two friends are in Wu Xianling's living-room. Wu's new baby is on her lap; the friends have been served tea, fruit, and some crackers.)

David:	Hǎo dà le, xiǎo wáwa.	*She's grown big, the little baby.*
Lǐ:	Zhēn kě'ài.	*She's really cute.*
Friend:	Tā jǐ ge yuè le?	*How many months is she?*
Wú:	Kuài jiǔ ge yuè le.	*Almost nine months.*
Zhāng:	Shénme shíhou kāishǐ zǒulù?	*When will she start to walk?*
Lǐ:	Kěnéng zài guò sì-wǔ ge yuè.	*Maybe in another four-five months.*
David:	Dàole míngnián jiù néng zǒu néng shuō le.	*By next year she'll be able to walk and talk.*
Wú:	Tā liǎng ge yuè yǐqián jiù kāishǐ pá le.	*She started to crawl two months ago.*
Lǐ:	*(to the baby)*	
	Nǐ huì shuō huà ma? Bǎobao jiào "āyí."	*Can you talk? Say "auntie," little one.*
Zhāng:	Hái xiǎo ne. Dàole chūntiān jiù huì jiào "āyí" le.	*She's too little, yet. By spring she'll know how to say "auntie."*

Culture notes

Chinese parents as a rule are very solicitous of their children. Babies are often dandled, carried, and otherwise fussed over. It is not unusual for a young child never to be put down or left alone as long as it is awake; even when a parent is busy with chores, the child may be strapped into a backpack on the parent's back, or tended by a friend, neighbor, older sibling, or other relative.

Children are encouraged to greet adults by stating ("calling out") their kinship titles —"auntie," "uncle," "older brother," etc. Parent's friends get honorary titles as well: women are generally called "auntie" (āyí) and men "uncle" (shūshu).

Structure notes

1. Following the principle of proceeding from the largest divisions to the smallest in stating time and place, an indication of the season would fall into position thus:

1994 nián chūntiān sìyuè èrshíjiǔ hào   *April 29, 1994, Spring*

2. The sentence <u>Nǐ jīnnián dào nǎr qù?</u> follows the basic sentence pattern given below, indicating movement from one place to another.

7. Subject + [<u>bú</u>] + <u>dào</u> + Place + <u>qù</u>

Wǒ dào Rìběn qù.	*I + to + Japan + to go*	*I'm going to Japan.*
Xiǎo Wáng dào Zhōngguó qù le.	*Xiao Wang + to + China + to go + le*	*Xiao Wang went to China.*
Nǐ dào nǎr qù?	*you + to + where + to go*	*Where are you going?*
Wǒ bú dào nǎr qù.	*I + not + to + anywhere + to go*	*I'm not going anywhere.*

Structure exercise

Fill in the blanks in the English translation of the passage below, which is a monologue about a possible trip to New York City.

Wǒ wǔ nián yǐqián qùguo Niǔyuē *(New York)*. Wǒ zài nàr zhǐ *(only)* zhùle liǎng ge xīngqī, juéde tài lěng le. Shàngge xīngqī, wǒ de péngyou gěi wǒ dǎle yí ge diànhuà, jiào wǒ zài dào Niǔyuē qù. Tā yào wǒ xiàge yuè shíwǔ hào zuǒyòu *(approximately)* qù. Tā jiào wǒ zài Niǔyuē zhù liǎng-sān ge yuè. Wǒ bù zhīdao yīnggāi *(ought to)* bù yīnggāi qù. Wǒ xiǎng hòutiān gēn wǒ fùmǔ shāngliang yíxià *(to talk it over)*, yì-liǎng ge xīngqī yǐhòu zài gěi wǒ péngyou dǎ diànhuà, gàosù ta. Wǒ hěn xiǎng dào Niǔyuē qù; kěnéng *(perhaps)* xiàge yuè zhēn de néng qù.

I went to New York _____. I only stayed for _____, since I thought it was too cold. _____ my friend gave me a call, asking me to go to New York again. He wants me to go again, _____, around the fifteenth. He wants me to live in New York for _____. I don't know whether or not I ought to go. I think I'll talk it over with my parents _____, and then call my friend _____, and tell him. I'd really like to go to New York; perhaps I can really go _____.

SEGMENT A
Skill: To manage simple monetary transactions

yí kuài qián   *one dollar/ $1.00*
yì máo qián   *ten cents/ $.10*
yì fēn qián   *one cent/ $.01*

liǎng kuài qián   *two dollars/ $2.00*
liǎng máo qián   *twenty cents/ $.20*
liǎng fēn qián   *two cents/ $.02*

shǎo   *few*
duóshao   *how much?*
piányi   *cheap, inexpensive*
guì   *expensive*

jiǔ kuài jiǔ máo jiǔ fēn qián   *$9.99*
jiǔ kuài jiǔ máo jiǔ   *$9.99*
jiǔ kuài jiǔ máo qián   *$9.90*
jiǔ kuài jiǔ   *$9.90*

yìbǎi kuài qián   *one hundred dollars*
yìqiān kuài qián   *one thousand dollars*
yíwàn kuài qián   *ten thousand dollars*
duō   *much, many*

Tā de qián hěn duō.   *S/he has a lot of money.*
Zhèige tài guì le!   *This is too expensive!*
(Yígòng) duóshǎo qián?   *How much is it (altogether)?*
Jǐ kuài qián?   *How many dollars is it?*
Piányi yìdiǎnr, hǎo ma?   *Make it cheaper, okay?*
Qǐng nǐ suàn yí suàn...   *Please figure it out (add it up)...*

Dialogue Practice

The following sets of dialogues presume normal behavior, no unusual circumstances, and no misunderstandings in the contexts indicated. "A" begins the dialogue, "B" responds, "A" responds to "B," etc. Where there is a choice of responses available, please circle the more appropriate one.

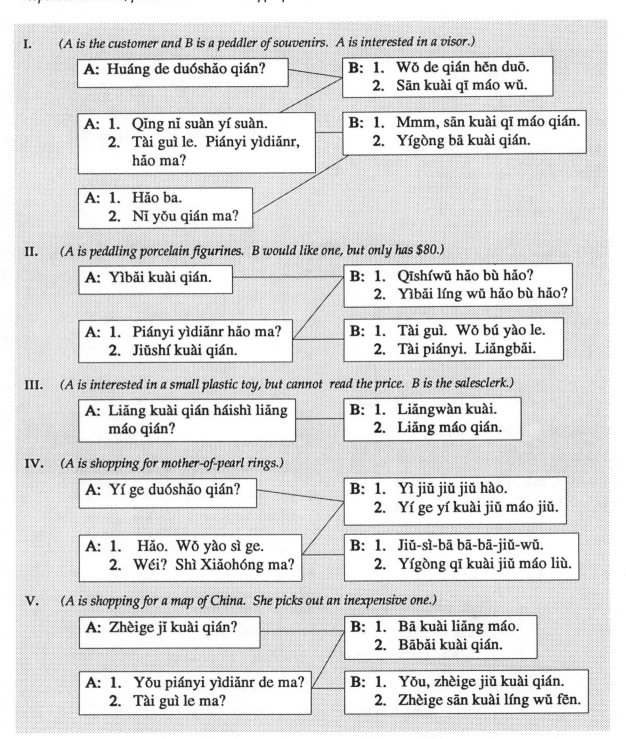

I.　　*(A is the customer and B is a peddler of souvenirs. A is interested in a visor.)*

A: Huáng de duóshǎo qián?

B: 1. Wǒ de qián hěn duō.
　　2. Sān kuài qī máo wǔ.

A: 1. Qǐng nǐ suàn yí suàn.
　　2. Tài guì le. Piányi yìdiǎnr, hǎo ma?

B: 1. Mmm, sān kuài qī máo qián.
　　2. Yígòng bā kuài qián.

A: 1. Hǎo ba.
　　2. Nǐ yǒu qián ma?

II.　　*(A is peddling porcelain figurines. B would like one, but only has $80.)*

A: Yìbǎi kuài qián.

B: 1. Qīshíwǔ hǎo bù hǎo?
　　2. Yìbǎi líng wǔ hǎo bù hǎo?

A: 1. Piányi yìdiǎnr hǎo ma?
　　2. Jiǔshí kuài qián.

B: 1. Tài guì. Wǒ bú yào le.
　　2. Tài piányi. Liǎngbǎi.

III.　　*(A is interested in a small plastic toy, but cannot read the price. B is the salesclerk.)*

A: Liǎng kuài qián háishì liǎng máo qián?

B: 1. Liǎngwàn kuài.
　　2. Liǎng máo qián.

IV.　　*(A is shopping for mother-of-pearl rings.)*

A: Yí ge duóshǎo qián?

B: 1. Yì jiǔ jiǔ jiǔ hào.
　　2. Yí ge yí kuài jiǔ máo jiǔ.

A: 1. Hǎo. Wǒ yào sì ge.
　　2. Wéi? Shì Xiǎohóng ma?

B: 1. Jiǔ-sì-bā bā-bā-jiǔ-wǔ.
　　2. Yígòng qī kuài jiǔ máo liù.

V.　　*(A is shopping for a map of China. She picks out an inexpensive one.)*

A: Zhèige jǐ kuài qián?

B: 1. Bā kuài liǎng máo.
　　2. Bābǎi kuài qián.

A: 1. Yǒu piányi yìdiǎnr de ma?
　　2. Tài guì le ma?

B: 1. Yǒu, zhèige jiǔ kuài qián.
　　2. Zhèige sān kuài líng wǔ fēn.

Comparisons

(David and Zhang are taking a break from studying.)

Zhāng:	Zài Měiguó dōngxi guì bú guì?	*Are things in America expensive (or not)?*
David:	Guì. Bǐ Zhōngguó guì.	*They are. More than in China.*
Zhāng:	*(pointing to an item on the desk)*	
	Zhèige zài Měiguó duóshǎo qián?	*How much would this be in America?*
David:	Mmm, kěnéng liù kuài qián, huòzhě qī kuài qián.	*Mmm, perhaps six dollars, or seven dollars.*
Zhāng:	Wa, hǎo guì. Zài Zhōngguó cái yí kuài, yí kuài wǔ.	*Wow, that's expensive. In China it's only one or one and a half dollars.*
	Méi guānxi, Měiguórén dōu hěn yǒuqián.	*It doesn't matter; all Americans are rich.*
David:	Bù, hěn duō Měiguórén dōu méiyǒu qián. Nǐ kàn, wǒ jiù méiyǒu qián le.	*No, lots of Americans don't have any money. Look at me, I don't have any money.*
Zhāng:	*(laughing)*	
	Nǐ shì Měiguórén háishì Zhōngguórén? Wǒ kàn nǐ háishì Zhōngguórén!	*Are you American or Chinese? I think (to my way of looking) you are still Chinese, (after all)!*

Culture notes

Many misconceptions exist in China about the nature of American society, primarily having to do with how materially rich and spiritually bankrupt Americans are. While Chinese typically envy the goods and services available to all in the West, some are wary of Western social values in general and Western morals in particular.

Chinese-Americans, to the Chinese, are Chinese people who happen to be living overseas. The common expectation is that all ethnic Chinese will want to continue to speak the language and follow the customs of the ancestral homeland. If a Chinese-American speaks Chinese well, is savvy of Chinese customs and mores, and overall can behave more or less like any other Chinese person in China, he or she often enjoys (sometimes too much) popularity and respect. On the other hand, Chinese-Americans who have "fallen" entirely into foreign ways are at best treated with tolerance, especially by cosmopolitan people who have had a good deal of contact with foreigners, and at worst with suspicion and some distaste by those who do not regularly interact with foreigners. In any case, Chinese-Americans are hardly ever seen as "real" Americans by the Chinese.

Structure notes

1. Sentence pattern #4: **Subject + Verb + Number + Measure + Noun** (see p. 60) is the basis of many structures involving the use of money. The measures used with money are fēn ($.01), máo ($.10), kuài ($1.00); the noun is qián "money."

Wǒ yǒu wǔ fēn qián.	*I + to have + five + fēn + money*	*I have five cents.*
Zhè shì sān máo qián.	*this + to be + three + máo + money*	*Here are thirty cents.*
Tā yào sānshí kuài qián.	*she + to want + thirty + kuài + money*	*She wants thirty dollars.*

2. Counting with the numeral two is complicated, because in some circumstances the èr changes to liǎng. Consider the following examples.

liǎng kuài qián	*$2.00*
shí'èr kuài qián	*$12.00*
èrshí kuài qián	*$20.00*
èrshí'èr kuài qián	*$22.00*
yìbǎi líng èr kuài qián	*$102.00*
liǎngbǎi kuài qián	*$200.00*
liǎngbǎi èrshí kuài qián	*$220.00*
yìqiān liángbǎi èrshí'èr kuài qián	*$1,222.00*
liǎngqiān kuài qián	*$2,000.00*
liǎngwàn kuài qián	*$20,000.00*

We can generalize that èr changes to liǎng under the following circumstances:

- when the numeral 2 appears as a single digit preceding a measure word (liǎng kuài qián, liǎng gè rén)
- when 2 modifies bǎi, qiān, or wàn, but not shí. Thus: liǎngbǎi, liǎngqiān, liǎngwàn, but èrshí.

In other contexts, such as when counting, in giving dates and telephone numbers, 2 remains èr.

3. There are two ways of asking "How much?" One is Jǐ kuài qián (how many + kuài + money); the other is Duóshǎo qián (how much + money). Duóshǎo qián generally refers to larger sums of money. Jǐ kuài qián specifies "How many kuài?" and is usually used with amounts under $10. To pinpoint "How many cents?" one can use Jǐ máo qián when talking in increments of 10, or Jǐ fēn qián in reference to pennies.

Structure exercise

Please write the amounts on the following price tags in pinyin.

$.25	_____	$1.89	_____
$2.75	_____	$9.99	_____
$10.05	_____	$11.50	_____
$45.75	_____	$222.22	_____
$2,924.00	_____	$3,547.00	_____
$20,000.00	_____	$40,000.00	_____

SEGMENT B
Skill: To specify color, size & shape of objects.

zhèige	*this, this one*
zhège	*this, this one*
nèige	*that, that one*
nàge	*that, that one*

dàxiǎo	*size*
dà (de)	*large*
zhōng (de)	*medium*
xiǎo (de)	*small*

yánse	*color*
hóng (de)	*red*
lán (de)	*blue*
bái (de)	*white*

xíngzhuàng	*shape*
yuán (de)	*round*
fāng (de)	*square*
chángfāng (de)	*rectangular*
sānjiǎo (de)	*triangular*

Nín yào mǎi shénme yàng de?	*What kind would you like to buy?*
Wǒ yào dà de, bái de, yuán de.	*I want a big, white, round one.*
Yánse zěnmeyàng?	*How's the color?*
Dàxiǎo xíng ma?	*Is the size okay?*
Nín yào fāng de háishì yuán de?	*Do you want the square one or the round one?*
Wǒ tīng bu dǒng; qǐng shuō màn yìdiǎnr.	*I don't understand; please speak more slowly.*

Dialogue Practice

The following sets of dialogues presume normal behavior, no unusual circumstances, and no misunderstandings in the contexts indicated. "A" begins the dialogue, "B" responds, "A" responds to "B," etc. Where there is a choice of responses available, please circle the one which is more appropriate.

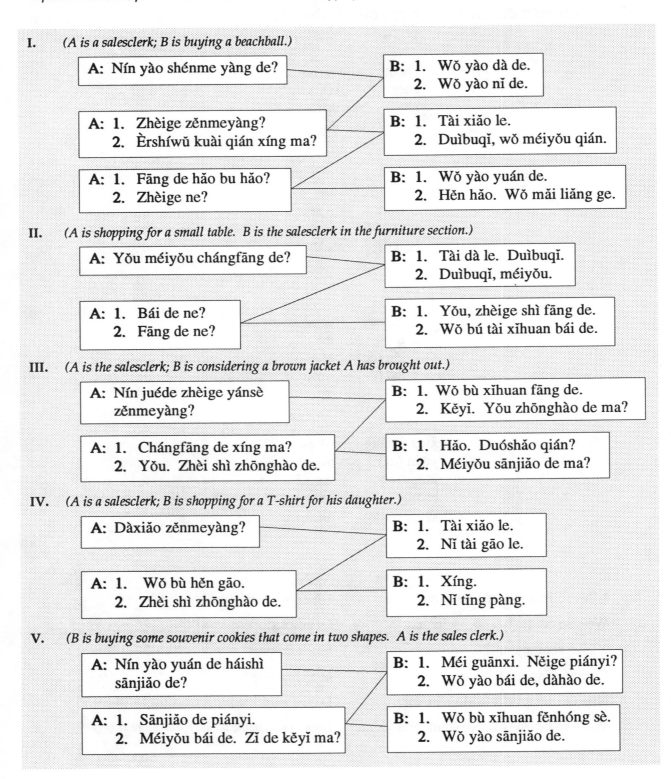

I.   *(A is a salesclerk; B is buying a beachball.)*

A: Nín yào shénme yàng de?

B: 1. Wǒ yào dà de.
   2. Wǒ yào nǐ de.

A: 1. Zhèige zěnmeyàng?
   2. Èrshíwǔ kuài qián xíng ma?

B: 1. Tài xiǎo le.
   2. Duìbuqǐ, wǒ méiyǒu qián.

A: 1. Fāng de hǎo bu hǎo?
   2. Zhèige ne?

B: 1. Wǒ yào yuán de.
   2. Hěn hǎo. Wǒ mǎi liǎng ge.

II.   *(A is shopping for a small table. B is the salesclerk in the furniture section.)*

A: Yǒu méiyǒu chángfāng de?

B: 1. Tài dà le. Duìbuqǐ.
   2. Duìbuqǐ, méiyǒu.

A: 1. Bái de ne?
   2. Fāng de ne?

B: 1. Yǒu, zhèige shì fāng de.
   2. Wǒ bú tài xǐhuan bái de.

III. *(A is the salesclerk; B is considering a brown jacket A has brought out.)*

A: Nín juéde zhèige yánsè zěnmeyàng?

B: 1. Wǒ bù xǐhuan fāng de.
   2. Kěyǐ. Yǒu zhōnghào de ma?

A: 1. Chángfāng de xíng ma?
   2. Yǒu. Zhèi shì zhōnghào de.

B: 1. Hǎo. Duóshǎo qián?
   2. Méiyǒu sānjiǎo de ma?

IV.   *(A is a salesclerk; B is shopping for a T-shirt for his daughter.)*

A: Dàxiǎo zěnmeyàng?

B: 1. Tài xiǎo le.
   2. Nǐ tài gāo le.

A: 1. Wǒ bù hěn gāo.
   2. Zhèi shì zhōnghào de.

B: 1. Xíng.
   2. Nǐ tǐng pàng.

V.   *(B is buying some souvenir cookies that come in two shapes. A is the sales clerk.)*

A: Nín yào yuán de háishì sānjiǎo de?

B: 1. Méi guānxi. Něige piányi?
   2. Wǒ yào bái de, dàhào de.

A: 1. Sānjiǎo de piányi.
   2. Méiyǒu bái de. Zǐ de kěyǐ ma?

B: 1. Wǒ bù xǐhuan fěnhóng sè.
   2. Wǒ yào sānjiǎo de.

A new baby

(Li and three of her roommates are chatting in their dorm room.)

Lǐ:	Wú Xiānlíng shēngle yí ge xiǎo wáwa.	*Wu Xianling has had a baby.*
Roommate 1:	Shì nán de háishì nǚ de?	*Is it a boy or a girl?*
Roommate 2:	Nǚ de. Sān diǎnr wǔ gōngjīn.	*A girl. Three point five kilograms.*
Lǐ:	Liǎn yuányuán de, yǎnjīng hěn dà, xiǎo hóng zuǐbā. Zhēn hǎowánr.	*(Her) face is roundish, (her) eyes are large, (she has a) small, red mouth. (She's) really cute.*
Roommate 3:	Yǒu yí wèi Yīngwén lǎoshī yě shēngle ge wáwa— hóng tóufa de.	*There is an English teacher who has just had a baby too—with red hair.*
Roommate 1:	Hóng tóufa?	*Red hair?*
Roommate 3:	Shì. Hóng tóufa, lǜ yǎnjing. Fāngfāng de liǎn dàdà de yǎnjing. Yě hěn hǎowánr.	*That's right. Red hair and green eyes. (It's got) a square face and large, large eyes. It's very cute too.*
Roommate 1:	Zhēnde ma?	*Really?*

Nǐ bù juéde wǒmen hěn hǎowánr ma?

Culture notes

A round or oval face, large, bright eyes, a small, well-formed nose, and small, red lips are characteristic of a charming child as well as a beautiful adult woman. Large eyes, dark, dense eyebrows, a full forehead, and a straight nose mark male beauty.

Structure notes

1. <u>Dà, xiǎo, yuán</u>, and the colors are **adjectives**, and can be used in pattern #2: **Subject + (hěn) + Adjective**. Thus:

Zhèige dōngxi hěn dà.	*this + ge + thing + very + to be big*	*This thing is very big.*
Nèige dōngxi yě bù xiǎo.	*that + ge + thing + also + not + too + to be small*	*That thing is not too small, either.*
Nǐ de liǎn hěn yuán.	*your + face + very + to be round*	*Your face is very round.*
Nǐ de liǎn yě hěn hóng.	*your + face + also + very + to be red*	*Your face is also very red.*

2. When words describing size, color, and shape are used to modify nouns, they are followed by the particle <u>de</u>.

Wǒ yào yí ge hóng de qìqiú.	*I + to want + one + ge + to be red + de + balloon*	*I want a red balloon.*
Wǒ yào yí ge dà de qìqiú.	*I + to want + one + ge + to be big + de + balloon*	*I want a big balloon.*

When the noun is stated, the <u>de</u> may also sometimes be omitted without affecting the meaning of the sentence:

Wǒ yào yí ge hóng qìqiú.	*I + to want + one + ge + to be red + balloon*	*I want a red balloon.*
Wǒ yào yí ge dà qìqiú.	*I + to want + one + ge + to be big + balloon*	*I want a big balloon.*

If however, the noun is omitted (because previous reference has been made to it), then the <u>de</u> must be retained.

Wǒ yào hóng de.	*I + to want + to be red + de*	*I want a red one.*
Wǒ yào dà de.	*I + to want + to be big + de*	*I want a big one.*

3. <u>Zhèi</u> "this," <u>nèi</u> "that," and <u>něi</u> "which" are **specifiers**, and appear in the following pattern:

4a. Subject + Verb + Specifier + (Number) + Measure + Noun

Wǒ xǐhuān nèi sān ge rén.	*I + to like + that + three + ge + person*	*I like those three people.*
Tāmen mǎile zhèi wǔ ge qìqiú.	*they + to buy + that + five + ge + balloon*	*They bought these five balloons.*

If a number is not stated, it is understood to be "one," and the phrase refers to the singular (except when the plural marker <u>xiē</u> is used; see Unit 5c).

Wǒ xǐhuān nèige rén.	*I + to like + that + ge + person*	*I like that person.*
Tā mǎile zhèige qìqiú.	*he + to buy + this + ge + balloon*	*He bought this balloon.*

4. The phrase **Number + Measure + Noun** can be used either as the subject or the object of the verb. Thus:

(as subject)

Zhèi wǔ ge qìqiú zuì hǎo. *this + five + ge + balloon +*   *These five balloons are the best.*
                                     most + to be good

(as object)

Wǒ yào zhèi ge qìqiú.   *I + to want + this + ge +*   *I want this balloon.*
                                     balloon

5. Zhèige and nèige are sometimes used as "pause fillers," while the speaker gropes for a word or a phrase. A speaker might say "Wǒ xiǎng zhèige, zhèige..hóng qìqiú tài..zhèige, zhèige..dà le" *(I think this..er, red balloon is too..er, er..big).*   Of course, fillers should not be overused in normal conversation.

Structure exercise

Fill in the blanks in the monologue below, based on the English translation. It is spoken by a elderly lady on her way to a toy store.

Wǒ xiǎng mǎi qìqiú. Wǒ yào _____, _____, _____.

_____ qìqiú hěn guì; sān kuài qián yí ge. _____ qìqiú piányi yìdiǎnr; yí

kuài wǔ yí ge. Bù zhīdao yǒu méi yǒu _____? Míngtiān wǒ de,

_____, zhízi *(nephew)* guò shēngri. Tā shí'èr _____. Suǒyǐ wǒ yào

mǎi _____ qìqiú. Wǒ yào liù ge _____, liù ge _____.

Wǒ juéde _____ zuì _____, kěshì wǒ zhízi xǐhuan

_____. Suǒyǐ wǒ liǎng yàng dōu mǎi. Bù zhīdao yígòng duóshǎo qián?

I think I'll buy (some) balloons. I want red ones, blue ones, and white ones. Big balloons are expensive; they are three dollars each. Small balloons are a little cheaper, a dollar fifty each. I wonder if they have big ones? Tomorrow my, er, nephew has a birthday. He'll be twelve. So I'll buy twelve balloons. I want six big ones and six little ones. I think little ones are best, but my nephew likes big ones. So I'll buy both kinds. I wonder how much it'll cost altogether?

Yào mǎi shénme?

Zhèr shénme dōu mài!

SEGMENT C

Skill: To request a specific number of some common objects.

Wǒ yào mǎi (yí)ge _____.	*I want to buy a _____.*
Wǒ yào mǎi yìxiē _____	*I want to buy some _____.*
Nǐmen mài _____ ma?	*Do you sell _____?*

hézi	*box(es)*
píngzi	*bottle(s)*
dàizi	*bag(s)*
qiú	*ball(s)*
wánjù	*toy(s)*

Wǒ yào mǎi _____.	*I want to buy _____.*

yì duǒ huā.	*a flower.*
yì běn shū.	*a book.*
yí fènr bàozhǐ.	*a newspaper.*
yì zhāng huàr.	*a painting.*
yí kuài táng.	*a piece of candy.*
yì tiáo shéngzi.	*a rope.*
yìxiē dōngxi.	*some things.*

Wǒ yào sòng péngyou de.	*I want (it) to give to a friend.*
Wǒ jízhe yào.	*I need (it) in a hurry.*
Nǐ yào mǎi jǐ yàng dōngxi?	*How many things do you have to buy?*
Nǐ yào mǎi jǐ ge?	*How many do you want?*
Nín zhǎo shénme?	*What are you looking for?*
Nǐ (shì) zhǎo Zhōngwén shū ma?	*Are you looking for Chinese books?*
Nǐ (shì) sònggěi shéi de?	*Who are you giving (it) to?*

Dialogue Practice

The following sets of dialogues presume normal behavior, no unusual circumstances, and no misunderstandings in the contexts indicated. "A" begins the dialogue, "B" responds, "A" responds to "B," etc. Where there is a choice of responses available, please circle the one which is more appropriate.

I. *(A is shopping for some toys. B is the salesclerk.)*

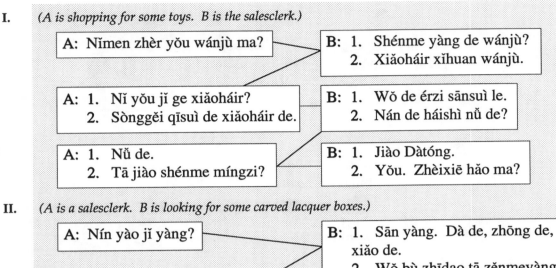

A: Nǐmen zhèr yǒu wánjù ma?

B: 1. Shénme yàng de wánjù?
    2. Xiǎoháir xǐhuan wánjù.

A: 1. Nǐ yǒu jǐ ge xiǎoháir?
    2. Sònggěi qīsuì de xiǎoháir de.

B: 1. Wǒ de érzi sānsuì le.
    2. Nán de háishì nǚ de?

A: 1. Nǚ de.
    2. Tā jiào shénme míngzi?

B: 1. Jiào Dàtóng.
    2. Yǒu. Zhèixiē hǎo ma?

II. *(A is a salesclerk. B is looking for some carved lacquer boxes.)*

A: Nín yào jǐ yàng?

B: 1. Sān yàng. Dà de, zhōng de, xiǎo de.
    2. Wǒ bù zhīdao tā zěnmeyàng.

A: 1. Yánsè yǒu guānxi ma?
    2. Nǐ yào píngzi háishi hézi?

B: 1. Píngzi gēn shéngzi.
    2. Méi guānxi. Dōu kěyǐ.

III. *(A and B are friends walking home after class.)*

A: Wǒ děi mǎi yìxiē dōngxi.

B: 1. Xiǎoháir dōu xǐhuan qiú.
    2. Nǐ yào mǎi shénme?

A: 1. Qiú háishì huàr?
    2. Yí ge dàizi, yí ge hézi.

B: 1. Wǒ gēn nǐ yíkuàir qù mǎi.
    2. Táng dōu shì hóngsè de.

IV. *(A and B are friends strolling together in a shopping district.)*

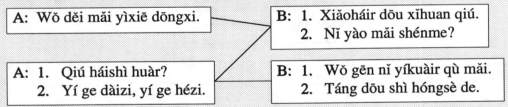

A: Nǐ bú shì yào mǎi bàozhǐ ma?

B: 1. Duì. Bàozhǐ zài nǎr?
    2. Bàozhǐ shì hēi-bái de.

A: 1. Zài nàr. Duóshao qián yí fènr?
    2. Méiyǒu hóng shéngzi ma?

B: 1. Zhèi tiáo shéngzi hěn cháng.
    2. Qī máo wǔ.

V. *(B is browsing in a gift store. A is the salesclerk.)*

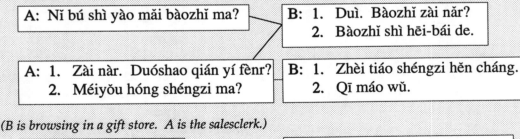

A: Nín zhǎo shénme?

B: 1. Nǐmen zhèr mài huār ma?
    2. Wǒ bù zhīdao tā shì shéi.

A: 1. Méiyǒu huār. Táng xíng ma?
    2. Tā zài mài huār.

B: 1. Sān duǒ hóng huār.
    2. Hǎo. Wǒ mǎi yì hé táng.

A gift for the baby

(David, Zhang, Li, and their friends are discussing buying a gift for Wu Xianling's new baby.)

Friend 1:	Mǎi yì hé táng gěi xīn māma.	*(We could) buy a box of candy for the new mother.*
Lǐ:	Tā bú yào táng. Gòu pàng le.	*She doesn't want candy. She's fat enough.*
David:	*(laughing)*	
	Táng gěi xiǎoháir chī ba.	*Let the child eat the candy.*
Lǐ:	Xiǎoháir hái bú huì chī táng ne!	*The child doesn't know how to each candy yet!*
Friend 2:	Mǎi jǐ yàng wánjù gěi xiǎoháir ba.	*Let's buy a few toys for the child.*
Lǐ:	Zài mǎi jǐ zhī xiān huā gěi mǔqīn.	*And a few fresh flowers for the mother.*
Zhang:	Hǎo! Jiù zhème bàn.	*Fine! Let's do it that way.*

Culture notes

The birth of a new baby sets off a flurry of activities on the part of family and friends of the arrival. In Southern China, gifts of food from the new parents or grandparents announce the birth. Everywhere, gifts of money, nourishing foods, clothing, or miscellaneous items for both mother and child are given. A gift of fresh flowers is an innovation borrowed from the West.

Two cautions regarding gift-giving in Taiwan: a gift of a clock or an umbrella is never appropriate. The Chinese word for "clock"—zhōng—is homophonous with the word for "death," while the word for "umbrella"—sǎn—sounds like the word for "parting" or "to separate"—sàn. Since these are unpleasant events, the gift of a clock or an umbrella are thought to portend misfortune.

Structure notes

1. Sentence pattern #4, **Subject + Verb + Number + Measure + Noun (see p. 60)**, forms the basis of the expressions in this lesson. **Measure words** are a characteristic of Chinese (and some other Asian languages). English uses measure words to some extent. One speaks of a <u>sheet</u> of paper, a <u>stick</u> of gum, a <u>piece</u> of candy, a <u>nugget</u> of gold, a <u>herd</u> of cattle, a <u>flock</u> of birds, a <u>school</u> of fish, a <u>horde</u> of people, a <u>bevy</u> of beauties, etc.

Chinese goes the distance on measure words. EVERY measured noun is marked by a measure word, and the measure word must be used whenever a number of units of the noun is stated or implied. Thus the measure word is not necessary when one speaks of humanity in general (<u>rén</u>), but is required in speaking of a number of people (<u>liǎng ge rén</u>). The measure word is unnecessary for books in general (<u>shū</u>), but must be used when referring to a certain book (<u>nǐde nèi běn shū</u>) or number of books (<u>zhèi sì běn shū</u>).

2. <u>Ge</u> and <u>xiē</u> are "general use" measures. <u>Ge</u> applies to a variety of nouns (including people); it marks a singular noun, or a specified number of the noun. <u>Xiē</u> marks the plural form of any noun, where the number is not specified. Thus:

yí ge rén	*one + ge + person*	*one person, a person*
sān ge rén	*three + ge + person*	*three people*
yìxiē rén	*one + xie + person*	*some people*

3. Some nouns take special measures. <u>Zhāng</u> marks objects with a flat surface, such as paper, paintings, maps, tables, chairs. <u>Běn</u> marks books. <u>Kuài</u> marks a piece or a segment of something that has been divided off from the whole, such as a piece of cloth, a piece of candy, a slice of watermelon, a chunk of meat, a unit of money, a piece of land. <u>Tiáo</u> marks long, winding things, such as rope, belts, neckties, rivers, roads, snakes, and inexplicably, cows. <u>Duǒ</u> marks flowers and clouds. <u>Fèn</u> marks material assembled together in a set, thus—newspapers, magazines, examinations, reports, etc.

These special measures should be learned together with the noun. If you are talking with a native speaker of Chinese and are unsure of which special measure to use with a specific noun, it would be safer to use <u>ge</u>: although <u>ge</u> may be wrong, it would be less jarring in conversation than the incorrect use of a special measure.

4. Basic sentence pattern #8 is as follows:

> ## 8. Subject + (shì) + adjunct + Verb + de
> or
> ## Subject + (shì) + Verb + adjunct + de

The **ADJUNCT** is any phrase that describes **time, place, purpose, agent, beneficiary** etc. of a specific action—in other words, the *circumstances under which* an action occurred. For example, if the basic action is tā lái le (he came), the examples below the adjuncts (underlined) that could describe some circumstances under which the action took place.

Tā shì zuótiān lái de.	he + shì + yesterday + to come + de	He came yesterday.
Tā shì gēn tā jiějie yíkuàr lái de.	he + shì + with + his + sister + together + to come + de	He came with his sister.
Tā shì kàn wǒ lái de.	he + shì + to see + me + to come + de	He came to see me.
Tā shì qí chē lái de.	he + shì + to ride + vehicle + to come + de	He came by bicycle.

In this lesson, the action involves shopping for some items, and the shì..de sentences used describe the **purpose** of the action. (The parentheses around shì in the pattern above indicate that its use is optional.)

Wǒ yào sòng péngyou de.	I + to want to + to present to + friend + de	I want it to give (as a present) to a friend.
Nǐ shì sònggěi shéi de?	You + shi + to present to + for + who + de	To whom are you giving this?

Structure exercise

The following is a monologue by a store-keeper as she adds up the purchases of a customer. Please write one appropriate word in each blank. The customer has bought flowers, bags, books, a newspaper, rope, and paintings.

Liǎng duǒ _____ wǔ kuài qián; yí_____ hóng dàizi, dà de, sān kuài qián; yí_____ hóng dàizi, xiǎo de, liǎng kuài qián; yī, èr, sān běn _____, yígòng shí kuài qián; yí fèn _____ wǔ máo qián; liǎng tiáo _____ sān kuài liǎng _____ wǔ; háiyǒu wǔ zhāng _____, yí kuài qián yì zhāng; yígòng shì èrshí _____ kuài qī máo wǔ.

Qǐng nǐ shuō shuō wǒmen shéi yīfu chuān de zuì hǎokàn?

SEGMENT D
Skill: To request specific items of clothing.

Wǒ chuān _____. *I wear/ am wearing _____.*

yīfu	*clothing*
(yí jiàn) chènshān.	*a shirt, blouse.*
(yí jiàn) T-xù shān.	*a T-shirt.*
(yì tiáo) kùzi.	*(a pair of) pants.*
(yì tiáo) chángkù.	*(a pair of) long pants.*
(yì tiáo) duǎnkù.	*(a pair of) shorts.*
(yì tiáo) niúzǎikù.	*(a pair of) blue-jeans.*
(yì tiáo) qúnzi.	*a skirt.*
(yí jiàn) máoyī.	*a sweater*
(yí jiàn) jiákè.	*a jacket.*
(yì shuāng) wàzi.	*(a pair of) socks.*
(yì shuāng) xiézi.	*(a pair of) shoes.*
(yì shuāng) liángxié.	*(a pair of) sandals.*
(yì shuāng) tuōxié.	*(a pair of) slippers.*

dàhào (de)   *large (size)*

zhōnghào (de)   *medium (size)*

xiǎohào (de)   *small (size)*

Nǐ chuān shénme?	*What are you wearing?*
Nèitiáo kùzi héshì ma?	*Does that pair of pants fit?*
Dàxiǎo héshì ma?	*Is the size okay (appropriate)?*
Nǐ chuān jǐ hào de?	*What size do you wear?*
Bā hào xíng ma?	*Is size eight okay?*
Wǒ de jiákè hǎokàn ma?	*Does my jacket look good?*
Chènshān duóshao qián?	*How much are the shirts?*
Nǐ yào chángkù yào duǎnkù?	*Do you want long pants or shorts?*

Dialogue Practice

The following sets of dialogues presume normal behavior, no unusual circumstances, and no misunderstandings in the contexts indicated. "A" begins the dialogue, "B" responds, "A" responds to "B," etc. Where there is a choice of responses available, please circle the more appropriate one.

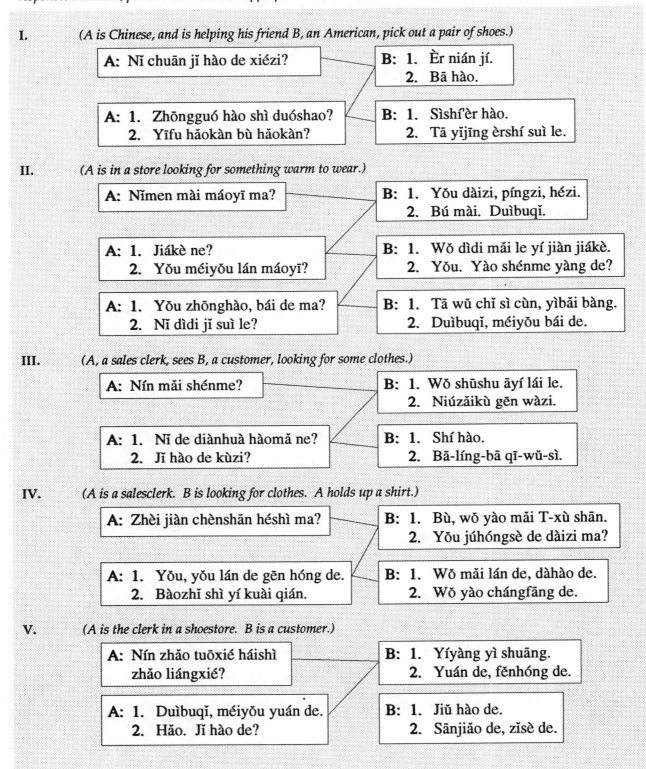

I.   *(A is Chinese, and is helping his friend B, an American, pick out a pair of shoes.)*

A: Nǐ chuān jǐ hào de xiézi?

B: 1. Èr nián jí.
    2. Bā hào.

A: 1. Zhōngguó hào shì duóshao?
    2. Yīfu hǎokàn bù hǎokàn?

B: 1. Sìshí'èr hào.
    2. Tā yǐjīng èrshí suì le.

II.   *(A is in a store looking for something warm to wear.)*

A: Nǐmen mài máoyī ma?

B: 1. Yǒu dàizi, píngzi, hézi.
    2. Bú mài. Duìbuqǐ.

A: 1. Jiákè ne?
    2. Yǒu méiyǒu lán máoyī?

B: 1. Wǒ dìdi mǎi le yí jiàn jiákè.
    2. Yǒu. Yào shénme yàng de?

A: 1. Yǒu zhōnghào, bái de ma?
    2. Nǐ dìdi jǐ suì le?

B: 1. Tā wǔ chǐ sì cùn, yìbǎi bàng.
    2. Duìbuqǐ, méiyǒu bái de.

III.   *(A, a sales clerk, sees B, a customer, looking for some clothes.)*

A: Nín mǎi shénme?

B: 1. Wǒ shūshu āyí lái le.
    2. Niúzǎikù gēn wàzi.

A: 1. Nǐ de diànhuà hàomǎ ne?
    2. Jǐ hào de kùzi?

B: 1. Shí hào.
    2. Bā-líng-bā qī-wǔ-sì.

IV.   *(A is a salesclerk. B is looking for clothes. A holds up a shirt.)*

A: Zhèi jiàn chènshān héshì ma?

B: 1. Bù, wǒ yào mǎi T-xù shān.
    2. Yǒu júhóngsè de dàizi ma?

A: 1. Yǒu, yǒu lán de gēn hóng de.
    2. Bàozhǐ shì yí kuài qián.

B: 1. Wǒ mǎi lán de, dàhào de.
    2. Wǒ yào chángfāng de.

V.   *(A is the clerk in a shoestore. B is a customer.)*

A: Nín zhǎo tuōxié háishì zhǎo liángxié?

B: 1. Yíyàng yì shuāng.
    2. Yuán de, fěnhóng de.

A: 1. Duìbuqǐ, méiyǒu yuán de.
    2. Hǎo. Jǐ hào de?

B: 1. Jiǔ hào de.
    2. Sānjiǎo de, zǐsè de.

Wash day

(Li Zhongying, her sister Li Zhongxiu, and an aunt from out of town are taking the daily laundry off the clothesline in their courtyard.)

Aunt:	Zhōngxiū, zhè shì nǐ de T-xù shān ma?	*Zhongxiu, is this your T-shirt?*
Zhōngxiū:	Bù, nèi jiàn lán de shì wǒ de.	*No, the blue one is mine.*
Aunt:	Zhèi jiàn fěnhóng de bú shì nǐ de ma?	*Isn't this pink one yours?*
Zhōngxiū:	Fěnhóng de? O, duì, fěnhóng de yě shì wǒ de.	*The pink one? Oh yes, the pink one is mine too.*
Lǐ:	*(laughing)*	
	Tā de yīfu tài duō le, dōu jì bù qīng la.	*She really has a lot of clothes; she can't keep track of them.*
Zhōngxiū:	Bù, bù, jiějie de yīfu bǐ wǒ duō. Māma jìng gěi tā mǎi hǎo yīfu. Nǐ kàn, niúzǎikù, duǎnkù, qúnzi, chènshān, dōu shì jiějie de.	*No, no; elder sister has more clothes than I do. Mom is always buying nice clothes for her. Look, the jeans, the shorts, the skirt, the shirt, they're all hers.*
Lǐ:	Nǎr de huà! Zhè bú shì nǐ de qúnzi ma? Zhèi tiáo chángkù, yī, èr, sān jiàn T-xù shān...Nǐ de yīfu hái bú gòu ma?	*What are you talking about! Isn't this your skirt? These pants, one, two, three T-shirts... Don't you have enough clothes?*
Aunt:	Hǎo le hǎo le, bié chǎo le. Yīfu duō jiù zěnmeyàng? Jiù bǐ biérén qiáng ma?	*Enough, enough, stop quarreling. So what if a person has a lot of clothes? Does that make her better than someone else?*

Culture notes

School-age children in Chinese communities are encouraged to make sure that they are clean and neat, but beyond that not to pay too much attention to physical appearance. Most schools through the secondary level and even some universities require that their students wear school uniforms. Excessive interest in clothing, as the sisters above demonstrate, is considered unhealthy—and the aunt's remonstration is typical.

Structure notes

1. Pants and skirts take the measure tiáo (for long and winding things); shirts, sweaters, jackets, coats etc. take the measure jiàn. Shuāng, meaning "double, twin, two, a pair," is the measure for things which come in pairs: shoes, socks, slippers, etc. (An exception is glasses: yí fù yǎnjìng.)

2. Héshì is an adjective, and as such can be used in pattern #2 **Subject + (hěn) + adjective** (see p. 28).

    Zhèijiàn chènshān hěn héshì. *this + jian + shirt + very + to be fitting*   *This shirt fits very well.*

3. Adjectives denoting opposites sometimes combine to form the abstract quality for which they signify opposing extremes:

dàxiǎo	*to be big + to be small*	*size*
chángduǎn	*to be long + to be short*	*length*

4. Repeating the verb phrase is the same as using háishì in an "either/or" question:

    Nǐ yào chángkù yào duǎnkù?   *you + to want + long pants + to want + short pants*   *Do you want long pants or shorts?*

    Nǐ yào chángkù háishì yào duǎnkù?   *you + to want + long pants+ or + to want + short pants*   *Do you want long pants or shorts?*

Structure exercise

Fill in each blank below with an appropriate word, based on the English equivalent. The questions are asked by a pesky but well-meaning new acquaintance, who is helping you with your shopping.

Nín jué_____ zhèi _____ chènshān zěnmeyàng? Yánsè

_____ bù hǎo? Dàxiǎo héshì _____? Jiàqián *(price)* _____?

Bú _____ guì le ba? Nín hái yào _____ shénme? Hái yào mǎi kùzi

_____? Yào chángkù _____ duǎnkù? Yào mǎi jǐ _____? Yào

_____ yánsè de? Bái sè _____ hǎo ma? Huī sè de _____? Nín

xǐhuan huī_____ ma? Kùzi wǔshí kuài qián yì_____ kěyǐ ma? Nín

háiyào mǎi shénme ma?

What do you think of this shirt? How's the color? Is the size all right? How's the price? It isn't too expensive, is it? What else would you like to buy? Do you want to buy some pants? Would you like long pants or short? How many pairs do you want? What color do you want? How about white ones? What about grey ones? Do you like the color grey? Would fifty dollars a pair for pants be all right? Would you like to buy anything else?

SEGMENT E
Skill: To request a different item than the one presented, specifying size, color, price & quantity.

Zhèige bùxíng.   *This one won't do.*

Qǐng gěi wǒ ＿＿ de.   *Please give me one that is ＿＿.*

dà yìdiǎnr *bigger* xiǎo yìdiǎnr *smaller*	cháng yìdiǎnr *longer* duǎn yìdiǎnr *shorter*
hòu yìdiǎnr *thicker , heavier (as in clothing)* báo yìdiǎnr *thinner, lighter (as in clothing)*	
	zhòng yìdiǎnr *heavier* qīng yìdiǎr *lighter*
yánsè qiǎn yìdiǎnr *lighter in color* yánsè shēn yìdiǎnr *darker in color*	cū yìdiǎnr *thicker, rougher* xì yìdiǎnr *finer, smoother*
hǎo yìdiǎnr *better*	piányi yìdiǎnr *cheaper* guì yìdiǎnr *more expensive*

Wǒ yào xīn de.   *I want a new one.*

Zhèige shì jiù de.   *This is (an) old (one).*

Qǐng nǐ duō gěi wǒ jǐ ge.   *Please give me a few more.*

Qǐng nǐ zài gěi wǒ yí ge.   *Please give me another one.*

Gòu le, xièxie.   *That's enough, thank you.*

Yǒu méi yǒu dà yìdiǎnr de?   *Do you have anything bigger?*

Qǐng zhǎo yí ge xīn de gěi wǒ.   *Please find me a new one.*

Dialogue Practice

The following sets of dialogues presume normal behavior, no unusual circumstances, and no misunderstandings in the contexts indicated. "A" begins the dialogue, "B" responds, "A" responds to "B," etc. Where there is a choice of responses available, please circle the one which is more appropriate.

I.   (*A is a salesclerk helping B, a customer, with a selection of pants.*)

> A: Zhèi tiáo kùzi zěnmeyàng?
>
> B: 1. Liángxié huòzhe wàzi.
>   2. Tài cháng le.
>
> A: 1. Qǐng duō gěi wǒ jǐ ge.
>   2. Zhèi tiáo duǎn yìdiǎnr.
>
> B: 1. Háishì tài cháng.
>   2. Méiyǒu zhòng yìdiǎnr de ma?
>
> A: 1. Wáng Xiǎoméi yào yì tiáo.
>   2. Zhèi tiáo ne?
>
> B: 1. Wáng Xiǎoméi tài pàng le.
>   2. Nnng. Zhèi tiáo héshì.

II.   (*A and B are husband and wife on a shopping expedition. He picks up a large white box.*)

> A: Zhèige hézi bú cuò, kěshì tài zhòng le yìdiǎnr.
>
> B: 1. Mǎi xiǎo de ba. Xiǎo de qīng.
>   2. Yánsè hěn hǎo, bú tài qiǎn.
>
> A: 1. Nǐ búshì xǐhuan guì de ma?
>   2. Mm, tài qīng le.
>
> B: 1. Ai, nǐ bié mǎi hézi le.
>   2. Wǒ bú yào jiù de, yào xīn de.

III. (*B is browsing in a hardware store. A is the salesclerk.*)

> A: Nín mǎi shénme?
>
> B: 1. Wǒ zhǎo yì tiáo shéngzi.
>   2. Tài báo le. Wǒ yào hòu de.
>
> A: 1. Yánsè shēn de bù xíng ma?
>   2. Cū de háishì xì de?
>
> B: 1. Cū yìdiǎnr de.
>   2. Wǒ yào dàdà de.

IV.   (*A and B are friends out shopping. A is trying to decide about a sweater.*)

> A: Nǐ juéde zhèi jiàn máoyī zěnmeyàng?
>
> B: 1. Hái kěyǐ. Tǐng hòu.
>   2. Mǎi. Dōu tǐng hòu de.
>
> A: 1. Yánsè ne? Tài qiǎn le ma?
>   2. Jiákè ma? Zhèr yǒu liǎng jiàn.
>
> B: 1. Yánsè qiǎn yìdiǎnr hǎokàn.
>   2. Gòu le. Xièxie.

V.   (*A is B's older sister, and is visiting B at school.*)

> A: Nǐ de xiézi tài jiù le. Qù mǎi yì shuāng xīn de ba.
>
> B: 1. Wàzi dōu tǐng piányi.
>   2. Tài guì le.
>
> A: 1. Wǒ mǎi yì shuāng gěi nǐ. Nǐ xǐhuan shénme yàng de?
>   2. Cū de yě hǎo, xì de yě hǎo.
>
> B: 1. Bù, zhēn de tài guì le. Bié mǎi le.
>   2. Bù, zhòng yìdiǎnr de hǎo.

Getting dressed

(Li Zhongying is helping her sister get dressed for a school excursion into the mountains.)

Sister:	Jiějie, wǒ chuān zhèi tiáo kùzi hǎo bù hǎo?
	Sister, what if I wear this pair of pants?
Lǐ:	Nèi tiáo tài báo le. Chuān hòu yìdiǎnr de hǎo.
	That pair is too thin. It would be better to wear something thicker.
Sister:	Wǒ bú yào hòu de. Yàoburán wǒ jiù chuān duǎnkù ba.
	I don't want a thick pair. Or else maybe I can wear shorts.
Lǐ:	Duǎnkù tài lěng le, Xiǎomèi. Nǐ háishì chuān niúzǎikù hǎo.
	Shorts would be too cold (cool), little sister. You'd best wear jeans.
Sister:	Wǒ de niúzǎikù tài duǎn le, wǒ bù xiǎng chuān. Wǒ yào chuān yánse qiǎn yìdiǎnr de kùzi hé bái chènshān.
	My jeans are too short; I don't feel like wearing them. I want to wear light colored pants and a white shirt.
Lǐ:	Nǐ de pífū zhème bái, yòu chuān qiǎn sè de kùzi hé bái chènshān, xiàng guǐ yíyàng!
	Your skin is so fair; if you wear light pants and a white shirt on top of that, you'll look like a ghost!
Sister:	*(pouting)* Jiějie bié kāi wǒ de wánxiào.
	Don't make fun of me, sister.
Lǐ:	*(laughing)* Hǎo ba. Nǐ chuān nǐ de ba. Wǒ bù guǎn nǐ le.
	Fine. You wear what you want. I won't bother with you anymore.
Sister:	Jiějie! Nǐ bié zǒu! Wǒ chuān niúzǎikù.
	Sister! Don't leave! I'll wear jeans.
Lǐ:	Nǐ bú shì shuō tài duǎn le ma?
	Didn't you say they were too short?
Sister:	Duǎn yìdiǎnr méi guānxi. Jiù zěnmeyàng?
	It doesn't matter if they are a little short. So what?
Lǐ:	Nà hǎo ba. Nǐ chuān shénme chènshān?
	Fine, then. What shirt will you wear?
Sister:	Hóng de, hǎo bù hǎo?
	The red one, okay?
Lǐ:	Hǎo!
	Fine!

Culture notes

Chinese children receive a fair amount of pampering at home. As a result, they are generally less independent and more compliant than their American counterparts. In this episode, Li is afraid the outfit her sister has selected is inappropriate—not warm enough—for the excursion. She puts some indirect pressure on her sister to accept her recommendation. "Well-brought-up" children will sooner or later come around to the older person's point of view.

Structure notes

1. Regarding sentence pattern #2 **Subject + (hěn) + Adjective** (<u>Tā hěn gāo</u>) (see p. 28), it was mentioned that the <u>hěn</u> has very little meaning. <u>Hěn</u> by itself means "very," but in most of these sentences does not carry much of that meaning: rather, it serves merely to ground the sentence in a non-comparative mode. That is to say, if <u>hěn</u> were not there, the sentence would imply a comparison.

Tā hěn gāo.	*she + <u>hěn</u> + to be tall*	*She is tall.*
Tā gāo.	*she + to be tall*	*She is taller.*
Zhèi jiàn chènshān hěn héshì.	*this + <u>jiàn</u> + shirt + <u>hěn</u> + to be suitable*	*This shirt fits fine.*
Zhèi jiàn chènshān héshì.	*this + <u>jiàn</u> + shirt + to be suitable*	*This shirt fits better.*

2. Adding <u>yìdiǎnr</u> to a comparative phrase carries the meaning "a little more (adjective);" adding <u>de duō</u> would mean "much more (adjective)."

13. Subject + Adjective + yìdiǎnr/de duō

Tā gāo yìdiǎnr.	*she + to be tall + a little*	*She's a little taller.*
Nǐ ǎi de duō.	*you + to be short + by much*	*You are much shorter.*
Zhèi jiàn chènshān héshì yìdiǎnr.	*this + <u>jiàn</u> + shirt + to be suitable + a little*	*This shirt fits a little better.*
Nèi jiàn chènshān héshì de duō.	*that + <u>jiàn</u> + shirt + to be suitable + by much*	*That shirt fits much better.*

3. In the sentence <u>Wǒ yào dà yìdiǎnr de</u>, the noun that is understood to follow <u>de</u> has been left out. If the interaction involved shirts, for instance, the full form of the sentence would be <u>Wǒ yào dà yìdiǎnr de chènshān</u>. The phrase pattern that applies to this sentence, involving the use of <u>de</u> between an adjective and the noun it modifies, has been discussed previously in connection with colors (see Unit 5b). It is as follows:

Adjective (yìdiǎnr) + de + Noun

báisè de kùzi	*to be white (color) + <u>de</u> + pants*	*white pants*
hěn hǎo de xiézi	*very + to be good + <u>de</u> + shoes*	*very good shoes*
dà yìdiǎnr de chènshān	*to be big + a little + <u>de</u> + shirt*	*a shirt that is a little bigger*
xīn de qúnzi	*to be new + <u>de</u> + skirt*	*a new skirt*

When the adjective used consists of only one syllable, and it does not occur with <u>hěn</u> or <u>yìdiǎnr</u>, the phrase is usually abbreviated and the <u>de</u> left off.

bái kùzi	*to be white + pants*	*white pants*
hǎo xiézi	*to be good + shoes*	*good shoes*
dà chènshān	*to be big + shirt*	*a big shirt*
xīn qúnzi	*to be new + skirt*	*a new skirt*

Structure exercise

Write Chinese equivalents of the sentences below.

Wǒ yào mǎi yí jiàn chènshān.   *I want to buy a shirt.*

_____   *I want to buy a big shirt.*

_____   *I want to buy a very big shirt.*

_____   *I want to buy a bigger shirt.*

SEGMENT A
Skill: To provide & obtain preferences in colors

yánsè	*color*
hóng (sè)	*(the color) red*
lán (sè)	*(the color) blue*
lǜ (sè)	*(the color) green*
huáng (sè)	*(the color) yellow*
júhóng (sè)	*(the color) orange*
fěnhóng (sè)	*(the color) pink*
kāfēi (sè)	*(the color) brown, coffee-colored*
zǐ (sè)	*(the color) purple*
hēi (sè)	*(the color) black*
bái (sè)	*(the color) white*
huī (sè)	*(the color) grey*
jīn (sè)	*(the color) gold*
yín (sè)	*(the color) silver*

xǐhuan	*to like*
bù xǐhuan	*to dislike*
ài	*to love*
tǎoyàn	*to hate*

Duì le.	*That's right*
Bú duì.	*That's not right.*

Nǐ xǐhuan shénme yánsè?	*What color do you like?*
Nǐ xǐhuan hóngsè ma?	*Do you like red?*
Shì shénme yánsè de?	*What color is it?*
Hóngsè hǎo <u>háishì</u> lánsè hǎo?	*Which is better, red <u>or</u> blue?*

Dialogue Practice

The following sets of dialogues presume normal behavior, no unusual circumstances, and no misunderstandings in the contexts indicated. "A" begins the dialogue, "B" responds, "A" responds to "B," etc. Where there is a choice of responses available, please circle the one which is more appropriate.

I. *(A is a student that Dr. Wang, B, has hired to make a poster. A is trying to decide what color to make a particular item. He points it out to Dr. Wang.)*

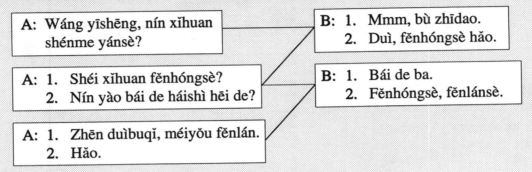

A: Wáng yīshēng, nín xǐhuan shénme yánsè?

B: 1. Mmm, bù zhīdao.
   2. Duì, fěnhóngsè hǎo.

A: 1. Shéi xǐhuan fěnhóngsè?
   2. Nín yào bái de háishì hēi de?

B: 1. Bái de ba.
   2. Fěnhóngsè, fěnlánsè.

A: 1. Zhēn duìbuqǐ, méiyǒu fěnlán.
   2. Hǎo.

II. *(A and B are trying to find their T-shirts in a bag of laundry.)*

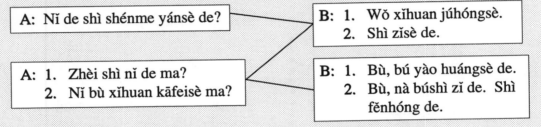

A: Nǐ de shì shénme yánsè de?

B: 1. Wǒ xǐhuan júhóngsè.
   2. Shì zǐsè de.

A: 1. Zhèi shì nǐ de ma?
   2. Nǐ bù xǐhuan kāfeisè ma?

B: 1. Bù, bú yào huángsè de.
   2. Bù, nà búshì zǐ de. Shì fěnhóng de.

III. *(A has picked out a style of wristwatch, and must decide on a color. B is the salesclerk.)*

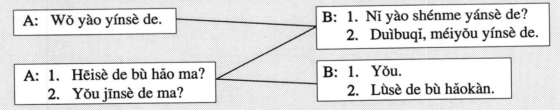

A: Wǒ yào yínsè de.

B: 1. Nǐ yào shénme yánsè de?
   2. Duìbuqǐ, méiyǒu yínsè de.

A: 1. Hēisè de bù hǎo ma?
   2. Yǒu jīnsè de ma?

B: 1. Yǒu.
   2. Lǜsè de bù hǎokàn.

IV. *(A and B, Chinese students in the US, are coloring a Halloween poster.)*

A: Huángsè hǎo háishì júhóngsè hǎo?

B: 1. Wǒ xǐhuan júhóngsè.
   2. Duìbuqǐ, méiyǒu hóng de.

A: 1. Hóng de hǎokàn, háishì lán de hǎokàn?
   2. Nǐ bù xǐhuan huángsè ma?

B: 1. Kāfēisè bù hěn hǎokàn.
   2. Bú tài xǐhuan.

V. *(A is selecting a shirt to buy, and holds one up for B's approval.)*

A: Nǐ xǐhuan fěnhóng ma?

B: 1. Wǒ tǎoyàn fěnhóng.
   2. Méiyǒu fěnhóng.

A Poster

(Li , Zhang, David, and several other students are huddled over a table, making a poster.)

Student 1:	Zhèr tú shénme yánsè?	*What color shall we put here?*
Zhāng:	Zǐsè ba.	*How about purple.*
Student 1:	Zǐsè ma? Zǐsè...	*Purple? Purple..*
Student 2:	Aiya, zǐsè bù hǎokàn.	*Aw, purple doesn't look good.*
Lǐ:	Zěnme bù hǎokàn!	*What do you mean it doesn't look good!.*
	Zǐsè hěn hǎo ma.	*Purple is very nice.*
David:	Wǒ yě tǎoyàn zǐsè..	*I hate purple too..make it yellow.*
	tú huáng de ba.	
Student 1:	Huángsè..jīnsè xíng ma?	*Yellow..how about gold?*
Lǐ:	Nǐ yǒu méiyǒu jīnsè?	*Do you have gold?*
Student 1:	Yǒu a.	*I do.*
Student 2:	Hǎo ba. Jiù tú jīnsè ba.	*Fine. Then make it gold.*
Zhāng:	*(sings)*	
	Jīnsè, jīnsè, shéi bú ài	*Gold, gold, who doesn't love the color gold..*
	jīnsè..	

(Li and the others laugh.)

Culture notes

The color red has particular significance in Chinese (particularly folk) tradition. It is the color of life—of flowing blood—as opposed to white which imbues the complexion when life leaves the body and blood ceases to flow. Thus red is the color of celebration, white the color of mourning. A young child is dressed in red or other bright colors, and brides traditionally wear red. As people age, they turn to blues, greys, and other more sombre colors. Old people are rarely seen wearing red or other vibrant colors. White is traditionally the color worn at funerals.

In the People's Republic of China, red was a particularly auspicious color, since it connoted a revolutionary spirit. Although political fervor has died down in the years since the end of the Great Proletarian Cultural Revolution and the deaths of Mao Zedong and Zhou Enlai in 1976, red continues to have good implications, in a political sense.

Members of the urban elite often prefer muted or staid colors, in rejection of village values, considered coarse or vulgar. Under Western influence, the preferred color of bridal gowns is now white, in urban areas, and black often appears at funerals.

Structure notes

1. When a color is used as a noun, as in "the color red," the equivalent phrase "color + sè" is used in Chinese. Thus, "I like the color red" is Wǒ xǐhuan hóngsè.

2. When a color modifies a noun, as in "the red object" hóng de dōngxi, the particle de is inserted between the two. The word sè is optional in this case: there is no difference in meaning between hóngsè de dōngxi and hóng de dōngxi.

3. Sometimes the noun that the color modifies is left off because it is understood. Thus, instead of saying "the red object" hóng de dōngxi, one can simply say "the red one" hóng de. Thus: Wǒ yào hóng de, bú yào lán de "I want the red one, not the blue one"—where the noun that "one" refers to is understood.

4. Xǐhuan "to like," ài "to love," and tǎoyàn "to detest, hate" can precede either verbs or nouns. Thus:

Wǒ tǎoyàn hóngsè.	*I + to hate + the color red*	*I hate the color red.*
Wǒ ài wǒ māma.	*I + to love + my + mother*	*I love my mother.*

Wǒ xǐhuan kànshū.	*I + to like to + to read*	*I like to read.*
Wǒ zuì tǎoyàn xǐzǎo.	*I + most + to hate to + to bathe*	*I hate to take a bath more than anything.*

5. Háishì means "or" in "either/or" questions.

Nǐ juéde hóngsè hǎo háishì lánsè hǎo?	*you + to feel + the color red + to be good + or + the color blue + to be good*	*Which do you think is better, red or blue?*
Nǐ shì lǎoshī háishì xuéshēng?	*you + to be + teacher + or + student*	*Are you a teacher or a student?*
Nǐ xiǎng hēchá háishì xiǎng hēshuǐ?	*you + to think/want + drink tea + or + to think/want + drink water*	*Would you like to drink tea or water?*

Repeating the verb after háishì is optional.

PLEASE NOTE: háishì means "or" in questions. "Or" in a statement generally requires something else; the term huòzhě is usually appropriate. Thus: "Either this one or that one will be fine" is Zhèige huòzhě nèige dōu hǎo, NOT *Zhèige háishì nèige dōu hǎo.

Structure exercise

Fill in the blanks in the monologue below, made by a garrulous person who doesn't wait for answers, based on the English equivalents provided.

Wǒ zuì xǐhuan _____. Wǒ yào yí ge _____. Nǐ ne? Nǐ xǐhuan shénme yánse? Lán _____ _____ huáng _____? Nǐ yào lán _____ _____ huáng _____? Nǐ bù tǎoyàn _____ ma? Wǒ juéde _____ bù hǎo.

I like the color blue best of all. I want a blue one. How about you? What color do you like? Blue or yellow? Do you want a blue one or a yellow one? Don't you hate the color purple? I think a purple one wouldn't be any good.

SEGMENT B
Skill: To provide & obtain preferences in pastimes.

Wǒ zuì xǐhuan _____ .	*I most like to _____ .*
Zánmen yíkuàir _____ ba.	*Let's _____ together.*
Wǒ gēn nǐ yíkuàir qù _____ .	*I'll go _____ with you.*
Bié _____ !	*Don't _____ .*

ba *(particle conveying a suggestion)*
gēn *with, together with, and*

yīngdāng *ought to*
yěxǔ *perhaps*

kàn shū	*to read a book*
kàn diànshì	*to watch television*
kàn diànyǐng	*to see a movie*
tīng yīngyuè	*to listen to music*
xiě xìn	*to write a letter*
sànbù	*to go for a walk*
guàngjiē	*to go window-shopping*
mǎi dōngxi	*to go shopping*
dǎ diànhuà	*to talk on the telephone/ make a telephone call*
dǎqiú	*to play ball (general)*
dǎpái	*to play cards*
yóuyǒng	*to swim*
zánmen	*we (includes the person addressed)*
yíkuàir	*together*

Nǐ xiǎng zuò shénme?	*What do you feel like doing?*
Nǐ zuì xǐhuan zuò shénme?	*What do you like best to do?*
Zánmen yào zuò shénme?	*What will we be doing?*
Wǒmen yīngdāng zuò shénme?	*What should we do?*
Wǒ yěxǔ qù kàn diànyǐngr. Nǐ qù ma?	*Maybe I'll go see a movie. Will you go?*
Nǐ gēn wǒ yíkuàir qù ma?	*Will you go with me?*

Dialogue Practice

The following sets of dialogues presume normal behavior, no unusual circumstances, and no misunderstandings in the contexts indicated. "A" begins the dialogue, "B" responds, "A" responds to "B," etc. Where there is a choice of responses available, please circle the one which is more appropriate.

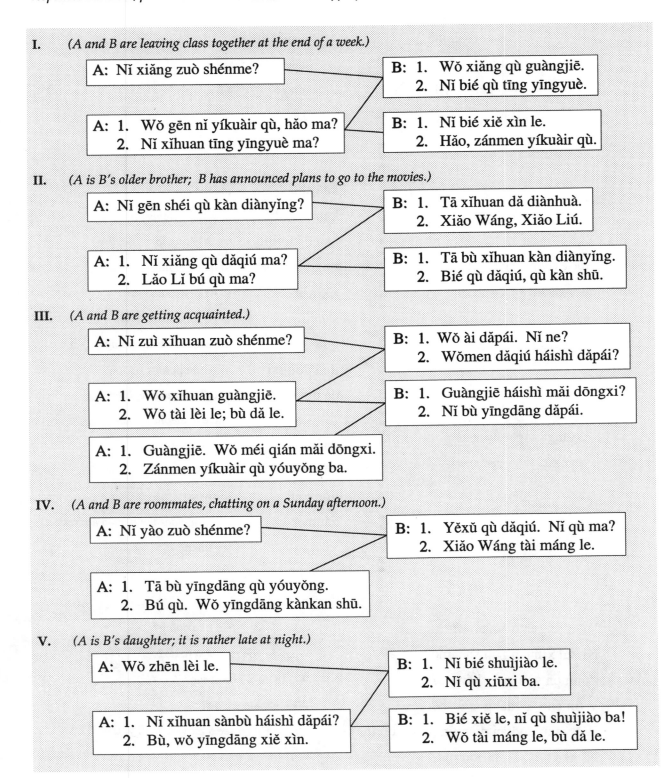

I.   (A and B are leaving class together at the end of a week.)

A: Nǐ xiǎng zuò shénme?

B: 1. Wǒ xiǎng qù guàngjiē.
   2. Nǐ bié qù tīng yīngyuè.

A: 1. Wǒ gēn nǐ yíkuàir qù, hǎo ma?
   2. Nǐ xǐhuan tīng yīngyuè ma?

B: 1. Nǐ bié xiě xìn le.
   2. Hǎo, zánmen yíkuàir qù.

II.   (A is B's older brother; B has announced plans to go to the movies.)

A: Nǐ gēn shéi qù kàn diànyǐng?

B: 1. Tā xǐhuan dǎ diànhuà.
   2. Xiǎo Wáng, Xiǎo Liú.

A: 1. Nǐ xiǎng qù dǎqiú ma?
   2. Lǎo Lǐ bú qù ma?

B: 1. Tā bù xǐhuan kàn diànyǐng.
   2. Bié qù dǎqiú, qù kàn shū.

III. (A and B are getting acquainted.)

A: Nǐ zuì xǐhuan zuò shénme?

B: 1. Wǒ ài dǎpái. Nǐ ne?
   2. Wǒmen dǎqiú háishì dǎpái?

A: 1. Wǒ xǐhuan guàngjiē.
   2. Wǒ tài lèi le; bù dǎ le.

B: 1. Guàngjiē háishì mǎi dōngxi?
   2. Nǐ bù yīngdāng dǎpái.

A: 1. Guàngjiē. Wǒ méi qián mǎi dōngxi.
   2. Zánmen yíkuàir qù yóuyǒng ba.

IV.   (A and B are roommates, chatting on a Sunday afternoon.)

A: Nǐ yào zuò shénme?

B: 1. Yěxǔ qù dǎqiú. Nǐ qù ma?
   2. Xiǎo Wáng tài máng le.

A: 1. Tā bù yīngdāng qù yóuyǒng.
   2. Bú qù. Wǒ yīngdāng kànkan shū.

V.   (A is B's daughter; it is rather late at night.)

A: Wǒ zhēn lèi le.

B: 1. Nǐ bié shuìjiào le.
   2. Nǐ qù xiūxi ba.

A: 1. Nǐ xǐhuan sànbù háishì dǎpái?
   2. Bù, wǒ yīngdāng xiě xìn.

B: 1. Bié xiě le, nǐ qù shuìjiào ba!
   2. Wǒ tài máng le, bù dǎ le.

After the poster

(Li, Zhang, David, and their friends finish a poster they have been making, and decide to spend the rest of the afternoon relaxing.)

Lǐ:	Zěnmeyàng? Zánmen zuò shénme?	*Well? Where shall we go?*
Zhāng:	Bù zhīdao. Lǐ Zhōngyīng, nǐ xiǎng zuò shénme?	*I don't know. Li Zhongying, what do you feel like doing?*
Lǐ:	Suíbiàn. Sànsanbù, dōudoufēng, kànkan diànyǐngr, dōu kěyǐ.	*I don't care. Go for a walk, go for a drive, anything's okay.*
David:	*(to the other people)* Xiǎo Bái, Lǎo Fāng, nǐmen tōngcháng xǐhuan zuò shénme?	*Bai, Fang, what do you usually like to do?*
Bái:	Shénme dōu xǐhuan. Kàn diànyǐngr, dǎqiú, guàngjiē.	*I like everything. See a movie, play ball, walk around town.*
Lǐ:	Lǎo Fāng, nǐ ne?	*Fang, what about you?*
Fāng:	Wǒ xǐhuan kàn diànyǐngr.	*I like seeing movies.*
Lǐ:	Nnng, kàn diànyǐngr hěn hǎo.	*Uh-huh, (seeing) movies are great.*
Zhāng:	Nnn, wǒ yě zuì xǐhuan kàn diànyǐngr.	*Yes, I like movies best too.*
David:	Nà wǒmen qù kàn diànyǐngr ba.	*In that case, let's go see a movie.*
Bái:	Hǎo! Zánmen yíkuàir qù kàn diànyǐngr.	*Great! Let's see a movie together.*

(They all get up and go out together.)

Culture notes

Chinese young people are more likely to do things in a group than their American counterparts. "Cliquing" is rare; individuals adapt to other individuals and the company of many people quite readily. Dating in the American sense, with a young man and woman seeing each other exclusively, does not occur until quite late in the Chinese social process. Generally, a couple that dates is considering marriage; and dating couples do not change partners very often.

Attaining **harmony** within a group is a central concept in Chinese society. Very often, individuals hesitate to assert strong personal preferences, without first ascertaining that these preferences are generally those of the group as a whole. The first few statements in any negotiation for a group concensus are likely to be tentative—"It doesn't matter to me, what do you think?"—until some parameters have been established for the group's preferences.

Another key principle in group dynamics is that of "democratic centralism." Decisions that effect the group are made democratically, with general participation, but the decision, once made, is likely to be accepted by all members of the group without demurral. Even if an individual initially opposed an idea, once it has been accepted by the group, he or she is likely to go along.

Structure notes

Zuì "most," yíkuàir "together," yīngdāng "ought to," and yěxǔ "perhaps" all modify verbs
and adjectives.   Thus:

zuì:

zuì hǎo	*most + to be good*	*best, the best*
Hēisè zuì hǎo.	*black + color + most + to be good*	*The color black is the best.*
Wǒ zuì xǐhuan shuìjiào.	*I + most + to like to + to sleep*	*I like to sleep best of all.*
Xiǎo Wáng zuì pàng.	*Xiao Wang + most + to be fat*	*Xiao Wang is the fattest.*

yíkuàir:

Zánmen yíkuàir kàn diànshì.	*we + together + to look at + television.*	*Let's watch television together.*
Nǐ gēn shéi yíkuàir niànshū?	*you + with + who + together + to study*	*Who do you study with?*

yīngdāng:

Nǐ yīngdāng shuìjiào le.	*you + to ought to + to sleep + le*	*You should go to sleep (now).*
Zánmen yīngdāng dǎdǎqiú.	*we + to ought to + play + play + ball*	*We ought to play some ball.*
Měiguórén yīngdāng huì shuō Yīngwén.	*Americans + to ought to + to know how to + to speak + English*	*Americans should know how to speak English.*

yěxǔ:

Tā yěxǔ ài kàn diànyǐngr.	*he + perhaps + to love to + to look at + movies*	*He might like to see movies.*
Tāmen yěxǔ chībǎo le.	*they + perhaps + eat till full + le*	*They may be full, now.*
Tā yěxǔ shì Xiǎo Lǐ de jiějie.	*she + perhaps + to be + Xiao Li + 's + older sister*	*She might be Xiao Li's older sister.*
Tā yěxǔ xìng Wáng.	*she + perhaps + to be surnamed + Wang*	*Her last name might be Wang.*

Structure exercise

Match the number of each Chinese sentences on the right with the equivalent English sentence on the left, and write it in the blank space provided.

1. Wǒ zuì xǐhuan dǎpái.

2. Wǒ zuì xǐhuan gēn Lǎo Wèi yíkuàir dǎpái.

3. Lǎo Wèi yīngdāng gēn wǒ yíkuàir dǎpái.

4. Wǒ yěxǔ huì gēn Lǎo Wèi yíkuàir dǎpái.

5. Lǎo Wèi zuì xǐhuan dǎqiú.

6. Lǎo Wèi zuì xǐhuan gēn wǒ yíkuàir dǎqiú.

7. Wǒ yīngdāng gēn Lǎo Wèi yíkuàir dǎqiú.

8. Wǒ zuì xǐhuan gēn Xiǎo Zhāng yíkuàir dǎqiú.

9. Wǒ bù yīngdāng gēn Xiǎo Zhāng yíkuàir dǎqiú.

10. Wǒ yěxǔ bú huì gēn Xiǎo Zhāng yíkuàir dǎqiú.

11. Xiǎo Zhāng zuì xǐhuan dǎpái.

12. Xiǎo Zhāng bù xǐhuān gēn Lǎo Wèi yíkuàir dǎpái.

13. Wǒ yěxǔ huì gēn Xiǎo Zhāng yíkuàir dǎpái.

14. Lǎo Wáng yěxǔ huì gēn Xiǎo Zhāng yíkuàir dǎqiú.

15. Yěxǔ Xiǎo Zhāng, Lǎo Wáng gēn wǒ huì zài yíkuàir dǎqiú.

16. Xiǎo Zhāng, Lǎo Wáng gēn wǒ bù yīngdāng zài yíkuàir dǎpái.

17. Xiǎo Zhāng, Lǎo Wáng gēn wǒ yīngdāng zài yíkuàir dǎqiú.

_____ *Lao Wei likes to play ball most of all.*

_____ *I most like to play ball with Xiao Zhang.*

_____ *I ought to play ball with Lao Wei.*

_____ *Perhaps I won't play ball with Xiao Zhang.*

_____ *Xiao Zhang, Lao Wang and I ought to play ball together.*

_____ *Most of all, Xiao Zhang likes to play cards.*

_____ *I like to play cards best of all.*

_____ *I may play cards with Xiao Zhang.*

_____ *Lao Wei should play cards with me.*

_____ *Perhaps Xiao Zhang, Lao Wang and I will play ball together.*

_____ *I like best to play cards with Lao Wei.*

_____ *Lao Wang may play ball with Xiao Zhang.*

_____ *I may play cards with Lao Wei.*

_____ *Xiao Zhang, Lao Wang and I should not play cards together.*

_____ *Most of all, Lao Wei likes to play ball with me.*

_____ *I shouldn't play ball with Xiao Zhang.*

_____ *Xiao Zhang doesn't like to play cards with Lao Wei.*

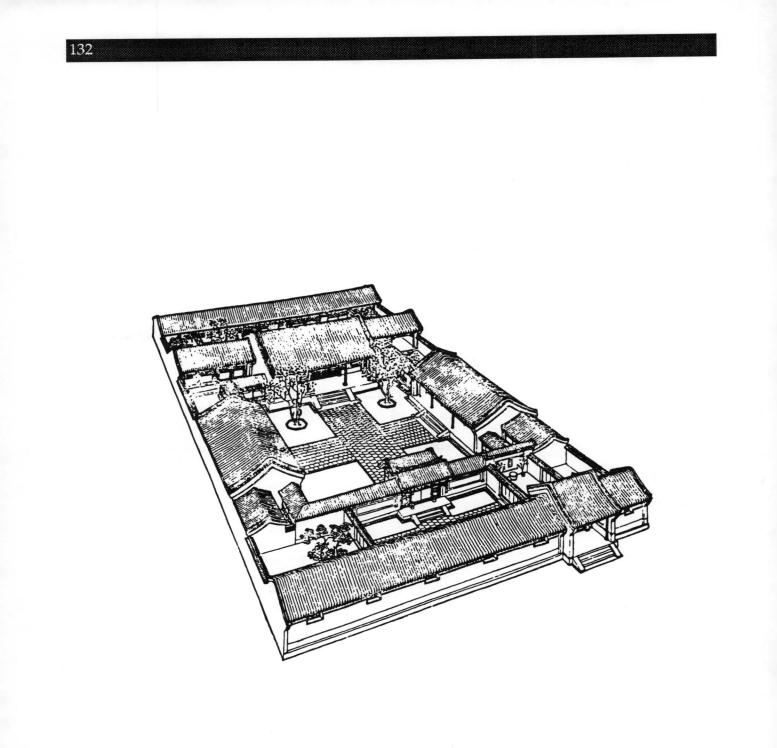

This diagram of a traditional Chinese *sìhéyuàn* (residential compound) shows a main gate (bottom right), a central courtyard, formal sitting rooms to the rear (near the top of the page), and living quarters on both sides.

SEGMENT A
Skill: To locate the home and items within the home.

Wǒ jiā zài_____.	*My home is (located at/in)_____.*
Fángzi zài _____.	*The house is (at)_____.*
Wǒ de dōngxi zài_____.	*My things are (at)_____.*

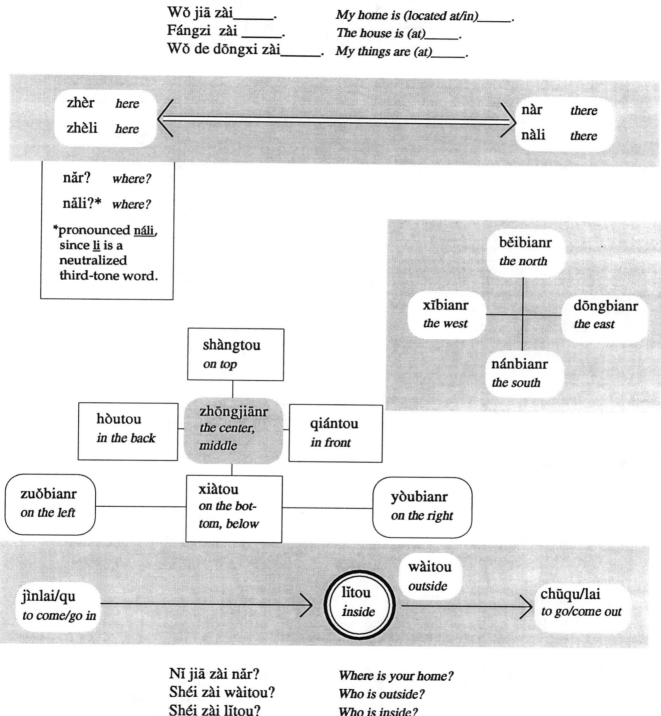

zhèr — *here*
zhèli — *here*

nàr — *there*
nàli — *there*

nǎr? — *where?*

nǎli?* — *where?*

*pronounced náli, since li is a neutralized third-tone word.

běibianr — *the north*

xībianr — *the west*   dōngbianr — *the east*

nánbianr — *the south*

shàngtou — *on top*

hòutou — *in the back*

zhōngjiānr — *the center, middle*

qiántou — *in front*

zuǒbianr — *on the left*

xiàtou — *on the bottom, below*

yòubianr — *on the right*

wàitou — *outside*

jìnlai/qu — *to come/go in*

lǐtou — *inside*

chūqu/lai — *to go/come out*

Nǐ jiā zài nǎr?	*Where is your home?*
Shéi zài wàitou?	*Who is outside?*
Shéi zài lǐtou?	*Who is inside?*
Shéi de jiā zài běibianr?	*Who's home is in the north?*
Wǒ de dōngxi zài nǎli?	*Where are my things?*

Dialogue Practice

The following sets of dialogues presume normal behavior, no unusual circumstances, and no misunderstandings in the contexts indicated. "A" begins the dialogue, "B" responds, "A" responds to "B," etc. Where there is a choice of responses available, please circle the one which is more appropriate.

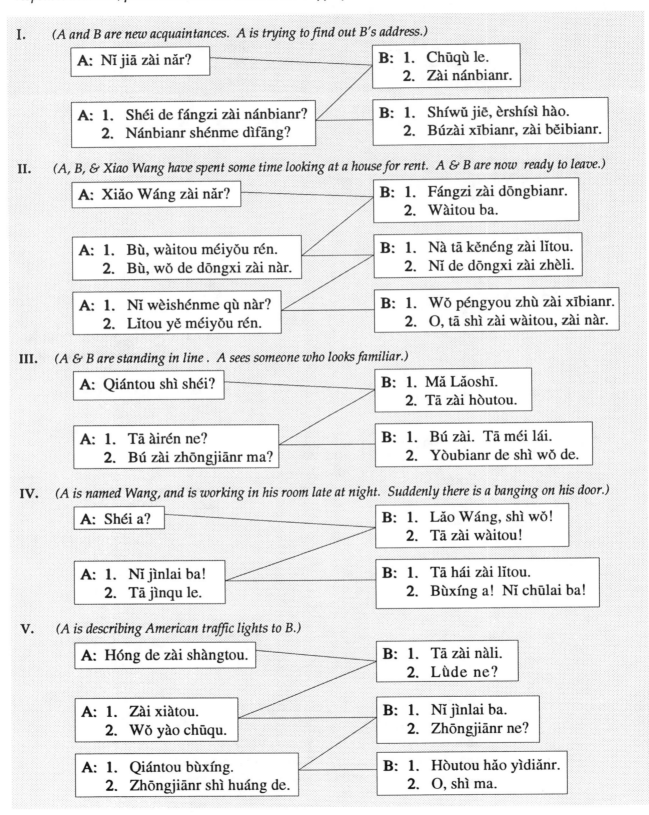

I.   *(A and B are new acquaintances. A is trying to find out B's address.)*

A: Nǐ jiā zài nǎr?

B: 1. Chūqù le.
   2. Zài nánbianr.

A: 1. Shéi de fángzi zài nánbianr?
   2. Nánbianr shénme dìfāng?

B: 1. Shíwǔ jiē, èrshísì hào.
   2. Búzài xībianr, zài běibianr.

II. *(A, B, & Xiao Wang have spent some time looking at a house for rent. A & B are now ready to leave.)*

A: Xiǎo Wáng zài nǎr?

B: 1. Fángzi zài dōngbianr.
   2. Wàitou ba.

A: 1. Bù, wàitou méiyǒu rén.
   2. Bù, wǒ de dōngxi zài nàr.

B: 1. Nà tā kěnéng zài lǐtou.
   2. Nǐ de dōngxi zài zhèli.

A: 1. Nǐ wèishénme qù nàr?
   2. Lǐtou yě méiyǒu rén.

B: 1. Wǒ péngyou zhù zài xībianr.
   2. O, tā shì zài wàitou, zài nàr.

III. *(A & B are standing in line . A sees someone who looks familiar.)*

A: Qiántou shì shéi?

B: 1. Mǎ Lǎoshī.
   2. Tā zài hòutou.

A: 1. Tā àirén ne?
   2. Bú zài zhōngjiānr ma?

B: 1. Bú zài. Tā méi lái.
   2. Yòubianr de shì wǒ de.

IV. *(A is named Wang, and is working in his room late at night. Suddenly there is a banging on his door.)*

A: Shéi a?

B: 1. Lǎo Wáng, shì wǒ!
   2. Tā zài wàitou!

A: 1. Nǐ jìnlai ba!
   2. Tā jìnqu le.

B: 1. Tā hái zài lǐtou.
   2. Bùxíng a! Nǐ chūlai ba!

V.   *(A is describing American traffic lights to B.)*

A: Hóng de zài shàngtou.

B: 1. Tā zài nàli.
   2. Lǜde ne?

A: 1. Zài xiàtou.
   2. Wǒ yào chūqu.

B: 1. Nǐ jìnlai ba.
   2. Zhōngjiānr ne?

A: 1. Qiántou bùxíng.
   2. Zhōngjiānr shì huáng de.

B: 1. Hòutou hǎo yìdiǎnr.
   2. O, shì ma.

Visiting Zhang

(David, Li, and several others are gathered on the lawn at school.)

Lǐ:	Jīntiān Xiǎo Zhāng zěnme méi lái?	*How come Zhang didn't come today?*
Friend:	Bù zhīdao. Xīwàng tā méi shì.	*I don't know. I hope nothing is wrong.*
David:	Tā zuótiān lái xuéxiào le ma?	*Did he come to school yesterday?*
Lǐ:	Wǒ méi kànjiàn tā.	*I didn't see him.*
David:	Ei, zánmen qù kànkan tā ba.	*Hey, let's go see him.*
Friend:	Tā zhù zài nǎr?	*Where does he live?*
David:	Tā zhù dì-wǔ sùshè, zài xiàoyuán nánbianr.	*He lives in Dorm #5, in the south of the campus.*
Lǐ:	Xiàoyuán nánbianr? Nǎli?	*The south of the campus? Where?*
Friend:	Jiù zài túshūguǎn hòutou.	*Right behind the library.*
David:	Duì. Tā de fángjiān zài zuì shàngtou, zài wǔ lóu.	*Right. His room is at the very top, on the fifth floor.*
Lǐ:	Hǎo ba. Nǐ dài lù. Zánmen qù ba.	*Fine. You lead the way. Let's go.*

(When they get to Zhang's room, they knock.)

Friend:	Wèi! Xiǎo Zhāng zài ma?	*Hello! Zhang!*
Zhāng:	Shéi a?	*Who is it?*
David:	Wǒmen lái la!	*We're here!*

(Zhang opens the door; he breaks into a smile.)

Zhāng:	Ai, bù hǎoyìsi, bù néng qǐng nǐmen jìnlai. Lǎo Fāng zài shuìjiào.	*Ah, how embarassing. I can't ask you to come in. Fang is sleeping.*
David:	Nǐ chūlai ba. Zánmen dào xiàtou qù zuò.	*Why don't you come out. Let's go sit downstairs.*
Zhāng:	Hǎo!	*Fine.*

Culture notes

Given crowded conditions in dormitories, friends often cannot be entertained in one's room. There are sitting areas provided for common use for socializing. On PRC campuses, students also bathe in a communal bath house that is separate from the dormitory.

Structure notes

1. This lesson primarily uses sentence structure #5 **Subject** + [**bú**] + **zài** + **place** (see p. 93), which is used to describe location at a place.

Tā bú zài jiā.	*he + not + to be at + home*	*He's not at home.*
Tā zài Zhōngguó.	*he + to be at + China*	*He's in China.*
Tā jiā zài Měiguó.	*he + home + to be at + America*	*His home is in America.*
Měiguó zài Zhōngguó de xībianr.	*America + to be at + China + 's the west (side)*	*America is to the west of China.*

2. The particle <u>de</u>, it has been mentioned, can act in the same fashion as the apostrophe-S in English, to mark a possessive.

Zhèi shì Xiǎo Wáng de shū.	*this + to be + Xiao Wang + 's + book*	*This is Xiao Wang's book.*

When a close relationship exists between the two nouns connected by <u>de</u>, the particle is often omitted. Some examples are <u>nǐ māma</u>, <u>tā bàba</u>, <u>wǒ jiějie</u>, <u>Xiǎo Wáng jiā</u>, etc.

Structure exercise

The following is a monologue by an idle person named Zhou, who is staring at a pile of books. Read the monologue, and then complete the task that follows it.

Wǒmen yǒu wǔ běn shū. Hóngsè de shū zài shàngtou, báisè de shū zài xiàtou, lán shū zài zuǒbianr, lǜ shū zài yòubianr. Hēisè de zài zhōngjiānr. Xiǎo Wáng de shū shì hēi de. Xiǎo Lǐ de shū shì bái de. Wǒ de shì lán de gēn lǜ de. Lǎo Fāng yǒu yì běn hóng shū. Wǒ xìng Zhōu.

Write five sentences stating the relative locations of the books belonging to Zhou, Fang, Wang, and Li. Whose is on top? Whose is on the bottom? Where is Zhou's book? Etc.

_____

_____

_____

_____

_____

SEGMENT B

Skill: To name & locate rooms in a house.

Wǒ jiāli yǒu _____. *In my home there is a _____.*

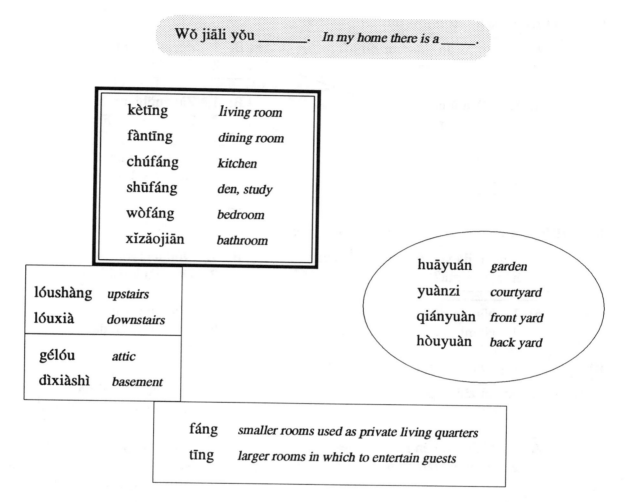

kètīng	*living room*
fàntīng	*dining room*
chúfáng	*kitchen*
shūfáng	*den, study*
wòfáng	*bedroom*
xǐzǎojiān	*bathroom*

lóushàng	*upstairs*
lóuxià	*downstairs*
gélóu	*attic*
dìxiàshì	*basement*

huāyuán	*garden*
yuànzi	*courtyard*
qiányuàn	*front yard*
hòuyuàn	*back yard*

fáng	*smaller rooms used as private living quarters*
tīng	*larger rooms in which to entertain guests*

Tā jiāli yǒu sān fáng èr tīng.	*His house has three bedrooms, a living room & a dining room.*
Wǒ de fángjiān zài lóushàng.	*My room is upstairs.*
Wǒ de fángjiān shì dì-yī jiān.	*My room is the first one.*
Shì wǒ zìjǐ yígerén de fángjiān.	*It's my own single (private) room.*
Shì wǒ gēn wǒ mèimei de fángjiān.	*It's my sister's and my room.*

- - - - - - - - - - - - - - - - - - -

Nǐ de fángjiān zài nǎr?	*Where is your room?*
Nǐ jiā yǒu dìxiàshì ma?	*Does your home have a basement?*
Nǐmen yǒu jǐ jiān fángjiān?	*How many rooms do you have?*
Nǐ gēn shéi yíge fángjiān?	*Who do you share a room with?*

Dialogue Practice

The following sets of dialogues presume normal behavior, no unusual circumstances, and no misunderstandings in the contexts indicated. "A" begins the dialogue, "B" responds, "A" responds to "B," etc. Where there is a choice of responses available, please circle the one which is more appropriate.

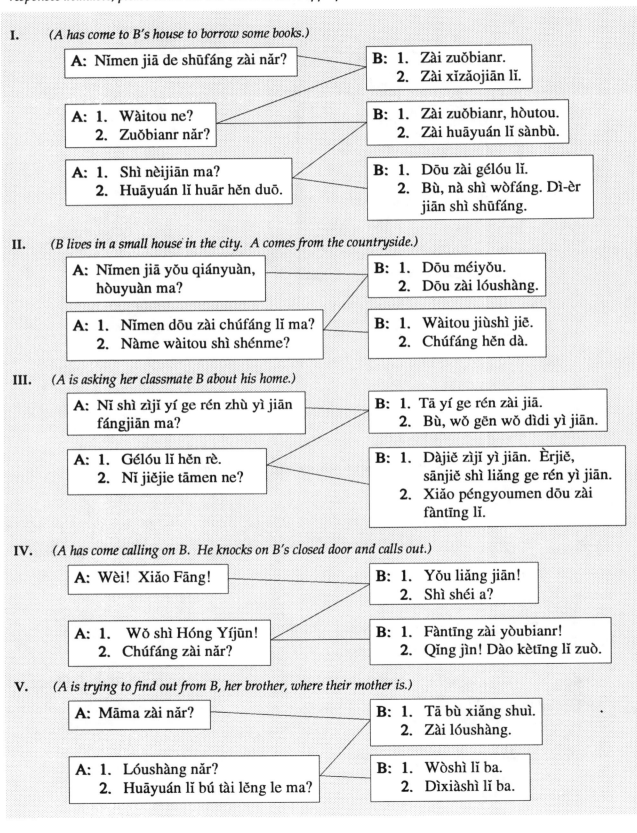

I.   (A has come to B's house to borrow some books.)

A: Nǐmen jiā de shūfáng zài nǎr?

B: 1. Zài zuǒbianr.
    2. Zài xǐzǎojiān lǐ.

A: 1. Wàitou ne?
    2. Zuǒbianr nǎr?

B: 1. Zài zuǒbianr, hòutou.
    2. Zài huāyuán lǐ sànbù.

A: 1. Shì nèijiān ma?
    2. Huāyuán lǐ huār hěn duō.

B: 1. Dōu zài gélóu lǐ.
    2. Bù, nà shì wòfáng. Dì-èr jiān shì shūfáng.

II.   (B lives in a small house in the city. A comes from the countryside.)

A: Nǐmen jiā yǒu qiányuàn, hòuyuàn ma?

B: 1. Dōu méiyǒu.
    2. Dōu zài lóushàng.

A: 1. Nǐmen dōu zài chúfáng lǐ ma?
    2. Nàme wàitou shì shénme?

B: 1. Wàitou jiùshì jiē.
    2. Chúfáng hěn dà.

III. (A is asking her classmate B about his home.)

A: Nǐ shì zìjǐ yí ge rén zhù yì jiān fángjiān ma?

B: 1. Tā yí ge rén zài jiā.
    2. Bù, wǒ gēn wǒ dìdi yì jiān.

A: 1. Gélóu lǐ hěn rè.
    2. Nǐ jiějie tāmen ne?

B: 1. Dàjiě zìjǐ yì jiān. Èrjiě, sānjiě shì liǎng ge rén yì jiān.
    2. Xiǎo péngyoumen dōu zài fàntīng lǐ.

IV.   (A has come calling on B. He knocks on B's closed door and calls out.)

A: Wèi! Xiǎo Fāng!

B: 1. Yǒu liǎng jiān!
    2. Shì shéi a?

A: 1. Wǒ shì Hóng Yíjūn!
    2. Chúfáng zài nǎr?

B: 1. Fàntīng zài yòubianr!
    2. Qǐng jìn! Dào kètīng lǐ zuò.

V.   (A is trying to find out from B, her brother, where their mother is.)

A: Māma zài nǎr?

B: 1. Tā bù xiǎng shuì.
    2. Zài lóushàng.

A: 1. Lóushàng nǎr?
    2. Huāyuán lǐ bú tài lěng le ma?

B: 1. Wòshì lǐ ba.
    2. Dìxiàshì lǐ ba.

Privacy

(David, Li, Zhang, and some others are sitting around a table studying.)

David:	Wa, Zhōngguó rén tài duō le.	*Wow, there are too many people in China.*
Zhāng:	Zěnme jiǎng?	*How do you mean?*
David:	Zài Zhōngguó dōu bù néng yǒu yìdiǎnr "privacy."	*You can't even have a little privacy in China.*
Friend:	Shénme jiàozuò "privacy"?	*What is "privacy"? (What is this that you call "privacy"?)*
Lǐ:	Shì "yǐnsīquán" de yìsi.	*It means "the right to be hidden and personal."*
David:	Yě bú shì. Jiùshì, yí ge fángjiān bā ge rén shízài tài duō le.	*It isn't really that, either. It's just that, eight people in one room is really too many.*
Zhāng:	Zài Měiguó zěnmeyàng?	*What's it like in America?*
David:	Zài wǒmen jiā měige rén yǒu yì jiān wòfáng.	*At our house we have a bedroom each.*
Lǐ:	Nǐmen jiā yǒu jǐ jiān wòfáng?	*How many bedrooms are in your house?*
David:	Sì jiān, háiyǒu shūfáng ne.	*Four, and a study in addition.*
Friend:	Wa, zhènme duō fángjiān. Nǐmen jiā cái sān kǒu rén ne.	*Wow, so many rooms. And there are only three people in your family.*
David:	Shì a; háiyǒu sān ge xǐzǎojiān.	*That's right; and there are three bathrooms too.*
Zhāng:	Fángzi nàme dà, cái sān ge rén, nǐ bú huì jìmò ma?	*With such a big house, and only three people, don't you get lonely?*
David:	Hái kěyǐ. Kěshì yǒu de shíhou huì wúliáo. Háishì Zhōngguó yǒu yìsi.	*(No,) it's alright. But it gets boring sometimes. China is more interesting, after all.*

Culture notes

One cannot always assume that a greater amount of personal living space and the freedom of the American lifestyle appeals to everyone. Although the abundance of material resources in America is usually exhilarating, the emptiness of many American residential streets and the lack of personal contact in some American homes can be disconcerting. Loneliness is a frequent complaint of many newcomers to America.

Structure notes

1. To say that something or someone exists or is available at a place, the following pattern is used.

9. (Zài +) Place + [méi] + yǒu + Noun

Měiguó yǒu hěn duō Zhōngguórén.	America + to have + very + to be many + Chinese people	There are many Chinese in America.
Zhèr méiyǒu yīshēng.	here + not + to have + doctor	There is no doctor here.
Zài tā jiālǐ yǒu liù jiān wòfáng.	at + her + house + in + to have + six + *jiān* + bedroom	She has six bedrooms in her house.

2. Wǒ de fángjiān zài lóushàng is an example of pattern #5, **Subject + [bú] + zài + place** (see p. 93).

3. An expanded version of pattern #5 involves sentences indicating location relative to a noun which may not be readily recognized as a place. That is to say, while "here" and "America" are readily identified as places, words such as "table" or "box," are usually considered objects rather than places, although they can function as place names in sentences such as "Put it on the table," or "I left it in the box." Sentences indicating location relative to a noun follow the pattern given below.

5a. Subject + [bú] + zài + Noun + Locational noun

A **locational noun** in this pattern indicates the position of the subject relative to the noun. Four useful locational nouns are lǐ or lǐtou (in, inside), wài or wàitou (outside), shàng or shàngtou (on, on top) and xià or xiàtou (under, below).

Zài fángzi lǐ.	to be at + house + in	It's in the house.
Māma zài shūfáng lǐtou.	Mom + to be at + study + inside	Mom is in the study.
Wǒ de xié zài xǐzǎojiān wàitou.	my + shoe + to be at + bathroom + outside	My shoes are outside the bathroom.
Tā de xìn zài xié xiàtou.	his + letter + to be at + shoe + under	His letter is under the shoes.

4. Wǒ de fángjiān shì dìyījiān follows sentence pattern #1, **Subject + equative verb + noun**, where wǒ de fángjiān "my room" is the subject and dìyījiān "the first room" is the noun to which the subject is being equated.

Shì wǒ zìjǐ yī ge rén de fángjiān and similar sentences follow pattern #1 as well, although this is not as evident. The subject here is understood to be Zhèi ge fángjiān, and is therefore omitted; in English the word "it" would take its place—"IT is my own private room." Wǒ zìjǐ yī ge rén de fángjiān (I + myself + one person + 's + room) "a room for me by myself" basically consists of the noun fángjiān, which is qualified (described) by everything that precedes it.

Structure exercise

Insert <u>zài</u>, <u>yǒu</u>, *or* <u>shì</u> *or their negative forms as appropriate in each of the sentences below. They form part of a rambling monologue by a young person looking at the dining room table.*

Bàba _____ wàitou.	*Father is outside.*
Lǐtou _____ rén.	*There is no-one inside.*
Rénren dōu _____ wàitou.	*Everyone is outside.*
Lǐtou _____ hěn duō dōngxi.	*There are a lot of things inside.*
Zhuōzi shàngtou _____ shū.	*There are books on the table.*
Zhuōzi xiàtou _____ yīfu.	*There are clothes under the table.*
Wǒ de hóng chènshān _____ zhuō xià.	*My red shirt is under the table.*
Lán xiézi _____ wǒ dìdi de.	*The blue shoes are my brother's.*
Hēi kùzi _____ wǒ bàba de.	*The black pants are my father's.*
Wǒ māma de máoyī _____ yǐzi shang.	*My mother's sweater is on the chair.*
Yǐzi xiàtou de máoyī _____ wǒ mèimei de.	*The sweater under the chair is my sister's.*
Yǐzi hòutou yě _____ máoyī.	*There is a sweater behind the chair, too.*
Wǒ de máoyī _____ zhèr.	*My sweater isn't here.*
Wǒ de máoyī _____ wǒ péngyou jiā.	*My sweater is at my friend's house.*
Zhèr de máoyī dōu _____ wǒ de.	*None of the sweaters here is mine.*

Péngyou, nǐ kàn wǒmen de
fángjiān zěnmeyàng?

SEGMENT C
Skill: To name & locate items in the interior of a room.

Wǒ fángjiān lǐtou yǒu _____. *In my room there is/are_____.*

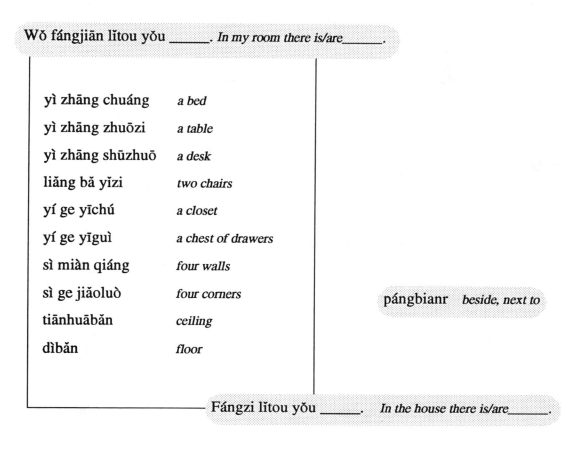

yì zhāng chuáng	*a bed*
yì zhāng zhuōzi	*a table*
yì zhāng shūzhuō	*a desk*
liǎng bǎ yǐzi	*two chairs*
yí ge yīchú	*a closet*
yí ge yīguì	*a chest of drawers*
sì miàn qiáng	*four walls*
sì ge jiǎoluò	*four corners*
tiānhuābǎn	*ceiling*
dìbǎn	*floor*

pángbianr   *beside, next to*

Fángzi lǐtou yǒu _____.   *In the house there is/are_____.*

liǎng zhāng shāfā	*two sofas*
yì zhāng fànzhuō	*a dining table*

Chuáng pángbianr yǒu yì bǎ yǐzi.	*Next to the bed there is a chair.*
Shūzhuō hòumiàn shì yīchú.	*Behind the desk is the closet.*
Fángjiān lǐtou yǒu shénme jiājù?	*What furniture iş in the room?*
Yǒu shāfā ma?	*Is there a sofa?*
Qiáng shì shénme yánsè de?	*What color are the walls?*
Mén yòubianr yǒu shénme?	*What's to the right of the door?*

Dialogue Practice

The following sets of dialogues presume normal behavior, no unusual circumstances, and no misunderstandings in the contexts indicated. "A" begins the dialogue, "B" responds, "A" responds to "B," etc. Where there is a choice of responses available, please circle the one which is more appropriate.

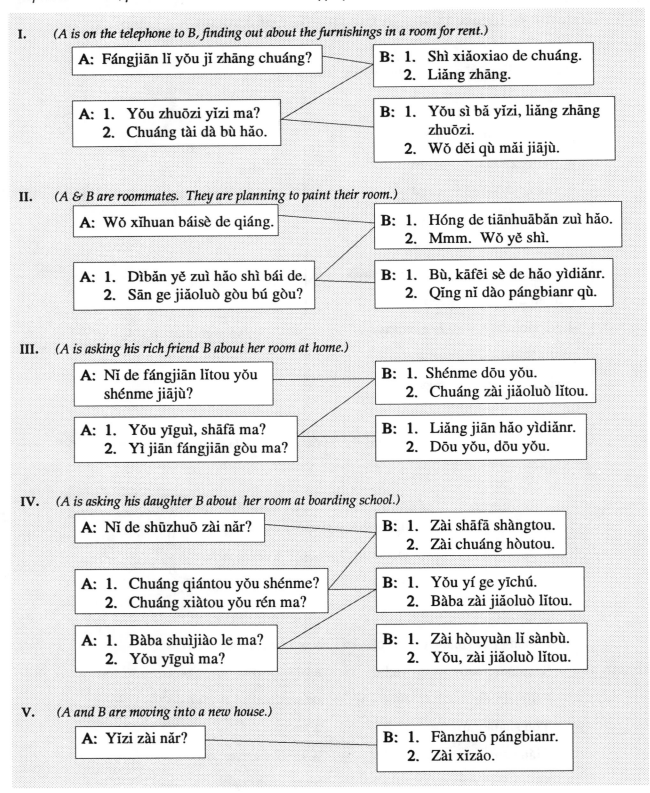

I.   *(A is on the telephone to B, finding out about the furnishings in a room for rent.)*

A: Fángjiān lǐ yǒu jǐ zhāng chuáng?

B: 1. Shì xiǎoxiao de chuáng.
    2. Liǎng zhāng.

A: 1. Yǒu zhuōzi yǐzi ma?
    2. Chuáng tài dà bù hǎo.

B: 1. Yǒu sì bǎ yǐzi, liǎng zhāng zhuōzi.
    2. Wǒ děi qù mǎi jiājù.

II.   *(A & B are roommates. They are planning to paint their room.)*

A: Wǒ xǐhuan báisè de qiáng.

B: 1. Hóng de tiānhuābǎn zuì hǎo.
    2. Mmm. Wǒ yě shì.

A: 1. Dìbǎn yě zuì hǎo shì bái de.
    2. Sān ge jiǎoluò gòu bú gòu?

B: 1. Bù, kāfēi sè de hǎo yìdiǎnr.
    2. Qǐng nǐ dào pángbianr qù.

III. *(A is asking his rich friend B about her room at home.)*

A: Nǐ de fángjiān lǐtou yǒu shénme jiājù?

B: 1. Shénme dōu yǒu.
    2. Chuáng zài jiǎoluò lǐtou.

A: 1. Yǒu yīguì, shāfā ma?
    2. Yì jiān fángjiān gòu ma?

B: 1. Liǎng jiān hǎo yìdiǎnr.
    2. Dōu yǒu, dōu yǒu.

IV.   *(A is asking his daughter B about her room at boarding school.)*

A: Nǐ de shūzhuō zài nǎr?

B: 1. Zài shāfā shàngtou.
    2. Zài chuáng hòutou.

A: 1. Chuáng qiántou yǒu shénme?
    2. Chuáng xiàtou yǒu rén ma?

B: 1. Yǒu yí ge yīchú.
    2. Bàba zài jiǎoluò lǐtou.

A: 1. Bàba shuìjiào le ma?
    2. Yǒu yīguì ma?

B: 1. Zài hòuyuàn lǐ sànbù.
    2. Yǒu, zài jiǎoluò lǐtou.

V.   *(A and B are moving into a new house.)*

A: Yǐzi zài nǎr?

B: 1. Fànzhuō pángbianr.
    2. Zài xǐzǎo.

Remembering Zhang's room

(Li Zhongying is telling her little sister Li Zhongxiu about the time she and the others went to Zhang Desheng's room.)

Sister:	Jiějie, tā de fángjiān lǐtou zěnmeyàng?	*Sister, what was the inside of his room like?*
Lǐ:	Hěn jǐ. Yǒu sì zhāng shàngxià pù, kěyǐ shuì bā ge rén. Háiyǒu sì zhāng xiǎo shūzhuō.	*It was very crowded. There were four bunk beds, that could sleep eight. There were also four small desks.*
Sister:	Háiyǒu ne?	*What else?*
Lǐ:	Méiyǒu le.	*There was nothing else.*
Sister:	Tā de fángjiān shì shénme yánse de?	*What color was his room?*
Lǐ:	Dìbǎn shì hēi de. Qiáng hé tiānhuābǎn shì...huīhui de—yīnwèi hěn zāng.	*The floor was black. The walls and the ceiling were...greyish—because they were dirty.*
Sister:	Tīng qǐlai bù zěnme hǎo.	*It doesn't sound too good.*

Culture notes

Food and housing for university students are modest, since the best and most prestigious universities in both the PRC and Taiwan are state-operated and rely on limited public funds. In the PRC, an average dorm room houses four to eight people. Furnishings include bunk bends and shared desks. Clothes often must be stored in suitcases since the room is unlikely to have a closet. Students may own radios, but other amenities (fan, television set) are rare. Conditions are better for foreign students, who normally live separately from local students.

Life in a tidy room in a graduate student dormitory at Peking (Beijing) University.

Structure notes

1. <u>Zhāng</u> is the measure for objects with a flat surface. Here it modifies bed, table, desk, chair, sofa, and dining room table. <u>Miàn</u> is used with very few objects, a wall and a flag among them. <u>Miàn</u> can also indicate one surface on an object that has two or more surfaces; an audiotape, for instance, would have <u>dì-yīmiàn</u> (side 1) and <u>dì-èrmiàn</u> (side 2).

2. The particle <u>de</u> often indicates that what **precedes** it modifies what **follows** it. In the phrases <u>wǒ de shū</u> "my book," <u>hóngsè de shū</u> "the red book," and <u>shàngtou de shū</u> "the book on top," the book is the topic of discussion. The words preceding <u>de</u> say something about that subject—that it is mine, red, and on top.

Constructions such as <u>zhuōzi de shàngtou</u> "on top of the table," <u>fángzi de wàitou</u> "outside the house," and <u>shūzhuō de pángbianr</u> "next to the desk" make similar use of the particle <u>de</u>. The focus is on the locations "on top," "outside," and "next to." What precedes <u>de</u> says something further about the locations—namely, on top of, outside, and next to WHAT?

<u>Zhuōzi de shàngtou</u> is usually abbreviated to <u>zhuōzi shàngtou</u>, or even <u>zhuōshàng</u>. Similarly, <u>fángzi de wàitou</u> becomes <u>fángzi wàitou</u> or <u>fángwài</u>, and <u>shūzhuō de pángbianr</u> becomes <u>shūzhuō pángbianr</u>.

Reversing the order of the items on either side of <u>de</u> would result in a significant change in meaning. Remember that what comes after <u>de</u> is the subject of the phrase. Thus in the phrases <u>shàngtou de zhuōzi</u>, <u>wàitou de fángzi</u>, <u>pángbianr de shūzhuō</u>, the focus would be on "table," "house," and "desk" respectively, and the words preceding <u>de</u> say something about those objects. Namely: "the table (which is) on top," "the house (which is) outside (of the city limits, perhaps)," and "the desk (which is) to the side."

In the examples below, the subject of the phrases are bold-faced in both the Chinese and English sentences.

fángzi (de) **wàitou**   *outside* the house _____ wàitou de **fángzi**   *the house which is outside*

zhuōzi (de) **shàngtou**   *on top* of the table ___ shàngtou de **zhuōzi**   *the table which is on top*

shūzhuō (de) **hòumiàn**   *behind* the desk ____ hòumiàn de **shūzhuō**   *the desk which is to the rear*

fángjiān **lǐtou**   *inside* the room _____ lǐtou de **fángjiān**   *the room(s) which are inside*

mén **yòubianr**   *to the right* of the door _____ yòubianr de **mén**   *the door which is to the right*

3. There is no difference between <u>wàitou</u>, <u>wàibianr</u>, and <u>wàimiàn</u>— they all mean "outside." <u>Tou</u>, <u>bianr</u>, and <u>miàn</u> all serve the same purpose as the "side" in "outside," and can be used interchangeably among all the locational nouns, except that <u>zuǒ</u> "left" and <u>yòu</u> "right" can only combine with <u>bianr</u>.

Structure exercise

Use the locations and nouns given below to translate each of the phrases into Chinese.

qiántou   hòutou   lǐtou   wàitou   shàngtou   xiàtou   zuǒbianr   yòubianr
chuáng   zhuōzi   shūzhuō   yǐzi   yīchú   yīguì   qiáng   shāfā   fànzhuō

in front of the table _____

behind the desk _____

to the right of the chair _____

under the chest _____

inside the wall _____

on top of the bed _____

outside the closet _____

to the left of the sofa _____

the chest to the right _____

the chair underneath _____

the closet outside _____

the sofa inside _____

the wall on the left _____

the bed on top _____

the dining table to the rear _____

the desk in front _____

in front of the wall _____

the sofa to the right _____

the chair in front _____

inside the chest _____

the closet in back _____

to the left of the sofa _____

under the bed _____

the chair on top _____

the bottom bed _____

behind the dining table _____

on top of the chest _____

the desk outside _____

the sofa inside _____

outside of the closet _____

*Wǒmen xǐ le liǎn, shū hǎo
tóufa yào chī zǎocān le.*

SEGMENT D
Skill: To specify routine activities at home.

Wǒ zài jiāli měitiān _____. *At home I _____ everyday.*

qī diǎn qǐchuáng   *get up at 7:00*

xǐliǎn   *wash (my) face*

xǐshǒu   *wash (my) hands*

shuāyá   *brush (my) teeth*

shū tóufa   *comb (my) hair*

guā húzi   *shave*

huàzhuāng   *put on make-up*

xǐwǎn	*wash the dishes*		
xǐ yīfu	*do the laundry*	zuò _____	*cook, fix_____*
zhěnglǐ fángjiān	*put (my) room in order*	chī _____	*eat _____*
zuò gōngkè	*do (my) homework*	zǎofàn	*breakfast*
xǐzǎo	*take a bath*	wǔfàn	*lunch*
shí diǎn shuìjiào	*go to sleep at 10:00*	wǎnfàn	*dinner*

píngcháng	*usually*		
chángcháng	*often*	chūmen	*leave the house*
yǒude shíhou	*sometimes*	huíjiā	*return home*

Wǒ píngcháng bā diǎn bàn chūmén.   *I generally leave the house at 8:30.*

Wǒ chángcháng bù chī zǎofàn.   *I often don't eat breakfast.*

Dialogue Practice

The following sets of dialogues presume normal behavior, no unusual circumstances, and no misunderstandings in the contexts indicated. "A" begins the dialogue, "B" responds, "A" responds to "B," etc. Where there is a choice of responses available, please circle the one which is more appropriate.

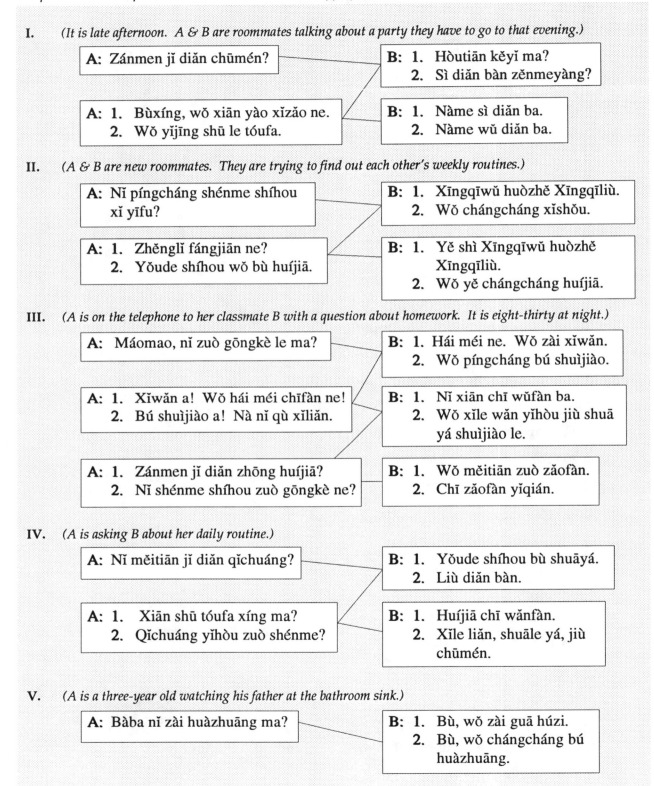

I.　(It is late afternoon. A & B are roommates talking about a party they have to go to that evening.)

A: Zánmen jǐ diǎn chūmén?

B: 1. Hòutiān kěyǐ ma?
　　 2. Sì diǎn bàn zěnmeyàng?

A: 1. Bùxíng, wǒ xiān yào xǐzǎo ne.
　 2. Wǒ yǐjīng shū le tóufa.

B: 1. Nàme sì diǎn ba.
　 2. Nàme wǔ diǎn ba.

II.　(A & B are new roommates. They are trying to find out each other's weekly routines.)

A: Nǐ píngcháng shénme shíhou xǐ yīfu?

B: 1. Xīngqīwǔ huòzhě Xīngqīliù.
　 2. Wǒ chángcháng xǐshǒu.

A: 1. Zhěnglǐ fángjiān ne?
　 2. Yǒude shíhou wǒ bù huíjiā.

B: 1. Yě shì Xīngqīwǔ huòzhě Xīngqīliù.
　 2. Wǒ yě chángcháng huíjiā.

III.　(A is on the telephone to her classmate B with a question about homework. It is eight-thirty at night.)

A: Máomao, nǐ zuò gōngkè le ma?

B: 1. Hái méi ne. Wǒ zài xǐwǎn.
　 2. Wǒ píngcháng bú shuìjiào.

A: 1. Xǐwǎn a! Wǒ hái méi chīfàn ne!
　 2. Bú shuìjiào a! Nà nǐ qù xǐliǎn.

B: 1. Nǐ xiān chī wǔfàn ba.
　 2. Wǒ xǐle wǎn yǐhòu jiù shuā yá shuìjiào le.

A: 1. Zánmen jǐ diǎn zhōng huíjiā?
　 2. Nǐ shénme shíhou zuò gōngkè ne?

B: 1. Wǒ měitiān zuò zǎofàn.
　 2. Chī zǎofàn yǐqián.

IV.　(A is asking B about her daily routine.)

A: Nǐ měitiān jǐ diǎn qǐchuáng?

B: 1. Yǒude shíhou bù shuāyá.
　 2. Liù diǎn bàn.

A: 1. Xiān shū tóufa xíng ma?
　 2. Qǐchuáng yǐhòu zuò shénme?

B: 1. Huíjiā chī wǎnfàn.
　 2. Xǐle liǎn, shuāle yá, jiù chūmén.

V.　(A is a three-year old watching his father at the bathroom sink.)

A: Bàba nǐ zài huàzhuāng ma?

B: 1. Bù, wǒ zài guā húzi.
　 2. Bù, wǒ chángcháng bú huàzhuāng.

Morning routines
(Zhāng and David are chatting.)

Zhāng:	Zāogāo, wǒ jīntiān zǎoshang shàngkè yòu chídào le.	*What a hassle. I was late to class again this morning.*
David:	Zěnme le?	*What happened?*
Zhāng:	Wǒ qǐchuáng wǎn le.	*I got up late.*
David:	Nǐ píngcháng jǐ diǎn qǐchuáng?	*When do you usually get up?*
Zhāng:	Qī diǎn bàn.	*Seven-thirty.*
David:	Qī diǎn bàn qǐ chuáng bā diǎn jiù néng shàngkè? Zěnme nàme kuài?	*You get up at seven-thirty and you can make it to class at eight? How (do you do it) so fast?*
Zhāng:	Wǒ shuā ge yá, xǐ ge liǎn, shū ge tóu jiù chūmen le. Nǐ zěnmeyàng?	*I give my teeth a brush, my face a wash, run a comb through my hair and I'm out the door. How about you?*
David:	Ou, wǒ bùxíng a. Wǒ zǎoshang háiyào xǐzǎo, xǐtóu, guā húzi ne.	*Oh, I can't do that. I have to take a bath, wash my hair and shave, in addition to that.*
Zhāng:	Tiāntiān xǐtóu duì shēntǐ bù hǎo a.	*It's not healthy to wash your hair everyday, you know.*
David:	*(laughing)* Nǎr de huà.	*Who says so!*

Culture notes

Chinese in major metropolitan areas all over the world with access to private bathrooms are often quite fastidious about bathing once a day before bed. Such urbanites are often puzzled by Americans who, even though they have access to bathing facilities, still retire without a proper bath.

Most people in the PRC, however, do not have modern, private bathrooms. Many urban dwellers frequent public neighborhood baths or the bathing facilities at their workplace once or twice a week. In the countryside, bathing is often accomplished at a bucket filled at a well or a pump, and is particularly difficult in the winter.

Many Chinese, even modern urbanites, do not feel comfortable about washing the hair too often. One regional belief is that washing one's hair more than at most twice a week will lead to headaches.

Chinese who have had occasion to compare do not as a rule consider their own body odor as pungent as that of foreigners—white, black, or brown. A whiff of run-of-the-mill "foreign body odor" leads some Chinese to believe that foreigners in general disdain baths.

Since Chinese as a rule have less facial and body hair than other races, not all Chinese men shave every day. Body hair is considered unattractive on both sexes—many Chinese find hair on the chest and back particularly distressing.

Structure notes

1. This lesson utilizes the following sentence pattern.

> **5b. Subject + [bú] + <u>zài</u> + Place/(Noun + Locational noun) + Verb phrase**

Tā zài jiālǐ chīfàn.	he + to be at + home + in + to eat	He eats at home.
Tā yě zài xuéxiào chīfàn.	he + also + to be at + school + in + to eat	He also eats at school.
Wǒ xǐhuan zài péngyou jiālǐ chīfàn.	I + to like + to be at + friend's house + to eat	I like to eat at my friend's house.
Wǒ yě xǐhuan zài péngyou jiālǐ dǎpái huòzhě kàn diànshì.	I + also + to like + to be at + friend's house + to play cards + or + to watch television	I also like to play cards or watch television at my friend's house.

2. <u>Píngcháng</u> "normally, usually, generally," <u>chángcháng</u> "often," and <u>yǒu de shíhou</u> "sometimes" go either directly before or directly after the subject of the sentence, in most cases.

Píngcháng wǒ bā diǎn zhōng chī zǎofàn.	normally + I + eight o'clock+ to eat + breakfast	I normally eat breakfast at eight o'clock.
Wǒ píngcháng bā diǎn bàn chūmén.	I + normally + eight thirty + to leave the house	I normally leave the house at eight thirty.
Yǒude shíhou wǒ bù chī zǎofàn jiù chūmén.	sometimes + I + not + to eat + breakfast + right away + to leave the house	Sometimes I leave the house without eating breakfast.

<u>Yǒude</u> is a useful term to mean "some," (literally "there are some..,") as in <u>yǒude rén</u> "some people," <u>yǒude shíhou</u> "sometimes," <u>yǒude dōngxi</u> "some things."

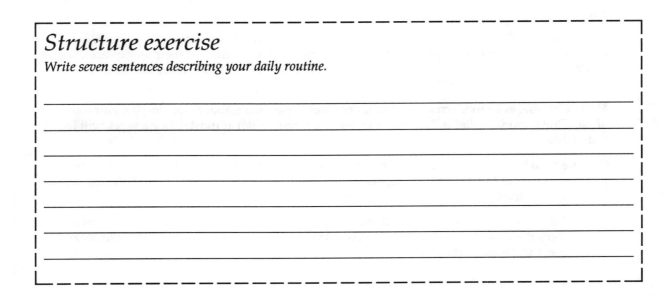

Structure exercise
Write seven sentences describing your daily routine.

_____

_____

_____

_____

_____

_____

_____

SEGMENT A
Skill: To name & locate items in a classroom.

Jiàoshì lǐtou yǒu_____.   *In the classroom is/are_____.*

(yí kuài) hēibǎn	*a blackboard*
(yí ge) bǎncā	*a board eraser*
(yí ge) zhōng	*a clock*
(yí ge) zhǐlǒu	*a wastebasket*
(yí ge) xiāobǐjī	*a pencil sharpener*
(yí ge) dìqiúyí	*a globe*
(yì zhāng) dìtú	*a map*
(yì zhāng) hǎibào	*a poster*
(yí ge) bùgàopái	*a bulletin board*
diànfēngshàn	*electric fan(s)*
kōngtiáo	*airconditioning (PRC)*
lěngqì	*airconditioning (Taiwan)*
mén	*door(s)*
chuānghù	*window(s)*

Wǒ de shūbāo lǐtou yǒu_____.   *In my bookbag there is/are_____.*

(yì zhī) qiānbǐ	*a pencil*
(yì zhī) yuánzhūbǐ	*a ball-point pen*
(yì zhī) qiānzìbǐ	*a fine-line, felt-tipped pen*
(yì bǎ) chǐzi	*a ruler*
(yí kuài) xiàngpí	*a rubber eraser*
jǐ ge bǐjìběn	*a few notebooks*
jǐ běn kèběn	*a few textbooks*
(yì běn) zìdiǎn	*a dictionary*

Qǐng bǎ nǐ de qiānbǐ jiègěi wǒ.   *Please lend me your pencil.*

Nǐ de jiàoshì shì jǐ hào fángjiān?   *What # is your classroom?*

Dialogue Practice

The following sets of dialogues presume normal behavior, no unusual circumstances, and no misunderstandings in the contexts indicated. "A" begins the dialogue, "B" responds, "A" responds to "B," etc. Where there is a choice of responses available, please circle the one which is more appropriate.

I.   (A & B are classmates. A is trying to borrow a writing implement from B.)

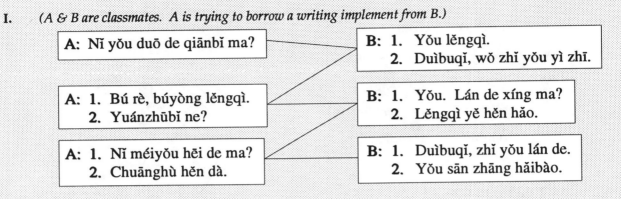

A: Nǐ yǒu duō de qiānbǐ ma?

B: 1. Yǒu lěngqì.
   2. Duìbuqǐ, wǒ zhǐ yǒu yì zhī.

A: 1. Bú rè, búyòng lěngqì.
   2. Yuánzhūbǐ ne?

B: 1. Yǒu. Lán de xíng ma?
   2. Lěngqì yě hěn hǎo.

A: 1. Nǐ méiyǒu hēi de ma?
   2. Chuānghù hěn dà.

B: 1. Duìbuqǐ, zhǐ yǒu lán de.
   2. Yǒu sān zhāng hǎibào.

II. (A calls her classmate B on the telephone, trying to remember if there is a map in their classroom.)

A: Wǒ wàng le, wǒmen jiàoshì lǐ yǒu dìtú ma?

B: 1. Yǒu. Zài hēibǎn pángbianr.
   2. Yǒu yì běn hěn dà de.

A: 1. Nǐ xǐhuan yòng chǐzi ma?
   2. Hēibǎn pángbianr? Nǎr?

B: 1. Chǐzi zài zhǐlǒu lǐ.
   2. Zài jiǎoluò nàr.

III. (A & B are classmates waiting at a bus-stop. A is curious about B's bulging book-bag.)

A: Nǐ shūbāo lǐ yǒu shénme?

B: 1. Chuānghù, mén, dōu yǒu.
   2. Yǒu kèběn gēn bǐjìběn.

A: 1. Duìbuqǐ, wǒ méiyǒu xiàngpí.
   2. Méiyǒu zìdiǎn ma?

B: 1. Qǐng jiè jǐ zhāng zhǐ gěi wǒ.
   2. Yǒu, yǒu yì běn xiǎo de.

IV. (A is new to class. Bored, he wonders when class is going to be over, and looks to find out the time. B is a regular student in this class.)

A: Zhōng zài nǎr?

B: 1. Zhǐlǒu lǐtou.
   2. Bùgàopái shàngtou.

V.   (A & B are getting acquainted at a party, and chat about their respective schools.)

A: Nǐmen jiàoshì yǒu kōngtiáo ma?

B: 1. Méiyǒu. Búyòng.
   2. Kěnéng yǒu hǎibào.

A: 1. Bǎncā bú zài hēibǎn nàr ma?
   2. Nǐ bù juéde rè ma?

B: 1. Wǒ yào yòng xiǎobǐjī.
   2. Bù. Yīnwèi yǒu diàn fēngshàn.

Cleaning the classroom

(Li Zhongying and her sister Li Zhongxiu are chatting in their bedroom before going to sleep.)

Sister: Jiějie, wǒmen jīntiān dǎsǎo le jiàoshì.
Sister, we cleaned the classroom today.

Lǐ: O? Nǐ zuò le shénme?
Oh? What did you do?

Sister: Wǒ cā le hēibǎn hé chuānghù.
I wiped the blackboard and the windows.

Lǐ: Zhēn hǎo. Qítā tóngxué zuò le shénme?
That's really good. What did the other students do?

Sister: Mmm, qīnglǐ bùgàopái, sǎodì, cā dìbǎn, cā zhuōzi yǐzi, dào zhǐlǒu...Máomao hé Jūnjun bāng wǒ cā ménchuāng.
Um, they cleaned off the bulletin board, swept and mopped the floor, wiped the tables and chairs, emptied the wastebaskets...Maomao and Junjun helped me wash the windows and doors.

Lǐ: Wa, hǎo máng o.
Wow, you were really busy.

Culture notes

As part of the training to turn young people into responsible adults, elementary and high school students spend 2-3 hours a week cleaning their classrooms and otherwise beautifying the campus. Since most schools do not have a cleaning staff, each classroom teacher is responsible for a share of the cleaning, and supervises his/her class in the task. Major clean-up chores (washing windows, planting trees) are handled on Saturday afternoons, when principals and other administrators participate. Even university students have a share of cleaning responsibilities on their campuses.

Children sometimes reduplicate one character in their name for a nickname. Li Zhongxiu for instance may have been called "Xiuxiu" by her friends.

Structure notes

1. The first basic pattern in this lesson is #9 <u>**Zài**</u> + **Place** + [<u>**méi**</u>] + <u>**yǒu**</u> + **Noun** (see p. 140). Sentences following this structure state whether or not particular items exist, or are located, at the place indicated.

> Wǒmen de jiàoshì lǐtou méiyǒu hēibǎn.
> *we + 's + classroom + inside + to not have + blackboard*
> *Our classroom does not have a blackboard.*

2. The second pattern is as follows.

> 10. **Subject** + <u>**bǎ**</u> + **Object** + **Verb phrase**

This structure is used to state that an action is/was/will be performed on a specified object: <u>Wǒ bǎ dìqiúyí ná huí jiā le</u> "I took the globe home." <u>Bǎ</u> highlights the object: the object in a <u>bǎ</u> sentence is always specific. The globe in the example sentence is a specific globe: this or that globe, and not just any globe. Even if <u>zhèi</u> or <u>nèi</u> is not stated in the Chinese, this specificity is still understood.

The verb phrase that comes at the end of a <u>bǎ</u> sentence must consist of something more than a single verb. In the example sentence above, <u>ná huí jiā le</u> "took the globe home" is the verb phrase. This lesson utilizes the verb phrase <u>jiègěi wǒ</u> "lend (to) me." <u>Gěi wǒ</u> by itself would me "give me."

Structure exercise

Some sentences that are usually expressed with <u>bǎ</u> also have non-<u>bǎ</u> equivalents. These are generally usually sentences involving short, simple verb phrases, such as the ones below. Please write the English translation for each sentence given in the space marked "E," and the <u>bǎ</u>-version of the sentence in the remaining space.

> Example: •Qǐng nǐ gěi wǒ nèige bǎncā. E: *Please give me that eraser.*
>
> bǎ: *Qǐng bǎ nèige bǎncā gěi wǒ.*
>
> •Qǐng gěi wǒ nèizhāng dìtú.   E:_____
>
> bǎ:_____
>
> •Qǐng gěi tā nèiběn zìdiǎn.   E:_____
>
> bǎ:_____
>
> •Qǐng jiè *(to loan)* wǒ nǐ de zìdiǎn.   E:_____
>
> bǎ:_____
>
> •Qǐng dǎkāi *(to turn on)* diànfēngshàn. E:_____
>
> bǎ:_____
>
> •Qǐng jiè wǒ nǐ de xiàngpí.   E:_____
>
> bǎ:_____
>
> •Tā gěi le wǒ tā de chǐzi.   E:_____
>
> bǎ:_____

SEGMENT B
Skill: To describe school routine.

dì-yī ge xuéqī	*the first semester*
hánjià	*winter recess*
chūnjià	*spring recess*
shǔjià	*summer vacation*

Wǒ dì-yí ge xuéqī xuǎn le _____.   *In the first semester I am taking_____.*

(yì mén) Zhōngwén (kè)	*(a) Chinese (class)*
(yì mén) kēxué (kè)	*(a) science (class)*
(yì mén) shùxué (kè)	*(a) mathematics (class)*
(yì mén) lìshǐ (kè)	*(a) history (class)*
(yì mén) dìlǐ (kè)	*(a) geography (class)*
(yì mén) shèhuì yánjiù (kè)	*(a) social studies (class)*
(yì mén) tǐyù (kè)	*(a) physical education (class)*

(Wǒmen xuéxiào) bā diǎn shàngkè.	*School starts at eight.*
Wǒ jiǔ diǎn shàng Zhōngwén kè.	*I go to my Chinese class at nine.*
Wǒ dì-yī jié shàng Zhōngwén kè.	*I have Chinese the first period.*
Wǒ shí diǎnzhōng xiàkè.	*My class is over at ten.*
(Wǒmen xuéxiào) sān diǎn fàngxué.	*School lets out at three.*

Nǐ niàn shénme?	*What are you studying?*
Nǐ jǐ diǎnzhōng yǒu kè?	*What time do you have class?*
Nǐ dì-yī jié shì shénme kè?	*What is your first period class?*
Zhōngwén kè jǐ diǎn <u>kāishǐ</u>?	*What time does Chinese <u>start</u>?*
Dì-yī ge xuéqī shénme shíhou <u>wán</u>?	*When does the first semester <u>end</u>?*

Dialogue Practice

The following sets of dialogues presume normal behavior, no unusual circumstances, and no misunderstandings in the contexts indicated. "A" begins the dialogue, "B" responds, "A" responds to "B," etc. Where there is a choice of responses available, please circle the one which is more appropriate.

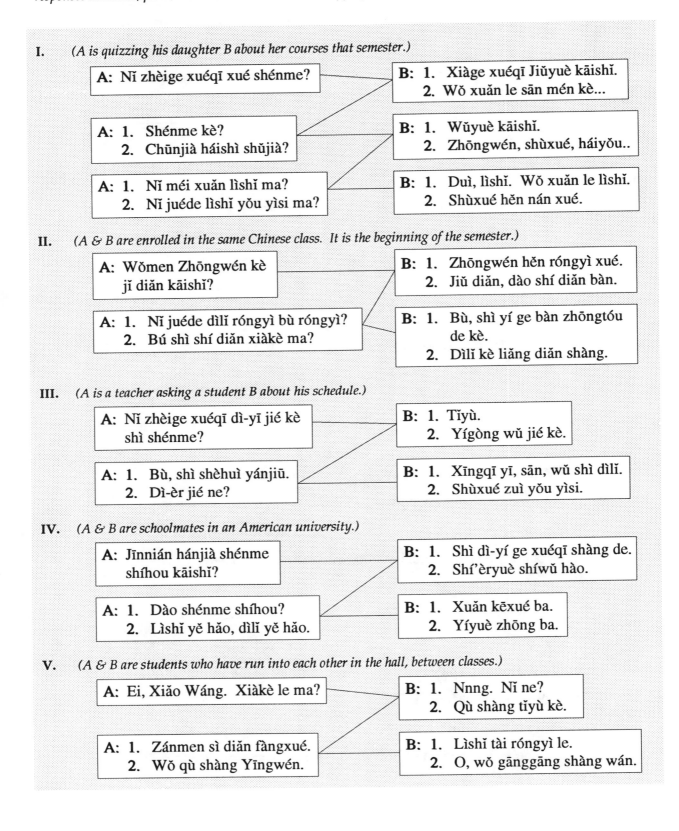

I.   (A is quizzing his daughter B about her courses that semester.)

A: Nǐ zhèige xuéqī xué shénme?

B: 1. Xiàge xuéqī Jiǔyuè kāishǐ.
   2. Wǒ xuǎn le sān mén kè...

A: 1. Shénme kè?
   2. Chūnjià háishì shǔjià?

B: 1. Wǔyuè kāishǐ.
   2. Zhōngwén, shùxué, háiyǒu..

A: 1. Nǐ méi xuǎn lìshǐ ma?
   2. Nǐ juéde lìshǐ yǒu yìsi ma?

B: 1. Duì, lìshǐ. Wǒ xuǎn le lìshǐ.
   2. Shùxué hěn nán xué.

II.   (A & B are enrolled in the same Chinese class. It is the beginning of the semester.)

A: Wǒmen Zhōngwén kè jǐ diǎn kāishǐ?

B: 1. Zhōngwén hěn róngyì xué.
   2. Jiǔ diǎn, dào shí diǎn bàn.

A: 1. Nǐ juéde dìlǐ róngyì bù róngyì?
   2. Bú shì shí diǎn xiàkè ma?

B: 1. Bù, shì yí ge bàn zhōngtóu de kè.
   2. Dìlǐ kè liǎng diǎn shàng.

III. (A is a teacher asking a student B about his schedule.)

A: Nǐ zhèige xuéqī dì-yī jié kè shì shénme?

B: 1. Tǐyù.
   2. Yígòng wǔ jié kè.

A: 1. Bù, shì shèhuì yánjiū.
   2. Dì-èr jié ne?

B: 1. Xīngqī yī, sān, wǔ shì dìlǐ.
   2. Shùxué zuì yǒu yìsi.

IV.   (A & B are schoolmates in an American university.)

A: Jīnnián hánjià shénme shíhou kāishǐ?

B: 1. Shì dì-yí ge xuéqī shàng de.
   2. Shí'èryuè shíwǔ hào.

A: 1. Dào shénme shíhou?
   2. Lìshǐ yě hǎo, dìlǐ yě hǎo.

B: 1. Xuǎn kēxué ba.
   2. Yíyuè zhōng ba.

V.   (A & B are students who have run into each other in the hall, between classes.)

A: Ei, Xiǎo Wáng. Xiàkè le ma?

B: 1. Nnng. Nǐ ne?
   2. Qù shàng tǐyù kè.

A: 1. Zánmen sì diǎn fàngxué.
   2. Wǒ qù shàng Yīngwén.

B: 1. Lìshǐ tài róngyì le.
   2. O, wǒ gānggāng shàng wán.

Plans

(Li and a friend leave class together.)

Friend: Kuài dào hánjià le. Zhōngyīng, nǐ
         xiàge xuéqī pái le shénme kè?

It's almost winter recess. Zhongying, what courses did you get next semester?

Lǐ: Shùxué, wùlǐ gēn Yīngyǔ. Nǐ ne?

Math, physics, and English. And you?

Friend: Hái bù zhīdao. Tāmen hái méi
         tōngzhī wǒ ne.

I don't know yet. They haven't contacted me yet.

(Zhang catches up with them.)

Zhāng: Xiǎo Lǐ.

Li.

Lǐ: Ei, Déshēng. Nǐ rènshi Wáng
         Huìlán ma?

Hi, Desheng. Do you know Wang Huilan?

Zhāng: Bú rènshi, nǐ hǎo. Wǒ shì
         Zhāng Déshēng.

No, how do you do. I'm Zhang Desheng.

(The friend smiles and nods.)

Lǐ: Xiǎo Zhāng, zěnmeyàng. Nǐ
         hánjià zuò shénme?

Zhang, how about it. What are you doing over winter break?

Zhāng: Wǒ huí jiā lo. Hǎohaor
         xiūxi xiūxi.

I'm going home! To have a good rest.

Culture notes

Students in schools and even universities in the PRC and Taiwan have some but not very much choice in which classes they take. The secondary school curriculum is more or less fixed; for the university level, students take entrance exams and place into courses of study. Classes are by and large determined by a course of study; students do not have many electives to choose from.

The winter recess in a Chinese academic calendar occurs at Chinese New Year (based on the lunar calendar)—which generally occurs between mid-January and mid-February. Winter recess lasts approximately a month. Summer vacation begins in early or mid-July and ends on September 1.

During school vacations, students generally either stay home with their families, or take special "cram" courses to catch up with or to get a head start on their school-work. Even students who stay at home often use the time to review or to read ahead. Since entrance into high schools and universities is by competitive examination, pressure on students to perform is intense.

Structure notes

1. Expressions such as <u>dì-yī ge xuéqī</u>, <u>dì-èr ge xuéqī</u>, <u>hánjià</u>, <u>shǔjià</u> etc. involve time, and as such go in the normal time expression position, either directly before or directly after the subject of the sentence.

2. Similarly, <u>dì-yī jié</u> (<u>dì-èr jié</u> etc.) "first period (second period etc.)," as time expressions, are used directly before or directly after the subject of the sentence. If both <u>dì yī ge xuéqī</u> and <u>dì-yī jié kè</u> are used in the same sentence, then the rule about larger divisions preceding smaller divisions in reference to time and place applies.

> Wǒ dì-yī ge xuéqī dì-yī jié kè shì Zhōngwén kè.
> *I + the first semester + the first period + to be + Chinese class*
> *I had Chinese in the first period of the first semester.*

3. <u>Xuéqī</u> "semester" is a noun that is modified by the measure <u>ge</u>. <u>Yí ge xuéqī</u> means "one semester." <u>Jié</u> is a measure word signifying one segment of the noun <u>kè,</u> for "class." Thus, "one period" is <u>yì jié kè</u>. Learners often erroneously say *<u>yí ge jié</u> to mean "one period," which attempts to treat the measure <u>jié</u> as a noun, which it is not, by modifying it with <u>ge</u>.

4. Any number prefixed with <u>dì</u> becomes an ordinal number, as in the following.

> dì-wǔ ge xuéxiào   *the fifth school*
> dì-sì jié kè   *fourth period, the fourth class*
> dì-èrbǎi ge rén   *the two hundredth person*

5. One attends class by "going up, ascending" (<u>shàng</u>) to it, and leaves class by "going down, descending" (<u>xià</u>) from it. Similarly, to attend school is <u>shàngxué</u> "ascend to school," but dismissal from school takes the verb <u>fàng</u> "to release, let go"—<u>fàngxué</u>.

Structure exercise

Please write the Chinese equivalents of the following phrases in the spaces provided.

my fifth period class	the second semester last year
the twentieth student	to let (school) out at 3:25 p.m.
my history class	my 9:30 class
to start at 12 noon	to be over at 1:00 pm (a class)

SEGMENT C
Skill: To describe motion around school.

(yì jiān) jiàoshì	*a classroom*
dàlǐtáng	*the auditorium*
shíyànshì	*the laboratory*
cāntīng	*the cafeteria*
tǐyùguǎn	*the gymnasium*
cāochǎng	*the (playing) field*
yóuyǒngchí	*the swimming pool*
bàngōngshì	*the office*
nǚshēng sùshè	*the girl's dormitory*
nánshēng sùshè	*the boy's dormitory*

Wǒ dào jiàoshì li qù shàngkè.	*I'm going to the classroom to attend class.*
Wǒ dào dàlǐtáng li qù tīng yǎnjiǎng.	*I'm going to the auditorium to listen to a lecture.*
Wǒ dào tǐyùguǎn li qù _____.	*I'm going to the gym to _____.*

dǎ lánqiú	*play basketball*
dǎ páiqiú	*play volleyball*
zuò tǐcāo	*do exercises*

Wǒ dào cāochǎng qù_____.   *I'm going to the field to_____.*

tī zúqiú	*play soccer*
tī Měishì zúqiú	*play (American) football*

Wǒ cānjiā tiánjìng duì.	*I'm on the track & field team.*
Wǒ cānjiā yóuyǒng duì.	*I'm on the swimming team.*
Wǒ dào bàngōngshì qù bànshì.	*I'm going to the office to do some business.*

Dialogue Practice

The following sets of dialogues presume normal behavior, no unusual circumstances, and no misunderstandings in the contexts indicated. "A" begins the dialogue, "B" responds, "A" responds to "B," etc. Where there is a choice of responses available, please circle the one which is more appropriate.

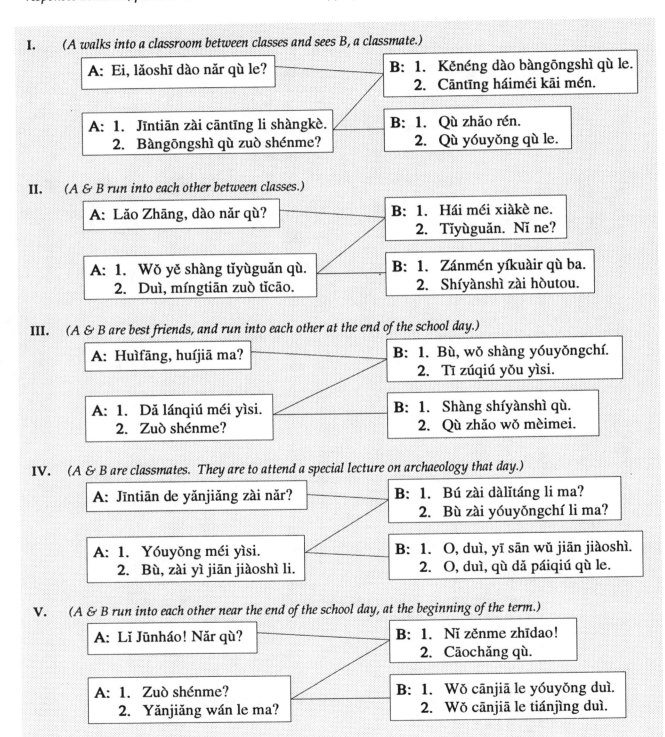

I. (A walks into a classroom between classes and sees B, a classmate.)

A: Ei, lǎoshī dào nǎr qù le?

B: 1. Kěnéng dào bàngōngshì qù le.
    2. Cāntīng háiméi kāi mén.

A: 1. Jīntiān zài cāntīng li shàngkè.
    2. Bàngōngshì qù zuò shénme?

B: 1. Qù zhǎo rén.
    2. Qù yóuyǒng qù le.

II. (A & B run into each other between classes.)

A: Lǎo Zhāng, dào nǎr qù?

B: 1. Hái méi xiàkè ne.
    2. Tǐyùguǎn. Nǐ ne?

A: 1. Wǒ yě shàng tǐyùguǎn qù.
    2. Duì, míngtiān zuò tǐcāo.

B: 1. Zánmén yíkuàir qù ba.
    2. Shíyànshì zài hòutou.

III. (A & B are best friends, and run into each other at the end of the school day.)

A: Huìfāng, huíjiā ma?

B: 1. Bù, wǒ shàng yóuyǒngchí.
    2. Tī zúqiú yǒu yìsi.

A: 1. Dǎ lánqiú méi yìsi.
    2. Zuò shénme?

B: 1. Shàng shíyànshì qù.
    2. Qù zhǎo wǒ mèimei.

IV. (A & B are classmates. They are to attend a special lecture on archaeology that day.)

A: Jīntiān de yǎnjiǎng zài nǎr?

B: 1. Bú zài dàlǐtáng li ma?
    2. Bù zài yóuyǒngchí li ma?

A: 1. Yóuyǒng méi yìsi.
    2. Bù, zài yì jiān jiàoshì li.

B: 1. O, duì, yī sān wǔ jiān jiàoshì.
    2. O, duì, qù dǎ páiqiú qù le.

V. (A & B run into each other near the end of the school day, at the beginning of the term.)

A: Lǐ Jūnháo! Nǎr qù?

B: 1. Nǐ zěnme zhīdao!
    2. Cāochǎng qù.

A: 1. Zuò shénme?
    2. Yǎnjiǎng wán le ma?

B: 1. Wǒ cānjiā le yóuyǒng duì.
    2. Wǒ cānjiā le tiánjìng duì.

Looking for David

(Zhang, Li, and some friends are working on an English lesson.)

Friend:	Aiya, wǒ zhēnde bù dǒng Yīngyǔ a.	*Arggh, I really don't understand English.*
Zhāng:	Zěnmele?	*What's wrong?*
Friend:	Yīngwén wénfǎ méi dàolǐ.	*English grammar makes no sense.*
Lǐ:	Shénme wèntí?	*What's the problem?*
Friend:	*The* gēn *a* yǒu shénme bù tóng?	*What's the difference between "the" and "a?"*
Zhāng:	Nà hěn jiǎndān ma. *The* jiùshi "nèige" de yìsi; *a* jiùshi "suíbiàn něige" de yìsi.	*But that's very simple. "The" means "that one"; "a" is just "whichever one."*
Friend:	Nàme wèishénme shuō *I am going to see a friend*—yòu bú shì suíbiàn yí ge péngyou; wǒ qù kàn de shì **nèige** péngyou. Yīngdāng shì *I am going to see the friend* ba.	*Then why say "I am going to see a friend"—it's not just any friend; the one I'm going to see is THAT (particular) friend. It should be "I am going to see the friend," (right)?*
Li:	Nnng. Zánmen qù wèn David ba.	*Hmm. Let's go ask David.*
Zhāng:	Tā hǎoxiàng dào bàngōngshì qù le.	*I think he went to the office. (He seems to have gone to the office.)*
Li:	Bù, wǒ gāngcái kànjian tā wǎng tǐyùguǎn nèibianr zǒu.	*No, I saw him just now going towards the gym.*
Friend:	Nà wǒmen dào tǐyùguǎn qù zhǎo tā ba.	*Then let's go to the gym to look for him.*
Zhāng:	Tā ài yùndòng. Bú zài tǐyùguǎn li jiù zài cāochǎng shang.	*He likes to exercise. If he's not in the gym, he'll be on the field.*
Friend:	Zài tǐyùguǎn li dǎ páiqiú ma?	*Does he play volleyball in the gym?*
Zhāng:	Bù, dǎ lánqiú.	*No, basketball.*

Culture notes

Chinese grammar, some say, is much simpler than the grammars of most other languages—there is no subject-verb agreement, for instance, and no modification of the verb for tense. English, since it derives from Greek, Latin, Celtic, Germanic and other sources, is particularly complex in its grammar and lexicon. Rules of English grammar and pronunciation exist, but so do many exceptions to the rules, and this is frustrating to people trying to learn it as a foreign language. The problem of when to use "a" versus "the" is particularly persistent.

English is the most popular foreign language in Taiwan and the PRC. Westerners living among the Chinese (including Europeans who may not speak English natively) are often sought out for English conversation and instruction.

Sports (ping-pong, volleyball, basketball, swimming, soccer, tennis) are popular among Chinese youth. Gymnastics and diving are popular as spectator sports.

Structure notes

1. The structure underlying this lesson is as follows.

> **7a.** Subject + [bú] + dào + Place + qù + Verb phrase

The verb phrase here is an activity that is carried out at the place in question. Generally, it consists of a verb plus its object, such as dǎ lánqiú "to play basket ball," or tīng yǎnjiǎng "to listen to a lecture."

The phrase structure dào + place + qù is frequently used with motion from one place to another. There is a variant that dispenses with dào and just treats "to go to a place" as a verb plus its object. Thus, qù xuéxiào is "to go to school"—qù xuéxiào is the same as dào xuéxiào qù. When the sentence is more complex, however, involving going to a place TO DO SOMETHING as in pattern #7a, for instance, dào is generally used for clarity. *Wǒ qù xuéxiào qù dǎ páiqiú is awkward; wǒ dào xuéxiào qù dǎ páiqiú "I'm going to school to play volleyball" is what is generally said.

"Going home" is always huí jiā—never *qù jiā or *dào jiā qù. This is idiomatic usage.

2. Dào by itself means "to arrive." Thus: Tā dào le "She has arrived," and Xiǎo Wáng wǔ diǎnzhōng dào "Xiao Wang will arrive at five."

3. Cānjiā means "to participate in"; cānjiā yóuyǒng duì is literally "to participate in the swim team."

Structure exercise

Fill in each blank below with an appropriate word, based on the English translation.

Wǒ _____ hěn máng. Bā diǎnzhōng wǒ děi _____sān hào jiàoshì qù
_____ lìshǐ kè. Xiàle kè yǐhòu, wǒ yào dào tǐyùguǎn _____ zuò tǐcāo.
Yào zuò yí ge zhōngtóu de tǐcāo. Ránhòu, wǒ děi dào shíyànshì qù shàng
_____. Xiàle kēxué kè yǐhòu, wǒ _____ péngyou yíkuàir qù chī wǔfàn.
Wǔfàn chīwán le yǐhòu, wǒ děi dào shí'èr _____jiàoshì qù shàng dìlǐ kè. Dìlǐ
kè jīntiān shì _____ge zhōngtóu. Wánle yǐhòu, wǒ děi qù _____.
Wǒ yǒu yìdiǎnr shì yào bàn. Yǐhòu wǒ kěyǐ _____ jiā le. Wǒ jīntiān dàgài
sì_____ zhōng dào jiā.

I'm very busy today. At eight I have to go to classroom 3 to attend a history class. After class, I'll go to the gym to do exercises. I'll exercise for an hour. After that, I have to go to the lab for a science class. After science class, I'll go eat lunch with a friend. After we've finished lunch, I have to go to classroom 12 for a geography class. This geography class is two hours today. After it's over, I have to go to the office. I have some things to take care of. After that I can go home. I will probably reach home at four today.

SEGMENT D
Skill: To identify people at school.

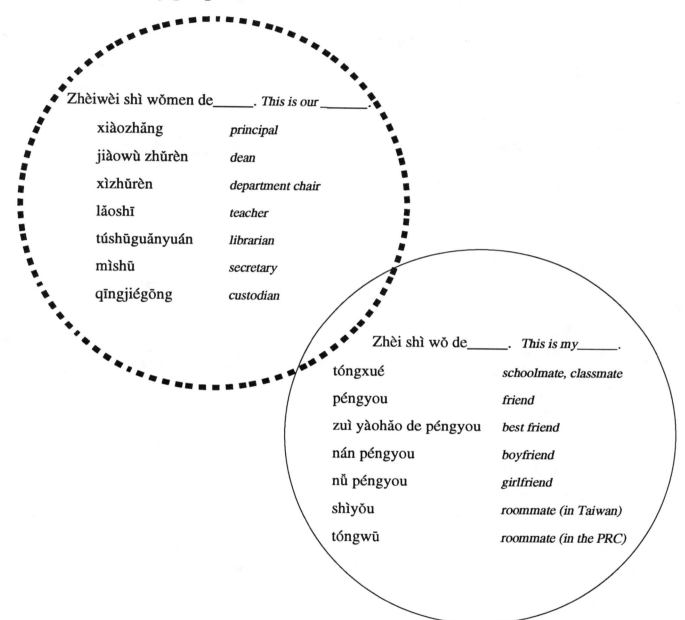

Zhèiwèi shì wŏmen de_____. *This is our _____.*

xiàozhăng	*principal*
jiàowù zhŭrèn	*dean*
xìzhŭrèn	*department chair*
lăoshī	*teacher*
túshūguănyuán	*librarian*
mìshū	*secretary*
qīngjiégōng	*custodian*

Zhèi shì wŏ de_____. *This is my_____.*

tóngxué	*schoolmate, classmate*
péngyou	*friend*
zuì yàohăo de péngyou	*best friend*
nán péngyou	*boyfriend*
nŭ péngyou	*girlfriend*
shìyŏu	*roommate (in Taiwan)*
tóngwū	*roommate (in the PRC)*

Nĭmen de xiàozhăng xìng shénme?	*What is your principal's name?*
Nĭ de tóngxué jiào shénme míngzi?	*What is your classmate's name?*
Shéi shì nĭ de shìyŏu?	*Who is your roommate?*
Nĭ péngyou cóng năr lái de?	*Where is your friend from?*
Wŏ bú shì nĭ zuì yàohăo de péngyou ma?	*Aren't I your best friend?*

Dialogue Practice

The following sets of dialogues presume normal behavior, no unusual circumstances, and no misunderstandings in the contexts indicated. "A" begins the dialogue, "B" responds, "A" responds to "B," etc. Where there is a choice of responses available, please circle the one which is more appropriate.

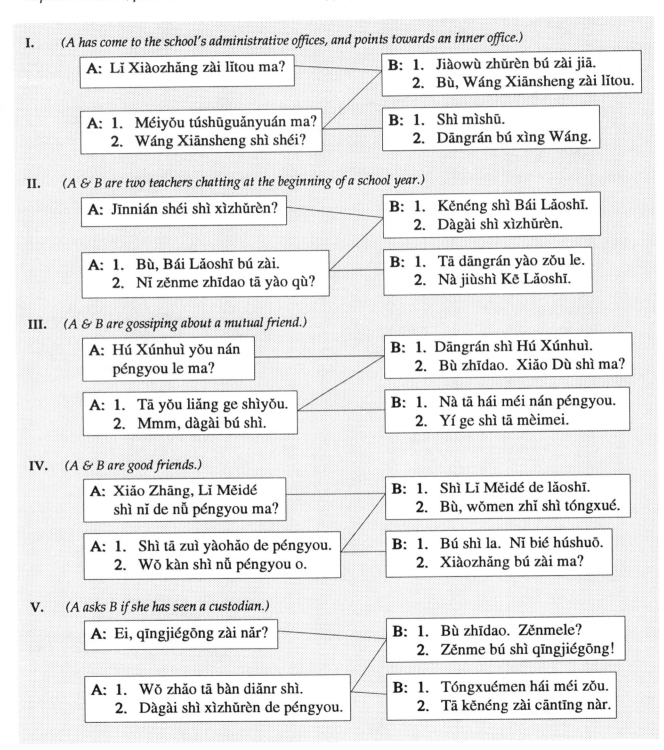

I. (A has come to the school's administrative offices, and points towards an inner office.)

A: Lǐ Xiàozhǎng zài lǐtou ma?

B: 1. Jiàowù zhǔrèn bú zài jiā.
   2. Bù, Wáng Xiānsheng zài lǐtou.

A: 1. Méiyǒu túshūguǎnyuán ma?
   2. Wáng Xiānsheng shì shéi?

B: 1. Shì mìshū.
   2. Dāngrán bú xìng Wáng.

II. (A & B are two teachers chatting at the beginning of a school year.)

A: Jīnnián shéi shì xìzhǔrèn?

B: 1. Kěnéng shì Bái Lǎoshī.
   2. Dàgài shì xìzhǔrèn.

A: 1. Bù, Bái Lǎoshī bú zài.
   2. Nǐ zěnme zhīdao tā yào qù?

B: 1. Tā dāngrán yào zǒu le.
   2. Nà jiùshì Kē Lǎoshī.

III. (A & B are gossiping about a mutual friend.)

A: Hú Xúnhuì yǒu nán péngyou le ma?

B: 1. Dāngrán shì Hú Xúnhuì.
   2. Bù zhīdao. Xiǎo Dù shì ma?

A: 1. Tā yǒu liǎng ge shìyǒu.
   2. Mmm, dàgài bú shì.

B: 1. Nà tā hái méi nán péngyou.
   2. Yí ge shì tā mèimei.

IV. (A & B are good friends.)

A: Xiǎo Zhāng, Lǐ Měidé shì nǐ de nǚ péngyou ma?

B: 1. Shì Lǐ Měidé de lǎoshī.
   2. Bù, wǒmen zhǐ shì tóngxué.

A: 1. Shì tā zuì yàohǎo de péngyou.
   2. Wǒ kàn shì nǚ péngyou o.

B: 1. Bú shì la. Nǐ bié húshuō.
   2. Xiàozhǎng bú zài ma?

V. (A asks B if she has seen a custodian.)

A: Ei, qīngjiégōng zài nǎr?

B: 1. Bù zhīdao. Zěnmele?
   2. Zěnme bú shì qīngjiégōng!

A: 1. Wǒ zhǎo tā bàn diǎnr shì.
   2. Dàgài shì xìzhǔrèn de péngyou.

B: 1. Tóngxuémen hái méi zǒu.
   2. Tā kěnéng zài cāntīng nàr.

Gossip

(Zhang , Li , and David are chatting over lunch in the cafeteria.)

David: Nǐmen jiànguo wómen xìzhǔrèn de   *Have you seen our department chair's son?*
         érzi ma?

Zhāng: Jiànguo. Ǎi'ǎi pàngpàng de yí ge xiǎoháir.   *I've seen him. A short(ish), fat(tish) kid.*

David: Qiántiān wǒ tīngjiàn tā zài bàngōngshì li   *The day before yesterday I heard him in the*
         mà xiàozhǎng tāmen.   *office, cursing out (criticizing) the principal and the*
                                                       others.

Lǐ: Zěnme? Xiǎoháizi zěnme mà dàrén na?   *What? How can a child (dare) scold an adult?*

Zhāng: Dāngmiàn mà xiàozhǎng?   *He criticized the principal to his face?*

David: Bù, xiàozhǎng bú zài. Tā shì gēn   *No, the principal wasn't there. He was*
         mìshūmen shuō de.   *talking to the secretaries.*

Zhāng: Tā shuō shénme?   *What did he say?*

David: Shuō xiàozhǎng chǒu, duì biérén yě   *He said the principal was ugly, and wasn't good to*
         bù hǎo.   *people.*

Lǐ: *(laughing)* Zhè shì zěnme shuō de?   *How did he mean that?*

David: Aiya, bù shuō le. Xiǎoháizi bù dǒng shì.   *Aw, I'm not saying anymore. Children don't*
                                                       know what they're doing. (Children don't
                                                       understand the ways of the world.)

Zhāng: Ei? Nǐ zěnme bù shuō le. Kuài shuō a!   *Huh? How can you not say anymore. Out with it!*

Lǐ: Nǐ shuō ya, David! Tā hái shuō shéi le?   *Tell us, David! Who else did he talk about?*

Culture notes

Traditionally, children were trained to be very deferential to adults. A child's virtue was to work hard and be obedient; "speaking one's own mind" or "being one's own person" was not encouraged. Therefore, it was rare to hear of a child with the audacity to criticize his elders.

However, with the current "one-child policy" in the PRC, many children are growing up more pampered and indulged than before. As a result, many are more independent and outspoken than was customary; some social critics worry that they will become monstrous adults who will always place their own needs above everyone else's.

Gossiping in general is a more influential activity in Chinese society than in American. People actually make decisions about what they will or will not do based on what other people have to say, or what they think other people might say.   Gossip sometimes serves as a social corrective: child or spouse abuse, for instance, is often mitigated by neighbors who talk about what is happening. These neighbors (or friends, relatives, and colleagues) might actually interfere with on-going abuse, and take turns "counseling" the perpetrators to make amends. In the case of the conversation above, word of general reaction to the child's behavior would likely eventually get back to the parents, who would then feel some pressure to take corrective action regarding the child. On the other hand, word might also reach the principal of the child's comments, and general reaction to those comments, which in turn might cause the principal to evaluate him/herself. The presence of the gossip mill can, of course, also be extremely intimidating, and prevent people from expressing themselves truthfully.

Structure notes

1. In speaking of one's school, principal, department chair, etc., the Chinese generally use wǒmen de rather than wǒ de—wǒmen de xuéxiào "our/my school," wǒmen de xiàozhǎng "our/my principal." Since schools, principals, and other officials exist for the benefit of a group rather than an individual, it is considered appropriate to make the possessive pronoun collective rather than singular.

2. It was mentioned previously that de is often used to indicate that what goes before it modifies the noun or noun phrase that comes after it. Thus, hěn dà de chènshān means "a very large shirt," with hěn dà modifying chènshān. The following examples further illustrate how de can be used to indicate modification of a noun. (The modifying phrases are underlined, and the noun modified is bold-faced.

Basic sentence:

Nèige rén shì wǒmen xiàozhǎng.	that + ge + person + to be + our + de + principal	**That person** is our principal.

With de modification:

Chuān hóng chènshān de **nèige rén** shì wǒmen xiàozhǎng.	to wear + red + shirt + de + that + ge + person + to be + our + principal	**The person** wearing a red shirt is our principal.
Zài shuōhuà de **nèige rén** shì wǒmen xiàozhǎng.	to be at + to speak + de + that + ge + person + to be + our + principal	**The person** speaking is our principal.
Hén ǎi, hén ǎi de **nèige rén** shì wǒmen xiàozhǎng.	very + to be short + very + to be short + de + that + ge + person + to be + our + principal	**That** very, very short **person** is our principal.
Xiǎo Wáng yòubianr de **nèige rén** shì wǒmen xiàozhǎng.	Xiao Wang + right side + de + that + ge + person + to be + our + principal	**The person** to the right of Xiao Wang is our principal.
Nèige rén shì wǒmen xīn lái de **xiàozhǎng**.	that + ge + person + to be + our + newly arrived + de + principal	That's our new **principal**.
Nèige rén shì wǒmen zuì xǐhuān de **xiàozhǎng**.	that + ge + person + to be + our + most + to like + de + principal	That's the **principal** we like best.

Structure exercise

Write in the modifying phrases below, based on the English equivalents provided.

Nèiběn shū hěn guì.		That book is expensive.
_____	nèiběn shū hěn guì.	The book that you bought is expensive.
_____	nèiběn shū hěn guì.	The book on the table is expensive.
_____	nèiběn shū hěn guì.	The thick book is expensive.
_____	nèiběn shū hěn guì.	The book that you want is expensive.

SEGMENT A
Skill: To identify food groups & order specific foods.

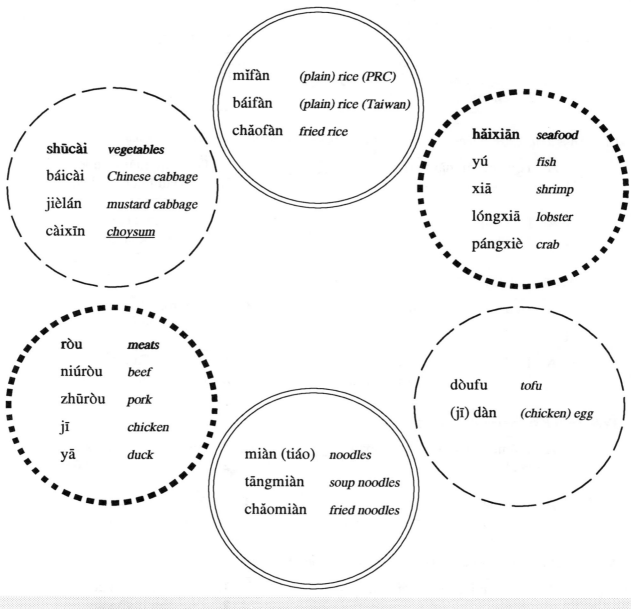

mǐfàn   (plain) rice (PRC)
báifàn   (plain) rice (Taiwan)
chǎofàn   fried rice

shūcài   *vegetables*
báicài   *Chinese cabbage*
jièlán   *mustard cabbage*
càixīn   *choysum*

hǎixiān   *seafood*
yú   *fish*
xiā   *shrimp*
lóngxiā   *lobster*
pángxiè   *crab*

ròu   *meats*
niúròu   *beef*
zhūròu   *pork*
jī   *chicken*
yā   *duck*

dòufu   *tofu*
(jī) dàn   *(chicken) egg*

miàn (tiáo)   *noodles*
tāngmiàn   *soup noodles*
chǎomiàn   *fried noodles*

Wǒ fēicháng xǐhuan chī pángxiè.	*I really love to eat crab.*
	(I like eating crabs extraordinarily well.)
Nǐ xiǎng chī shénme?	*What do you feel like eating?*
Wǒmen jiào (xie) shénme cài?	*What dishes shall we order?*
Tāmen zhèr yú zuò de hěn hǎo.	*They make fish really well here.*

Dialogue Practice

The following sets of dialogues presume normal behavior, no unusual circumstances, and no misunderstandings in the contexts indicated. "A" begins the dialogue, "B" responds, "A" responds to "B," etc. Where there is a choice of responses available, please circle the one which is more appropriate.

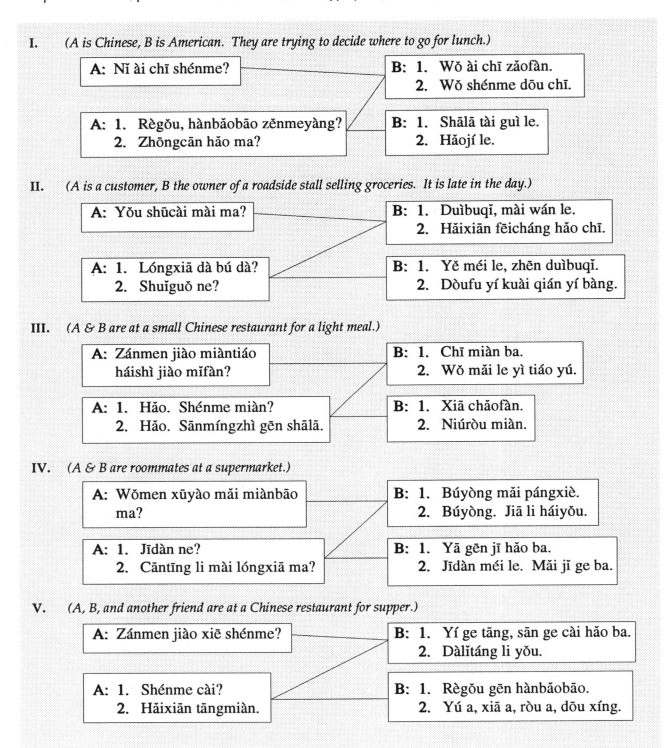

I.　(A is Chinese, B is American. They are trying to decide where to go for lunch.)

A: Nǐ ài chī shénme?

B: 1. Wǒ ài chī zǎofàn.
　 2. Wǒ shénme dōu chī.

A: 1. Règǒu, hànbǎobāo zěnmeyàng?
　 2. Zhōngcān hǎo ma?

B: 1. Shālā tài guì le.
　 2. Hǎojí le.

II.　(A is a customer, B the owner of a roadside stall selling groceries. It is late in the day.)

A: Yǒu shūcài mài ma?

B: 1. Duìbuqǐ, mài wán le.
　 2. Hǎixiān fēicháng hǎo chī.

A: 1. Lóngxiā dà bú dà?
　 2. Shuǐguǒ ne?

B: 1. Yě méi le, zhēn duìbuqǐ.
　 2. Dòufu yí kuài qián yí bàng.

III.　(A & B are at a small Chinese restaurant for a light meal.)

A: Zánmen jiào miàntiáo háishì jiào mǐfàn?

B: 1. Chī miàn ba.
　 2. Wǒ mǎi le yì tiáo yú.

A: 1. Hǎo. Shénme miàn?
　 2. Hǎo. Sānmíngzhì gēn shālā.

B: 1. Xiā chǎofàn.
　 2. Niúròu miàn.

IV.　(A & B are roommates at a supermarket.)

A: Wǒmen xūyào mǎi miànbāo ma?

B: 1. Búyòng mǎi pángxiè.
　 2. Búyòng. Jiā li háiyǒu.

A: 1. Jīdàn ne?
　 2. Cāntīng li mài lóngxiā ma?

B: 1. Yā gēn jī hǎo ba.
　 2. Jīdàn méi le. Mǎi jǐ ge ba.

V.　(A, B, and another friend are at a Chinese restaurant for supper.)

A: Zánmen jiào xiē shénme?

B: 1. Yí ge tāng, sān ge cài hǎo ba.
　 2. Dàlǐtáng li yǒu.

A: 1. Shénme cài?
　 2. Hǎixiān tāngmiàn.

B: 1. Règǒu gēn hànbǎobāo.
　 2. Yú a, xiā a, ròu a, dōu xíng.

Food for dinner

(Li's mother and father have come home from work. Her father is unpacking a fish he bought; her mother is washing rice.)

Father:	Jīntiān shìchǎng dōu mǎi bú dào ròu.	*I couldn't find any pork to buy at the market today.*
Mother:	Nà yě méi guānxi. Chī tài duō ròu duì shēntǐ bù hǎo. Mǎi bú dào ròu zánmen jiù duō chī yìdiǎnr yú.	*That doesn't matter. Eating too much pork is bad for your health. If we can't buy pork we'll just eat a little more fish.*
Father:	Duì, nǐ kàn, zhèi tiáo yú hái tǐng xīnxiān de.	*Right. See, this fish is still very fresh.*
Mother:	Mǎi dào shénme qīngcài le?	*What vegetables did you buy?*
Father:	Yǒu yì kē báicài...zài nàr. Bā máo yì jīn. Háiyǒu...xīhóngshì.	*(There's) a head of Chinese cabbage...over there. Eighty cents a jin (a Chinese measure of weight equivalent to .5 kg or 1.1 lbs). And there are...tomatoes.*
Mother:	Bīngxiāng li háiyǒu jīdàn ma?	*Are there any more eggs in the refrigerator?*
Father:	*(looking in the refrigerator)* Yǒu. Zuò ge fānqié chǎo jīdàn ba.	*Yes. Why don't we make eggs scrambled with tomatoes?*
Mother:	Nnng. Wǒ bǎ mǐ xǐ hǎo jiù lái zuò. Yú, báicài, chǎo jīdàn. Jīntiān yǒu de chī le.	*Uh-huh. As soon as I'm done washing the rice I'll make it. Fish, Chinese cabbage, scrambled eggs. We have plenty of food today.*

Culture notes

Chinese as a rule prefer to shop for food everyday, primarily because most foods are sold fresh, not frozen. Vegetables and fruit in season are plentiful, but meats are expensive and are consumed in far lesser quantity than is common in the U.S.

Ròu by itself generally refers to pork, although technically pork is zhūròu, just as chicken is jīròu (chicken meat) and beef is niúròu (cattle meat).

Most household chores continue to be performed by wives, in spite of the fact that, in most Chinese communities, women as well as men now hold down full-time jobs.

Structure notes

1. <u>Tāmen zhèr</u>, <u>nǐmen nàr</u>, <u>Xiǎo Wáng nàr</u> are examples of a stylistic use of <u>zhèr</u> and <u>nàr</u> that is very common in Chinese. When appended to nouns and pronouns, it indicates the general vicinity of that noun or pronoun.

(said about a mouse on the loose)

Tā dào wǒ zhèr lái le. *it + to + I + here + to come + <u>le</u>* *It's come over to where I am.*

(said about an absent brother)

Dìdi zài pópo nàr chīfàn. *brother + to be at + grandma + there + to eat* *Brother is eating at Grandma's.*

(said about a classmate's family)

Tāmen nàr shuō Rìwén. *they + there + to speak + Japanese* *There they speak Japanese.*

(said in a favorite restaurant)

Tāmen zhèr miàn chǎo de hěn hǎo. *they + here + noodles + to fry + <u>de</u> + very + to be good* *Here they fry noodles very well.*

2. Adjectives used to describe the fashion in which a verb is performed require the use of <u>de</u>, following the pattern below. (Remember that <u>hěn</u> has very little meaning, besides to indicate that the adjective is not being used in a comparative sense.)

11. Subject + Verb + <u>de</u> + [bù] + Adjective

Tā chī de hěn duō. *he + to eat + <u>de</u> + very + to be much* *He eats a lot.*

Tā zǒu de hěn màn. *he + to walk + <u>de</u> + very + to be slow* *He walks slowly.*

Tā shuō de hěn hǎo. *he + to speak + <u>de</u> + very + to be good* *He speaks well.*

Tā xiě de bù hǎo. *he + to write + <u>de</u> + not + to be good* *He doesn't write well.*

3. In cases where an object of the verb is specified, the following additions to the pattern occur.

> **11a. Subject + (Verb +) Object + Verb + de + [bù] + Adjective**

Tā fàn chī de hěn duō.	he + rice + to eat + <u>de</u> + very + to be much	He eats a lot of rice.
Tā Zhōngwén shuō de hěn hǎo.	he + Chinese + to speak + <u>de</u> + very + to be good	He speaks Chinese very well.
Tā xiě xìn xiě de bù hǎo.	he + to write + letter + to write + <u>de</u> + not + to be good	He doesn't write letters very well.
Tā yú zuò de hěn hǎo.	he + fish + to cook + <u>de</u> + very + to be good	He cooks fish very well.
Tā chǎo miàn chǎo de bù hǎo.	he + to fry + noodles + to fry + not + to be good	He doesn't fry noodles very well.

Structure exercise

Complete the sentences below, based on the English on the right.

Wǒ Zhōngwén shuō de bù hěn hǎo.	I don't speak Chinese very well.
Wǒ niúròu_____.	I eat a lot of beef.
Wǒ miàntiáo_____.	I cook noodles really well.
Wǒ jīdàn_____.	I don't eat many eggs.
Wǒ chá_____.	I drink a lot of tea.
Wǒ diànshì_____.	I don't watch much television.

Question:

Nǐ cāi zhè shì shénme dìfāng?

Zhèige rén zài zuò shénme?

Answer:

Zhè shì Zhōngguó cānguǎn (restaurant) lǐ de chúfáng.
Chúshī (chef) zài zuò dāoxiāomiàn (hand-shaved noodles).

SEGMENT B
Skill: To specify style of preparation.

Lái yìdiǎnr ____ ròu ba.   *Let's have some ____ pork.*

jiān	*fried (pan-fried)*
chǎo	*scrambled (stir-fried)*
zhá	*deep-fried (in batter)*
zhǔ	*boiled*
zhēng	*steamed*
lǔ	*stewed (in gravy)*
kǎo	*baked, grilled*
hóngshāo	*red-cooked (stewed in soy sauce)*

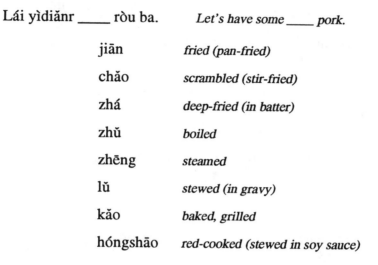

(jī) sī
slivers (of
chicken)

(jī) dīng
*small cubes
(of chicken)*

(jī) piàn
*slices (of
chicken)*

(jī) kuài
*large pieces
(of chicken,
with bones)*

Ròupiàn chǎo cài hǎo ma?	*Is slivers of pork stirfried with vegetables okay?*
Dàn yào chǎo de háishì jiān de?	*Do you want your egg scrambled or fried?*
Yú kǎo de hǎochī ma?	*Is fish good to eat when it's baked?*
Zhèige ròu shì lǔ de ma?	*Is this pork stewed?*
Yǒu méiyǒu zhēng de?	*Do you have any that is steamed?*

Dialogue Practice

The following sets of dialogues presume normal behavior, no unusual circumstances, and no misunderstandings in the contexts indicated. "A" begins the dialogue, "B" responds, "A" responds to "B," etc. Where there is a choice of responses available, please circle the one which is more appropriate.

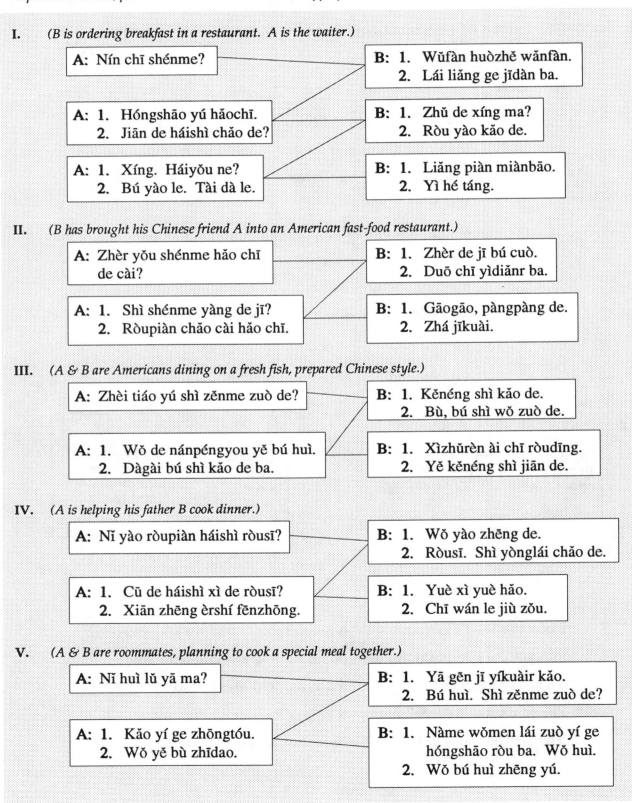

I. (B is ordering breakfast in a restaurant. A is the waiter.)

A: Nín chī shénme?

B: 1. Wǔfàn huòzhě wǎnfàn.
   2. Lái liǎng ge jīdàn ba.

A: 1. Hóngshāo yú hǎochī.
   2. Jiān de háishì chǎo de?

B: 1. Zhǔ de xíng ma?
   2. Ròu yào kǎo de.

A: 1. Xíng. Háiyǒu ne?
   2. Bú yào le. Tài dà le.

B: 1. Liǎng piàn miànbāo.
   2. Yì hé táng.

II. (B has brought his Chinese friend A into an American fast-food restaurant.)

A: Zhèr yǒu shénme hǎo chī de cài?

B: 1. Zhèr de jī bú cuò.
   2. Duō chī yìdiǎnr ba.

A: 1. Shì shénme yàng de jī?
   2. Ròupiàn chǎo cài hǎo chī.

B: 1. Gāogāo, pàngpàng de.
   2. Zhá jīkuài.

III. (A & B are Americans dining on a fresh fish, prepared Chinese style.)

A: Zhèi tiáo yú shì zěnme zuò de?

B: 1. Kěnéng shì kǎo de.
   2. Bù, bú shì wǒ zuò de.

A: 1. Wǒ de nánpéngyou yě bú huì.
   2. Dàgài bú shì kǎo de ba.

B: 1. Xìzhǔrèn ài chī ròudīng.
   2. Yě kěnéng shì jiān de.

IV. (A is helping his father B cook dinner.)

A: Nǐ yào ròupiàn háishì ròusī?

B: 1. Wǒ yào zhēng de.
   2. Ròusī. Shì yònglái chǎo de.

A: 1. Cū de háishì xì de ròusī?
   2. Xiān zhēng èrshí fēnzhōng.

B: 1. Yuè xì yuè hǎo.
   2. Chī wán le jiù zǒu.

V. (A & B are roommates, planning to cook a special meal together.)

A: Nǐ huì lǔ yā ma?

B: 1. Yā gēn jī yíkuàir kǎo.
   2. Bú huì. Shì zěnme zuò de?

A: 1. Kǎo yí ge zhōngtóu.
   2. Wǒ yě bù zhīdao.

B: 1. Nàme wǒmen lái zuò yí ge hóngshāo ròu ba. Wǒ huì.
   2. Wǒ bú huì zhēng yú.

Eating out

(Li, David, and Zhang are eating in a restaurant near their campus.)

Zhāng:	Jiào shénme cài?	*What dishes shall we order?*
Lǐ:	Lái ge yú ba.	*Let's have a fish dish.*
Zhāng:	Shénme yú? Zhēng de? Chǎo de? Hóngshāo de? Quányú háishì yúkuàir?	*What kind of fish? Steamed? Stir-fried? Red-cooked? A whole fish or pieces of fish?*
Lǐ:	Zhēng yú, yào quányú.	*Steamed, a whole fish.*
David:	Hǎo. Yú...zài jiào ge chǎo jīdīng ba.	*Okay. Fish...next let's have stir-fried chicken (cubes).*
Zhāng:	Gōngbǎojīdīng. Nǐ ài chī là de ma?	*Gongbao chicken (a hot dish). Do you like to eat hot food?*
David:	Yí, wǒ bù zěnme néng chī là de.	*Yuck, I can't much stand hot food.*
Lǐ:	*(laughing)*	
	Xiǎo Zhāng tā shì Húnán rén, néng chī hǎo là hǎo là de.	*(Now) Zhang, he's a Hunanese (person). He can eat really really hot food.*
Zhāng:	Duì. Wǒ lián hóng làjiāo dōu néng chī...zhēng de, zhá de, kǎo de, lǔ de, dōu xíng.	*Right. I can even eat red chili-peppers... steamed, deep-fried, baked or stewed, any way is fine.*
David:	Zhēng làjiāo? Lǔ làjiāo?	*Steamed chili-peppers? Stewed chili-peppers?*
Lǐ:	*(laughing)*	
	Nǐ bié tīng tā húshuō. Méiyǒu de shìr.	*Don't listen to his nonsense. There's no such thing.*
Zhāng:	Zhēn de. Wǒ zhǐ bù néng chī shēng de làjiāo.	*It's true. I just (only) can't eat raw chili-peppers.*
	(They all laugh.)	

Culture notes

There are major zones in Chinese regional cooking. Conventional wisdom states that northern food is salty, southeast is sweet, and southwest is hot (spicy). Southern cuisine is based on rice culture and northern on wheat. Thus at a Cantonese meal there are likely to be several dishes to accompany rice, while Northerners often eat noodles, jiǎozi (meat dumplings), or steamed buns.

In any culture, indigenous humor is sometimes hard to understand. Americans often complain that Chinese jokes aren't funny (and vice versa). Jokes generally hinge on a distortion of social convention, and unless the person hearing the joke understands the underlying convention(s), s/he will not appreciate it. Conventions underlying the "joke" in this conversation are twofold: 1) in China, red peppers are often used as one ingredient among many, in a dish, and 2) Hunan cooking is thought to make more extensive use of peppers than other regional cuisine. The absurd notion of having red peppers as the *main* ingredient in a dish, however, was concocted to poke some fun at David as the gullible outsider, as well as to exaggerate the stereotype that Hunan people love hot food.

Structure notes

1. <u>Lái</u> here has the idiomatic meaning of "let there come." <u>Lái yìdiǎnr ròu</u> roughly means "Let there come some pork—bring some pork." Another example of this usage of <u>lái</u> is the call of distress or authority, <u>Lái rén a</u>! "Somebody come (to help)!"

2. The sentence <u>Dàn yào chǎo de ma</u> illustrates a common procedure in Chinese, that of highlighting the object of a verb by moving it to the head of a sentence. The original structure of the sentence would be <u>Nǐ yào chǎo (de) dàn ma</u>, which follows a familiar phrase pattern for modifying a noun with a verb.

nǐ zuò de fàn	you + to make/do + <u>de</u> + food	the food you cooked
chǎo de dàn	to stir-fry + <u>de</u> + egg	stir-fried eggs
tā yào de shū	he + to buy + <u>de</u> + book	the book he wants

Foregrounding the object of the verb makes it the *topic* of the sentence. Thus:

Fàn shì nǐ zuò de ma?	food + to be + you + to make/do + <u>de</u> + ma	Was it you who made the food? (As for this food, was it you who made it?)
Dàn yào chǎo de ma?	egg + to want + to stir-fry + <u>de</u> + ma	Do you want the egg scrambled? (As for the egg, do you want it scrambled?)
Shū shì tā yào de ma?	book + to be + she + to want + <u>de</u> + ma	Was it she who wanted this book? (As for this/that book, was it she who wanted it?)

Structure exercise

The following is a dialogue between a waiter (A) and a customer (B). Fill in the blanks with a word or a phrase as appropriate, using the English as a guide.

A: Jī yào _____ ma? — *Would you like the chicken deep-fried?*

B: Wǒ bù xǐhuan _____. Chǎo jīdīng ba. — *I don't like it fried. Let's have stir-fried chicken (cubes).*

A: _____ ne? — *How about the pork?*

B: _____ hǎo bù hǎo? — *Would stewing it be all right?*

A: Kěyǐ. _____? — *Okay. How about the duck?*

B: _____ yā hǎo bù hǎo? — *Would roast duck be all right?*

A: _____ de...hǎo. Yú yě shì kǎo de _____? — *Roasted...fine. Would it be all right to bake the fish too?*

B: Yú _____ hǎo chī. Lái ge zhēng yú ba. — *Fish is better steamed. Let's have a steamed fish.*

A: Hǎo. — *Okay.*

SEGMENT C
Skill: To specify a dish.

Wǒ zuì ài chī_____.   *My favorite dish is_____. (I most love to eat _____.)*

qīngzhēngyú	*steamed fish*
zhájī	*deep-fried chicken*
jiāngcōngjī	*chicken with ginger & green onion*
hóngshāo niúròu	*red-cooked beef*
tángcù (zhū)ròu	*sweet-sour pork*
mùxūròu	*pork & vegetables with crepe-like wrappers*
Běijīng kǎoyā	*Peking duck (baked)*
jiǎozi	*gyoza; meat-filled dumplings, boiled*
ròusī shíjǐn cài	*slivers of pork w/mixed vegetables*
shíjīnmiàn	*noodles with mixed meats & vegetables*
guōbātāng	*sizzling rice soup*
húndūntāng	*won-ton soup*
suānlàtāng	*hot-sour soup*

Zhèige cài tài ____ le.   *This dish is too _____.*

xián	*salty*
tián	*sweet*
suān	*sour*
dàn	*bland*

Yǒu jǐ dào cài?	*How many courses are we having?*
Yào jǐ ge cài?	*How many dishes shall we have?*
Sān ge cài yí ge tāng hǎo ma?	*How about three dishes & a soup?*
Yǒu méiyǒu tángcùyú?	*Do you have sweet-sour fish?*
Nǐ ài chī là de ma?	*Do you like hot food?*
Nǐ ài chī tián de ma?	*Do you like sweets (desserts)?*

Dialogue Practice

The following sets of dialogues presume normal behavior, no unusual circumstances, and no misunderstandings in the contexts indicated. "A" begins the dialogue, "B" responds, "A" responds to "B," etc. Where there is a choice of responses available, please circle the one which is more appropriate.

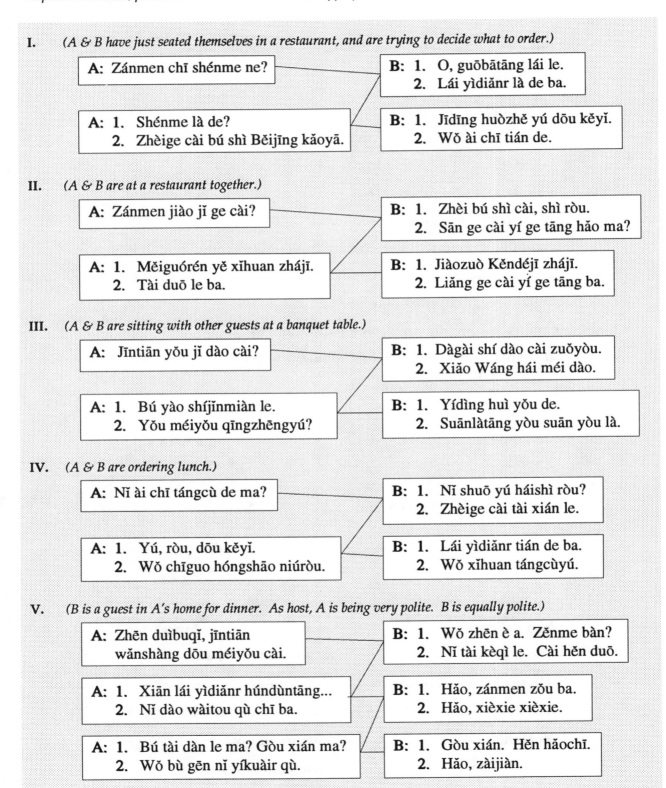

I.   *(A & B have just seated themselves in a restaurant, and are trying to decide what to order.)*

A: Zánmen chī shénme ne?

B: 1. O, guōbātāng lái le.
    2. Lái yìdiǎnr là de ba.

A: 1. Shénme là de?
    2. Zhèige cài bú shì Běijīng kǎoyā.

B: 1. Jīdīng huòzhě yú dōu kěyǐ.
    2. Wǒ ài chī tián de.

II.   *(A & B are at a restaurant together.)*

A: Zánmen jiào jǐ ge cài?

B: 1. Zhèi bú shì cài, shì ròu.
    2. Sān ge cài yí ge tāng hǎo ma?

A: 1. Měiguórén yě xǐhuan zhájī.
    2. Tài duō le ba.

B: 1. Jiàozuò Kěndéjī zhájī.
    2. Liǎng ge cài yí ge tāng ba.

III.   *(A & B are sitting with other guests at a banquet table.)*

A: Jīntiān yǒu jǐ dào cài?

B: 1. Dàgài shí dào cài zuǒyòu.
    2. Xiǎo Wáng hái méi dào.

A: 1. Bú yào shíjǐnmiàn le.
    2. Yǒu méiyǒu qīngzhēngyú?

B: 1. Yídìng huì yǒu de.
    2. Suānlàtāng yòu suān yòu là.

IV.   *(A & B are ordering lunch.)*

A: Nǐ ài chī tángcù de ma?

B: 1. Nǐ shuō yú háishì ròu?
    2. Zhèige cài tài xián le.

A: 1. Yú, ròu, dōu kěyǐ.
    2. Wǒ chīguo hóngshāo niúròu.

B: 1. Lái yìdiǎnr tián de ba.
    2. Wǒ xǐhuan tángcùyú.

V.   *(B is a guest in A's home for dinner. As host, A is being very polite. B is equally polite.)*

A: Zhēn duìbuqǐ, jīntiān wǎnshàng dōu méiyǒu cài.

B: 1. Wǒ zhēn è a. Zěnme bàn?
    2. Nǐ tài kèqì le. Cài hěn duō.

A: 1. Xiān lái yìdiǎnr húndùntāng...
    2. Nǐ dào wàitou qù chī ba.

B: 1. Hǎo, zánmen zǒu ba.
    2. Hǎo, xièxie xièxie.

A: 1. Bú tài dàn le ma? Gòu xián ma?
    2. Wǒ bù gēn nǐ yíkuàir qù.

B: 1. Gòu xián. Hěn hǎochī.
    2. Hǎo, zàijiàn.

Eating out (continued)

(Li, David and Zhang are still in the process of deciding what to order at a restaurant near their campus.)

Lǐ:	Ei, ei, ei. Dàodǐ zěnmeyàng. Zánmen jiào shénme cài ya?	*Hey, hey, hey. So what are we doing? (Finally, how will it be?) What dishes are we ordering?*
Zhāng:	Yǒu le yú, jiào shénme jī ne? Bú'ài chī là de, lái ge jiāngcōngjī ba.	*We have fish, what kind of chicken shall we have? If you don't like hot food, let's order a ginger-green onion chicken.*
David:	Xíng.	*Fine.*
Lǐ:	Hóngshāo de zěnmeyàng?	*How about something red-cooked?*
Zhāng:	Hǎo a. Hóngshāoròu?	*Alright. Red-cooked pork?*
Lǐ:	Kěyǐ. Yàoburán bǎ yú huànchéng hóngshāoyú.	*Okay. Or else we can change the fish to a red-cooked fish.*
Zhāng:	Ya. Nǐ bù chī Guǎngdōng qīngzhēng yú, huànchéng Shànghǎi de hóngshāo yú a.	*Huh? So you don't want the Canton steamed fish, and you are changing to a Shanghai red-cooked fish?*
Li:	Nnng. Huànhuan wèir ma.	*Uh-huh. For a change of taste, you see.*
Zhāng:	Xíng. Zánmen hái shǎo yí ge cài.	*Okay. We are still short a dish.*
David:	Hái méi jiào qīngcài. Sùshíjǐn hǎo ma?	*We haven't ordered a vegetable. Would mixed vegetables (vegetarian mixed medley) be alright?*
Lǐ:	Xíng. Yǒu le sān ge cài, hái yào tāng ma?	*Okay. We have three dishes, do we want soup too?*
David:	Búyòng le.	*No (there's no need for soup).*
Zhāng:	*(to waiter)*	
	Qǐng lái yí ge hóngshāo quányú..	*Please bring us a red-cooked whole fish...*
Waiter:	Aiya. Zhēn dùibuqǐ, yú jīntiān méi le.	*Aaa..I'm really sorry, there's no more fish today.*
Lǐ:	Méiyǒu jiù bù chī le. Huàn mùxūròu zěnmeyàng?	*If there isn't any we won't have any. How about changing to a muxu pork?*
Zhāng:	Xíng. Nàme jiùshì mùxūròu, jiāngcōngjī, sùshíjǐn, hé mǐfàn.	*Fine. In that case, it'll be muxu pork, ginger-green onion chicken, mixed vegetables, and rice.*

Culture notes

A guideline for ordering in a Chinese restaurant is to select one dish for each person present, taking care to maintain a balance among meat, fish, poultry and vegetable dishes, as well as to vary the style of preparation—so that steamed dishes will balance stirfried, stewed, or deep-fried. Dessert is not traditionally a part of the meal, but soup is.

In the PRC, rice is ordered by the ounce (<u>liǎng</u>). Most people eat one to three <u>liǎng</u> per meal. Taiwan and overseas Chinese communities provide rice either in individual bowls or in a large bowl for all at the table to share. There may or may not be an additional charge for the rice.

Structure notes

1. In the sentences <u>Nǐ ài chī là de ma</u> and <u>Nǐ ài chī tián de ma</u>, the adjectives <u>là</u> "to be spicy" and <u>tián</u> "to be sweet" modify an object that has been omitted—either <u>dōngxi</u> "things" or <u>cài</u> "dishes." The full form of the <u>de</u>-modification phrase would be, for example, <u>là de dōngxi</u> or <u>là de cài</u>. The object is understood in the abbreviated form.

2. When <u>tài</u> "too, excessively" modifies an adjective, <u>le</u> usually follows the adjective. <u>Le</u> does not add any meaning to the phrase, and it would not be wrong to leave the <u>le</u> off, but native speakers generally include it.

Tài hǎo le!	*too + to be good + le*	*That's great! (idiomatic)*
Zhèi běn shū tài guì le; wǒ bù mǎi.	*this + <u>ben</u> + book + too + to be expensive + <u>le</u> + I + not + to buy*	*This book is too expensive; I won't buy it.*
Nèi tiáo qúnzi tài cháng le.	*that + <u>tiao</u> + skirt + too + to be long + <u>le</u>*	*That skirt is too long.*

Structure exercises

1. *The sentences below are quoted out of context, but for each it is possible to guess the omitted object, that in the full form of the sentence would directly follow <u>de</u>. These objects have been listed to the right, but in scrambled order. Match each object with its sentence by writing the appropriate numeral in the blank provided.*

1. Xiǎo Wáng zuì ài chī là de.	_____ huār
2. Wǒ jīntiān mǎi de shì yì běn zìdiǎn.	_____ xiézi
3. Tā shuō de shì Yīngwén.	_____ cài
4. Wǒ chuān bā hào de.	_____ huà
5. Wǒ mǎi le liù duǒ hóng de.	_____ shū

2. *The monologue below is said by a student to his father, as he is about to leave the house for a few hours. There are seven occurences of <u>le</u> in it. To date we have discussed the following three uses of <u>le</u>: a) to indicate **completed action** (see p. 78), b) to indicate a **change of state or condition** (see pp. 42, 64), and c) to follow <u>tài</u>. For each occurence of <u>le</u> below, indicate which of these three uses applies, by drawing a <u>triangle</u>, a circle, or a <u>square</u> around each le, following these guidelines:*

    triangle = *completed action*

    circle = *change of status or condition*

    square = *following* <u>tài</u>

Zhāng Lǎoshi lái le. Wǒ xiǎng gēn tā yíkuàir qù mǎi dōngxi. Xiǎo Wáng běnlái (*originally*) yě gēn wǒmen yíkuàir qù, kěshì tā lèi le, suǒyǐ bù xiǎng qù le.

Zhāng Lǎoshī yào dào Měiguó qù. Wǒ gēn tā yíkuàir qù mǎi yīfu. Tā yào zài Zhōngguó mǎi yīfu, yīnwei tīngshuō (*it is said that, we hear that*) Měiguó de yīfu tài guì le. Wǒmen mǎi le yīfu yǐhòu, dào Jīngdū Fànguǎn (*The Capital Restaurant*) qù chīfàn. Qíshí (*actually*) wǒ bù xǐhuan Jīngdū Fànguǎn. Tāmen de cài tài dàn le. Kěshì Zhāng Lǎoshī xǐhuan, suǒyǐ wǒ yě gēn tā yíkuàir qù. Chī le fàn yǐhòu, wǒmen jiù huíjiā.

SEGMENT D
Skill: To request drinks, a menu, cutlery, the check.

Qǐng gěi wǒ yìdiǎnr _____.   *Please give me some_____.*

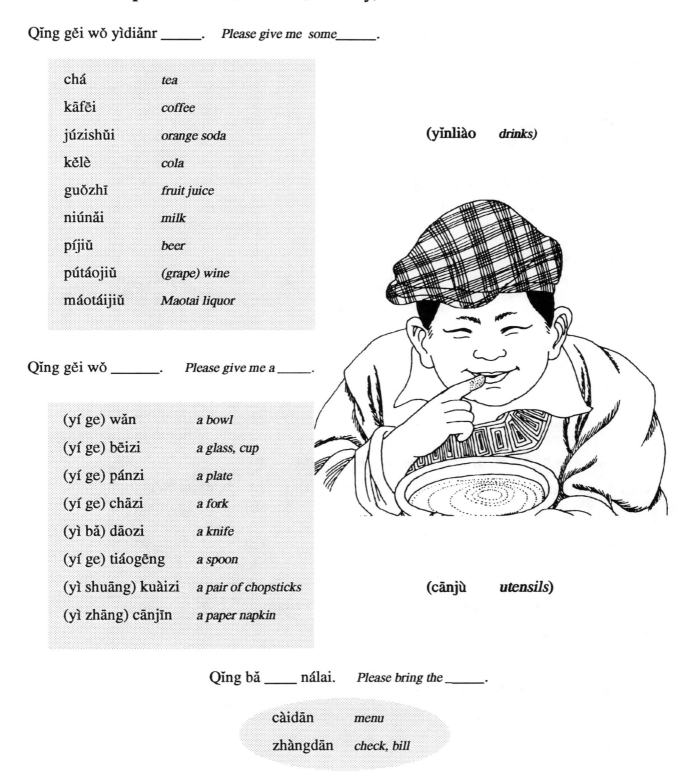

chá	*tea*
kāfēi	*coffee*
júzishǔi	*orange soda*
kělè	*cola*
guǒzhī	*fruit juice*
niúnǎi	*milk*
píjiǔ	*beer*
pútáojiǔ	*(grape) wine*
máotáijiǔ	*Maotai liquor*

(yǐnliào   *drinks*)

Qǐng gěi wǒ _____.   *Please give me a _____.*

(yí ge) wǎn	*a bowl*
(yí ge) bēizi	*a glass, cup*
(yí ge) pánzi	*a plate*
(yí ge) chāzi	*a fork*
(yì bǎ) dāozi	*a knife*
(yí ge) tiáogěng	*a spoon*
(yì shuāng) kuàizi	*a pair of chopsticks*
(yì zhāng) cānjīn	*a paper napkin*

(cānjù   *utensils*)

Qǐng bǎ ____ nálai.   *Please bring the _____.*

| càidān | *menu* |
| zhàngdān | *check, bill* |

Dialogue Practice

The following sets of dialogues presume normal behavior, no unusual circumstances, and no misunderstandings in the contexts indicated. "A" begins the dialogue, "B" responds, "A" responds to "B," etc. Where there is a choice of responses available, please circle the one which is more appropriate.

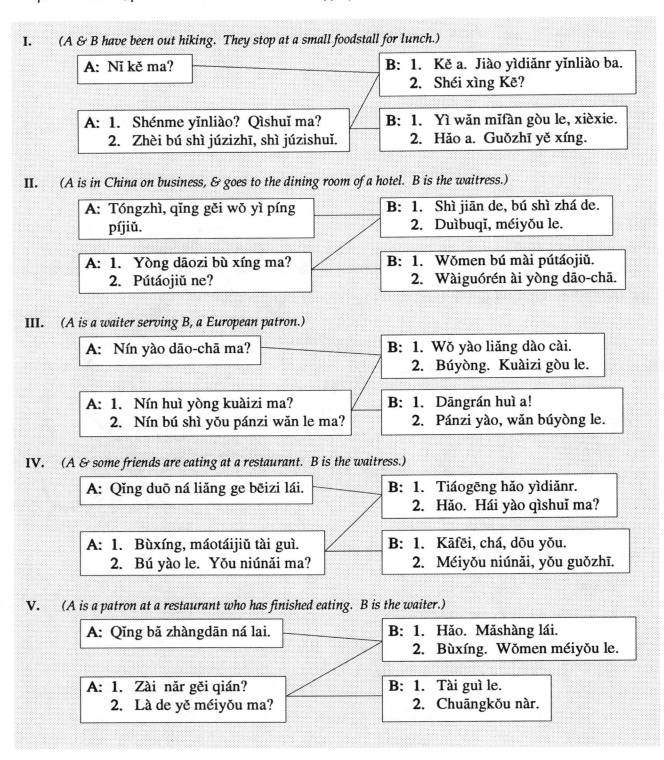

I.   (A & B have been out hiking. They stop at a small foodstall for lunch.)

A: Nǐ kě ma?

B: 1. Kě a. Jiào yìdiǎnr yǐnliào ba.
   2. Shéi xìng Kě?

A: 1. Shénme yǐnliào? Qìshuǐ ma?
   2. Zhèi bú shì júzizhī, shì júzishuǐ.

B: 1. Yì wǎn mǐfàn gòu le, xièxie.
   2. Hǎo a. Guǒzhī yě xíng.

II.   (A is in China on business, & goes to the dining room of a hotel. B is the waitress.)

A: Tóngzhì, qǐng gěi wǒ yì píng píjiǔ.

B: 1. Shì jiān de, bú shì zhá de.
   2. Duìbuqǐ, méiyǒu le.

A: 1. Yòng dāozi bù xíng ma?
   2. Pútáojiǔ ne?

B: 1. Wǒmen bú mài pútáojiǔ.
   2. Wàiguórén ài yòng dāo-chā.

III. (A is a waiter serving B, a European patron.)

A: Nín yào dāo-chā ma?

B: 1. Wǒ yào liǎng dào cài.
   2. Búyòng. Kuàizi gòu le.

A: 1. Nín huì yòng kuàizi ma?
   2. Nín bú shì yǒu pánzi wǎn le ma?

B: 1. Dāngrán huì a!
   2. Pánzi yào, wǎn búyòng le.

IV.   (A & some friends are eating at a restaurant. B is the waitress.)

A: Qǐng duō ná liǎng ge bēizi lái.

B: 1. Tiáogēng hǎo yìdiǎnr.
   2. Hǎo. Hái yào qìshuǐ ma?

A: 1. Bùxíng, máotáijiǔ tài guì.
   2. Bú yào le. Yǒu niúnǎi ma?

B: 1. Kāfēi, chá, dōu yǒu.
   2. Méiyǒu niúnǎi, yǒu guǒzhī.

V.   (A is a patron at a restaurant who has finished eating. B is the waiter.)

A: Qǐng bǎ zhàngdān ná lai.

B: 1. Hǎo. Mǎshàng lái.
   2. Bùxíng. Wǒmen méiyǒu le.

A: 1. Zài nǎr gěi qián?
   2. Là de yě méiyǒu ma?

B: 1. Tài guì le.
   2. Chuāngkǒu nàr.

Eating Western style

(Zhang, Li, Li's little sister Zhongxiu, and David have gone to a Western-style dining room to celebrate the end of the semester.)

Sister: Jiějie, zhèi xiē cānjù zěnme yòng a?

Sister, how do you use these utensils?

Lǐ: Hěn jiǎndān. Chāzi ná zài zuǒshǒu li, dāozi ná zài yòushǒu li, ránhòu...

It's really simple. Take the fork in your left hand, take the knife in your right hand, and then..

David: Nà shì Yīngguórén de yòngfǎ. Měiguórén bǎ chāzi ná zài yòushǒu li.

That's British usage. Americans take the fork in the right hand.

Lǐ: Nàme yào qiē dōngxi de shíhou zěnme bàn?

Then what do you do when you want to cut something?

David: Xiān bǎ chāzi fàng xiàlai, bǎ dāozi ná qǐlai, qiē hǎo le yǐhòu zài huàn.

First put down the fork, (then) pick up the knife, and after you've done the cutting, change again.

Lǐ: Duō máfan a.

What a bother.

Sister: Jiějie, méiyǒu chá. Zánmen hē shénme?

Sister, there's no tea. What will we drink?

Zhāng: Xiǎomèi, nǐ hē yìdiǎnr júzishuǐ huòzhě kělè ba.

Little sister, have some orange soda or cola.

David: Zài Měiguó xiǎoháir dōu hē niúnǎi de.

In America, all kids drink milk.

Sister: Wǒ bú'ài hē niúnǎi. Wèidào guàiguài de.

I don't like milk. It tastes funny (strange).

Zhāng: Zěnmeyàng, jiào shénme cài?

How about it, what dishes shall we order?

Sister: Jiějie, zěnme yǒu liǎng ge pánzi méiyǒu wǎn ne?

Sister, how come there are (we have) two plates and no bowl?

Zhāng: Yí ge pánzi shì chī shālā, yí ge shì chī zhǔcài de.

One plate is for the salad, and one is for the main dish.

Lǐ: Xiǎomèi, nǐ shǎo wèn jǐ ge wèntí, hǎo bù hǎo?

Little sister, ask a few fewer questions, okay?

Sister: Hnng.

Humph.

Culture notes

Western food is popular in urban Chinese communities. However, as Chinese food in America is often changed to conform to Western tastes, American food in China is sometimes influenced by Chinese cooking, and might taste unusual to Westerners. Hamburger flavored with ginger or meat loaf with a hint of five-spice is not uncommon.

The use of a knife (reminiscent of a sword) and fork (reminiscent of a pitch-fork) takes some getting used to, for Chinese unacquainted with such utensils. By Chinese custom, cutting and chopping are accomplished in the kitchen; equipping the diner with knife and fork and asking them to do at the table the job of the cook in the kitchen strikes many Chinese as slightly uncivilized.

Many Chinese cannot tolerate lactose, and are therefore not fond of milk. Milk-based products such as yogurt and ice-cream, however, are growing in popularity in many urban Chinese communities.

Structure notes

1. Please note that the construction <u>Qǐng gěi wǒ chá</u> "Please give me tea" or <u>Qǐng gěi wǒ yì bēi chá</u> "Please give me a cup of tea" or <u>Qǐng gěi wǒ yìdiǎnr chá</u> "Please give me some tea" contrasts with <u>Qǐng bǎ chá ná lai</u> "Please bring the tea" in the degree of specificity of the object.

In <u>Qǐng gěi wǒ (object)</u>, the object is unspecified—thus "some (object)" or "an (object)" rather than "**the** object." In reference to tea, it would work in a Chinese restaurant to say either <u>Qǐng gěi wǒmen yìdiǎnr chá</u> "Please give us some tea" (i.e., any tea that the restaurant happens to have), or <u>Qǐng bǎ chá ná lai</u> "Please bring the tea," since Chinese restaurants usually serve tea as a matter of course, and will generally have a pot prepared for your table. "The tea" then would refer to the pot of tea designated for your table.

On the other hand, it would be inappropriate to walk into a Chinese restaurant without having made any prior arrangements, sit down, and request, "<u>Qǐng bǎ niúnǎi ná lai</u>" (Please bring the milk). The waiter would wonder, "What milk?" since no specific portion of milk is waiting for you. If however, you request "<u>Qǐng gěi wǒ yìdiǎnr niúnǎi</u>" (Please give me some milk), the waiter would readily understand that you would like some milk. (Unfortunately, however, your chances of getting some milk in an average Chinese restaurant are not very good.)

Similarly, native speakers are more likely to say <u>Qǐng bǎ càidān ná lai</u> and <u>Qǐng bǎ zhàngdān ná lai</u>, than <u>Qǐng gěi wǒ càidān</u> or <u>Qǐng gěi wǒ zhàngdān</u>—since it is understood that what is being requested is not just any menu but the current menu of that particular restaurant, and not just any check but the check for your specific meal.

Structure exercise

How would you say the following in Chinese? (Be appropriate, not literal.)

pánzi

Please give me a plate. _____

Please give me your plate. _____

píjiǔ

Give us some beer . _____

Bring us the beer now. _____

cānjīn

Please give me a paper napkin. _____

Please give me that paper napkin. _____

guǒzhī

Is there any juice? _____

Please bring us the juice. _____

júzishuǐ

He wants some orange soda. _____

Please give him the orange soda. _____

SEGMENT A
Skill: To specify establishments in a town.

Wŏmen dào _____ qù ba. *Let's go to the _____.*

fēijīchǎng	*airport*
huŏchēzhàn	*train station*
gōnggòng qìchēzhàn	*bus stop*
fànguăn	*restaurant*
diànyĭngyuàn	*movie theater*
xìyuàn	*theater, playhouse*
lŭguăn	*hotel*
xuéxiào	*school*

túshūguăn	*library*
shūdiàn	*bookstore*
yóujú	*post office*
yínháng	*bank*
shìchǎng	*market*
jiāyóuzhàn	*gas station*
jĭngchájú/ pàichūsuŏ	*police station*
yīyuàn	*hospital*

Xìyuàn lí zhèr bù yuăn.	*The theatre is not far from here.*
Lí zhèr hĕn jìn.	*It is near here.*
Lí zhèr yì lĭ lù.	*It is one mile away.*
Túshūguăn zài năr?	*Where is the library?*
Lí zhèr yuăn ma?	*Is it far from here?*
Lí zhèr jĭ lĭ lù?	*How many miles away is it?*

Dialogue Practice

The following sets of dialogues presume normal behavior, no unusual circumstances, and no misunderstandings in the contexts indicated. "A" begins the dialogue, "B" responds, "A" responds to "B," etc. Where there is a choice of responses available, please circle the one which is more appropriate.

I.   (A and B are arriving at school in the morning, A by car and B by bicycle.)

   A: Nǐ jiā zài nǎr?

   B: 1. Zài xìyuàn li.
      2. Zài běibianr.

   A: 1. Yínháng bùxíng ma?
      2. Lí zhèr yuǎn ma?

   B: 1. Yínháng li méiyǒu qián.
      2. Wǔ lǐ lù zuǒyòu.

   A: 1. Bú tài yuǎn.
      2. Qù jiāyóuzhàn ba.

   B: 1. Jiāyóuzhàn li méiyǒu yóu.
      2. Gòu yuǎn le!

II. (A is walking down a city street. B is minding a souvenir stand on the street.)

   A: Qǐngwèn, yóujú zài nǎr?

   B: 1. Jiù zài qiántou.
      2. Bú zài yīyuàn li.

   A: 1. Shìchǎng ne?
      2. Jǐngchájú háishì pàichūsuǒ?

   B: 1. Jiù zài yóujú de yòubianr.
      2. Lǚguǎn ba.

III. (A has to find her friend Wang on some extremely urgent business. B is Wang's roommate.)

   A: Xiǎo Wáng dào nǎr qù le?

   B: 1. Jiāyóuzhàn lí zhèr shí lǐ lù.
      2. Tā qù kàn diànyǐngr le.

   A: 1. Diànyǐngyuàn zài nǎr?
      2. Shí lǐ lù hěn yuǎn.

   B: 1. Tā huíjiā shuìjiào le.
      2. Zài nánbianr, lí zhèr yì lǐ lù.

IV. (A is trying to locate an old friend, and has just been advised by B to go to the friend's home.)

   A: Wǒ wàng le, tā jiā lí xuéxiào yuǎn ma?

   B: 1. Kěnéng sān, sì lǐ lù ba.
      2. Wǒ xiān qù xìyuàn.

   A: 1. Ránhòu ne?
      2. Méiyǒu nàme jìn ba.

   B: 1. Tā yǐjīng qù fēijīchǎng le.
      2. Shì ma? Yěxǔ shì wǔ, liù lǐ.

V.   (A needs a certain book. She is trying to decide whether to buy or to borrow it.)

   A: Shūdiàn jìn háishì túshūguǎn jìn?

   B: 1. Gōnggòng qìchēzhàn zài nàr.
      2. Shūdiàn jìn yìdiǎnr.

   A: 1. Túshūguǎn lí zhèr duó yuǎn?
      2. Huǒchēzhàn bùxíng ma?

   B: 1. Zhèi jiā yīyuàn hěn guì.
      2. Liǎng, sān lǐ lù ba.

Visitors

(David's parents are coming to visit him. Zhang, Li, and some friends are planning their visit.)

David:	Tāmen Xīngqīwǔ wǎnshang liù diǎn bàn dào.	*They are arriving on Friday, at 6:30 in the evening.*
Lǐ:	Hǎojí le. Zánmen dào fēijīchǎng qù jiē tāmen ma?	*That's great. Shall we go to the airport to meet them?*
Zhāng:	Qù ba. Tāmen zhù zài nǎr?	*Let's. Where will they live?*
David:	Wǒ hái bù zhīdao shénme lǚguǎn lǐtou. Shì tāmen de lǚxíngshè ānpái de.	*In some hotel I don't know about yet. It was arranged by their travel agency.*
Friend:	Tāmen zhù duó jiǔ?	*How long will they stay?*
David:	Yí ge xīngqī. Tāmen lái kànkan zánmen xuéxiào. Ránhòu bàba yào cānguān zhèr de xiǎoxué gēn zhōngxué; māma yào cānguān jǐ jiā yīyuàn.	*A week. They'll come to see our school. After that, Dad wants to visit some primary and secondary schools here; Mom wants to visit a few hospitals.*
Friend:	Nǐ fùmǔ shì zuò shénme de?	*What do your parents do?*
David:	Bàba shì gāozhōng lǎoshī; māma shì hùshi.	*Dad's a high-school teacher; Mom's a nurse.*
Friend:	O, guàibude tāmen yào cānguān xuéxiào gēn yīyuàn.	*Oh, no wonder they want to visit schools and hospitals.*

Culture notes

Since Chinese society tends to be group-oriented, particularly in the PRC but to an extent in Taiwan as well, it is generally better equipped to handle foreign visitors, tourists or otherwise, in groups rather than individually. Travel alone is possible, certainly in Taiwan and even in the PRC, but handling logistics on one's own is sometimes an enormous problem. Most visitors to the PRC go in a group of one sort or another. Individuals who travel to the PRC generally have an institutional sponsor in China, which has a special department to make arrangements for foreigners.

Structure notes

1. <u>Wǒmen dào fēijīchǎng qù ba</u> follows sentence pattern #7 **Subject** + [**bú**] + <u>dào</u> + **Place** + <u>qù</u>, introduced in Unit 4e, which expresses movement from one place to another.

2. To indicate distance between two geographical points, the following patterns are used.

12. Place$_1$ + <u>lí</u> + Place$_2$ + [<u>bù</u>] + <u>yuǎn/jìn</u>

Fēijīchǎng lí wǒ jiā hěn yuǎn.	*airport* + *lí* + *my* + *home* + *very* + *to be far*	*The airport is far from my home.*
Wǒ jiā lí tā jiā bù yuǎn.	*my* + *home* + *lí* + *her home* + *not* + *to be far*	*My home isn't far from her home.*
Tā jiā lí fànguǎn hěn jìn.	*her* + *home* + *lí* + *restaurant* + *very* + *to be close*	*Her home is very near the restaurant.*

12a. Place$_1$ + <u>lí</u> + Place$_2$ + Number + <u>lǐ lù</u>

Fēijīchǎng lí wǒ jiā èrshí lǐ lù.	*airport* + *lí* + *my* + *home* + *20* + *mile* + *road*	*The airport is 20 miles from my home.*
Fēijīchǎng lí fànguǎn èrshí duō lǐ lù.	*airport* + *lí* + *restaurant* + *20* + *more* + *mile* + *road*	*The airport is over 20 miles from the restaurant.*

3. <u>Túshūguǎn zài nǎr?</u> is based on sentence pattern #5, **Subject** + [**bú**] + <u>zài</u> + **place** (see 93).

Túshūguǎn jiù zài qiántou.	*library* + *right* + *to be at* + *ahead*	*The library is right ahead.*
Yóujú yě zài qiántou.	*post office* + *also* + *to be at* + *ahead*	*The post office is up ahead, too.*

Structure exercise

The following is a rambling monologue by a student who is planning to see his friend off at the airport the next day. Fill in the blanks with appropriate words or phrases, based on the English translation.

Chén Xiǎofāng shì _____ péngyou. Tā shì cóng Běijīng _____ de. Tā míngtiān yào _____ Xiānggǎng qù jǐ tiān. Wǒ sòng tā _____ fēijīchǎng _____. Wǒ xiān dào _____ qù, ránhòu wǒmen yíkuàir _____ fēijīchǎng. Tā jiā _____ fēijīchǎng bù yuǎn, hěn kuài jiù kěyǐ dào le. Wǒ jiā _____ yìdiǎnr, yào bàn ge zhōngtóu cái néng dào fēijīchǎng. Tā jiā lí _____ dàgài zhǐ yǒu liǎng _____ lù. Wǒ jiā lí _____ dàgài yǒu wǔ lǐ lù. Tā míngtiān _____ shí diǎnzhōng bìxū dào fēijīchǎng. Wǒ děi bā diǎn bàn chūmén qù _____. Ránhòu _____ tā jiā dào fēijīchǎng qù, zuì wǎn yě yào jiǔ diǎn _____ jiù děi chūmén le.

Chen Xiaofang is my friend. She comes from Beijing. Tomorrow, she will go to Hong Kong for a few days. I'll take her to the airport. I'll go to her house first, and then we'll go to the airport together. Her house isn't far from the airport; we can get there quickly. My house is a little further; it would take a half hour to get to the airport. Her house is probably only two miles from the airport. My house is probably five miles from her house. She has to get to the airport by ten o'clock tomorrow morning. I will need to leave home at eight thirty to go to her house. Then from her house to the airport, we will need to leave the house by nine fifteen at the latest.

SEGMENT B
Skill: To specify points in & beyond the community.

Wǒmen dào _____ qù wánr ba.   Let's go (have fun) _____.

shān shang	*in (on) the mountains, hills*
hé shang	*on the river*
hú bianr	*by the lake*
hǎi bianr	*by the sea (ocean)*
shātān shang	*on the beach*
gōngyuán li	*in the park*
huāyuán li	*in the garden*
sēnlín li	*in the forest*
jiē shang	*in town (on the street)*
chéng li	*down town*

chángcháng	*often*
yǒude shíhou	*sometimes*

wánr qù (qù wánr)	*to go have a good time*
sànbù	*to take a walk*
páshān	*to go hiking (in the hills)*
guàngjiē	*to go window-shopping*
huáchuán	*to row a boat*

Zhè shì Táiwān de hǎi bianr.

Xīwàng nǐ wánr de yúkuài!	*Have a good time!*
Yǒu kòng lái wánr!	*Come over (& relax w/me) when you have time.*
Wǒmen gēn tā yíkuàir wánr qù ba.	*Let's go relax (together) with him/her.*
Wǒmen dào nǎr qù wánr?	*Where shall we go (to have fun)?*
Dào hé shang huáchuán qù hǎo ma?	*How about going boating on the river?*
Hé shang chángcháng rén hěn duō.	*There are often many people on the river.*
Yǒude shíhou méiyǒu chuán.	*Sometimes there are no boats (available).*

Dialogue Practice

The following sets of dialogues presume normal behavior, no unusual circumstances, and no misunderstandings in the contexts indicated. "A" begins the dialogue, "B" responds, "A" responds to "B," etc. Where there is a choice of responses available, please circle the one which is more appropriate.

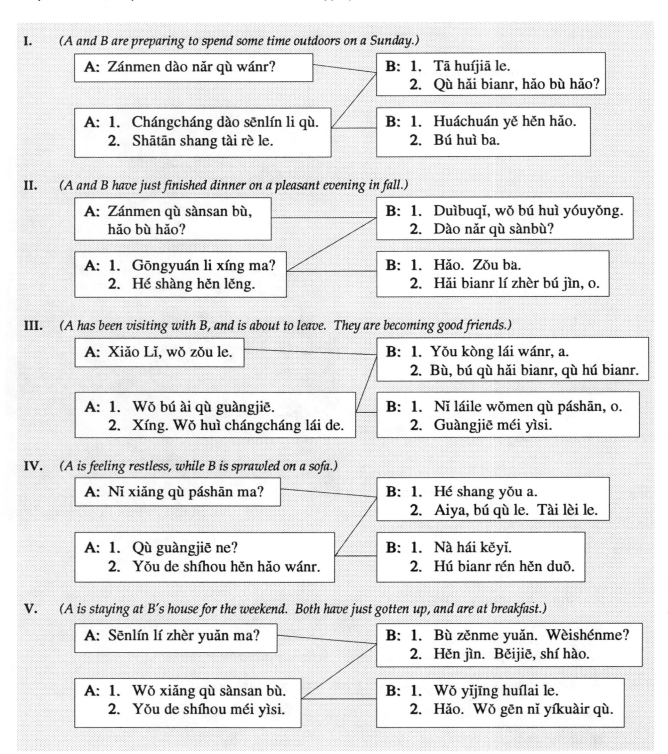

I.   (A and B are preparing to spend some time outdoors on a Sunday.)

A: Zánmen dào nǎr qù wánr?

B: 1. Tā huíjiā le.
   2. Qù hǎi bianr, hǎo bù hǎo?

A: 1. Chángcháng dào sēnlín li qù.
   2. Shātān shang tài rè le.

B: 1. Huáchuán yě hěn hǎo.
   2. Bú huì ba.

II.   (A and B have just finished dinner on a pleasant evening in fall.)

A: Zánmen qù sànsan bù, hǎo bù hǎo?

B: 1. Duìbuqǐ, wǒ bú huì yóuyǒng.
   2. Dào nǎr qù sànbù?

A: 1. Gōngyuán li xíng ma?
   2. Hé shàng hěn lěng.

B: 1. Hǎo. Zǒu ba.
   2. Hǎi bianr lí zhèr bú jìn, o.

III. (A has been visiting with B, and is about to leave. They are becoming good friends.)

A: Xiǎo Lǐ, wǒ zǒu le.

B: 1. Yǒu kòng lái wánr, a.
   2. Bù, bú qù hǎi bianr, qù hú bianr.

A: 1. Wǒ bú ài qù guàngjiē.
   2. Xíng. Wǒ huì chángcháng lái de.

B: 1. Nǐ láile wǒmen qù páshān, o.
   2. Guàngjiē méi yìsi.

IV.   (A is feeling restless, while B is sprawled on a sofa.)

A: Nǐ xiǎng qù páshān ma?

B: 1. Hé shang yǒu a.
   2. Aiya, bú qù le. Tài lèi le.

A: 1. Qù guàngjiē ne?
   2. Yǒu de shíhou hěn hǎo wánr.

B: 1. Nà hái kěyǐ.
   2. Hú bianr rén hěn duō.

V.   (A is staying at B's house for the weekend. Both have just gotten up, and are at breakfast.)

A: Sēnlín lí zhèr yuǎn ma?

B: 1. Bù zěnme yuǎn. Wèishénme?
   2. Hěn jìn. Běijiē, shí hào.

A: 1. Wǒ xiǎng qù sànsan bù.
   2. Yǒu de shíhou méi yìsi.

B: 1. Wǒ yǐjīng huílai le.
   2. Hǎo. Wǒ gēn nǐ yíkuàir qù.

David's parents

Father:	Dào gōngyuán li qù zǒuzou ba.	*Let's go to the park for a walk.*
Mother:	Ei, tài rè le. Xiànzài shì tàiyáng zuì lìhai de shíhou.	*Nah, it's too hot. Now is when the sun is at its harshest (when the sun is strongest).*
Father:	O, zěnme le. Nǐ háishì ge xiǎojiě pà shài tàiyáng ma?	*Oh, what's wrong. Are you still like a young girl afraid of the sun?*
Mother:	Nǐ shuō nǎr de huà. Xiàwǔ shéi yuànyi dào wàitou qù zǒu? Chī le wǎnfàn yǐhòu zài qù sànbù ba.	*What nonsense. Who wants to go out walking in the afternoon? Let's (wait until) after we've eaten dinner to go for a walk.*
Father:	Tiān hēi yǐhòu shéi dào gōngyuán li qù sànbù a!	*Who goes walking in the park after dark!*
Mother:	Bú qù gōngyuán jiù dào jiē shang qù guàngguang yě hěn hǎo a.	*So if we don't go to the park it would be very nice to go walk around the streets (go window-shopping) in town, too.*
Father:	Duó méi yìsi.	*How boring.*
Mother:	David, nǐ shuō ne?	*David, what do you say?*
David:	Nǐmen bié wèn wǒ. Wǒ wúsuǒwèi.	*Don't ask me. I don't care.*

Culture notes

Chinese-American children seldom speak entirely in Chinese at home—the influence of the English-speaking environment is too pervasive. Even first generation offspring of Chinese immigrants have often given up speaking Chinese by the time they reach their teens, especially if their parents are able to converse in English. Very few children grow up truly bilingually, like David. Those who do have generally spent a significant amount of time in a native Chinese community.

Generally Chinese prefer not to move about under a harsh mid-day sun. A deep tan is considered coarse and unattractive. Cosmopolitan young Asian women in particular are often careful to use a parasol when they must be under a strong sun.

Most Chinese cities have a night market, especially in the early part of the evening. Many local inhabitants emerge after dinner in the summertime, to catch some evening breezes and to enjoy the bustle on the street.

Although arguments between spouses are as common in Chinese communities as in American, the divorce rate is lower, in large part because expectations of marriage partners are not generally as high as in the West. A spouse is primarily a help-mate in China, a "co-parent" for the child (or children). The further (unrealistic) expectation that a spouse be a romantic partner on top of that often exceeds the capability of the spouse, and thus precipitates a divorce—or so many Chinese believe.

Structure notes

1. <u>Shān shang</u> is the contraction of the less commonly used <u>shān de shàngtou</u>, where <u>shàng</u> or <u>shàngtou</u> are **locational nouns**, here serving to indicate the destination of the subject relative to the place-noun. Following the principle discussed earlier (Unit 7c), what precedes <u>de</u> modifies what follows—"the top" is modified by "of the mountain"—thus: "on top of the mountain." In the sentence <u>Wǒ dào shān shang qù wánr</u> "I'm going up the mountain (for fun)," <u>shàng</u> indicates that the subject "I" will be going *onto* the mountain or *up* the mountain, rather than, say, to the foot of the mountain—<u>shān xià</u>. Other expanded forms are <u>hú de pángbianr</u> for <u>hú bianr</u>, and <u>gōngyuán de lǐtou</u> for <u>gōngyuán li</u>. The expanded forms are implied but hardly ever used.

In discussing movement to a place for a particular purpose, note the following pattern.

> **7b. Subject + [bú] + dào + Noun + Locational noun + qù + Verb phrase**

The location of the verb-phrase can be interchanged with the location of <u>qù</u> without affecting meaning—<u>qù wánr</u> has the same meaning as <u>wánr qù</u>.

Wǒ dào hú bianr qù kàn shū.	*I + to + lake + side + to go + to read*	*I'm going to the lake to read.*
Zánmen dào huāyuán li qù chī, hǎo ma?	*we + to + garden + in + to go + to eat + to be okay + ma*	*Let's go to the garden to eat, okay?*
Nǐmen dào jiē shang qù zǒuzou ba.	*you + to + street + on + to go + to walk + walk + ba*	*Why don't you go to town to walk around.*

2. In sentence pattern #7 **Subject + [bú] + dào + Place + qù** (see p. 98), the destination of the subject, a **place**, does not need to be followed by a **locational noun**. "Places" include geographic and social organizations, such as a particular country, city, school, company, store, etc. Thus, a Chinese would say "<u>Wǒ dào Rìběn qù</u>," not *"<u>Wǒ dào Rìběn li qù</u>." Countries and cities are never followed by locational nouns. For other "places" the locational noun is optional. It would be possible but not common to say "<u>Wǒ dào xuéxiào li qù</u>"; "<u>Wǒ dào xuéxiào qù</u>" suffices.

3. Nouns, however, are physical objects rather than social organizations—a house, a garden, a beach, a mountain— for which a **locational noun** is required. Some locations are difficult to identify either as "places" or "nouns"; "downtown" for instance should simply be remembered as <u>chéng li</u>—a noun plus a locational noun.

4. In the frequently used expression <u>Yǒu kòng lái wánr</u>, literally "Have free time come have fun," the pairing off of the two components <u>yǒu kòng</u> and <u>lái wánr</u> implies an "if..then" situation: "if you have free time then come over." The full form of the construction would be "<u>Yàoshi nǐ yǒu kòng, qǐng nǐ guò lai wánr</u>," where <u>yàoshi</u> means "if."

Structure exercise

Based on the English given, write in the appropriate equivalents in the spaces within the sentences; then number each of the sentences, starting with the earliest occurence and ending with the latest.

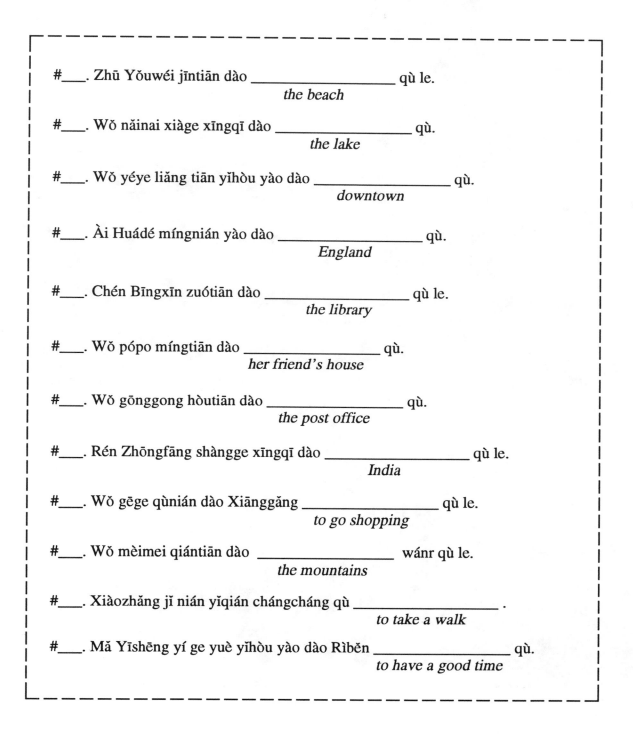

#____. Zhū Yǒuwéi jīntiān dào _____ qù le.
                                    the beach

#____. Wǒ nǎinai xiàge xīngqī dào _____ qù.
                                    the lake

#____. Wǒ yéye liǎng tiān yǐhòu yào dào _____ qù.
                                        downtown

#____. Ài Huádé míngnián yào dào _____ qù.
                                    England

#____. Chén Bīngxīn zuótiān dào _____ qù le.
                                    the library

#____. Wǒ pópo míngtiān dào _____ qù.
                                her friend's house

#____. Wǒ gōnggong hòutiān dào _____ qù.
                                    the post office

#____. Rén Zhōngfāng shàngge xīngqī dào _____ qù le.
                                            India

#____. Wǒ gēge qùnián dào Xiānggǎng _____ qù le.
                                        to go shopping

#____. Wǒ mèimei qiántiān dào _____ wánr qù le.
                                    the mountains

#____. Xiàozhǎng jǐ nián yǐqián chángcháng qù _____ .
                                                to take a walk

#____. Mǎ Yīshēng yí ge yuè yǐhòu yào dào Rìběn _____ qù.
                                                    to have a good time

Zhè shì Táiběi.

Zhè shì Běijīng.

Zhè shì Xiānggǎng.

SEGMENT C
Skill: To give & follow simple directions around town.

yánzhe zhèitiáo lù zǒu	*follow this road*
yìzhí zǒu	*go straight*
zǒu dào X jiē/lù	*go to X street/road*
zuǒ zhuǎn/guǎi	*turn left*
yòu zhuǎn/guǎi	*turn right*
guò liǎng ge jiēkǒu	*go through two intersections*
zǒu dào dì-yī ge hónglù dēng	*go to the first traffic light*
wǎnghuí zǒu	*turn around and go back*
shàng gāosù gōnglù	*get on the freeway*
xià gāosù gōnglù	*get off the freeway*
jīngguò X	*pass by X*

wèn lù   *ask for directions*

xiān (zuò zhèige)	*first (do this)*
ránhòu zài (zuò nèige)	*then after that, (do that)*
zuìhòu zài (zuò nèige)	*finally, (do that)*

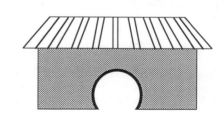

Láojià!	*Excuse me!*
Qǐngwèn, X zài nǎr?	*May I ask where the X is?*
Cóng zhèr zěnme zǒu?	*How do I go from here?*
X zài zhèige fāngxiàng ma?	*Is X in this direction?*
Bìxū zhuǎnwān ma?	*Do I have to turn?*
Qǐng zài shuō yí cì.	*Please say it again.*
Qǐng shuō màn yìdiǎnr.	*Please say it slower.*
Xièxie nín bāngmáng!	*Thank you for your help!*

Dialogue Practice

The following sets of dialogues presume normal behavior, no unusual circumstances, and no misunderstandings in the contexts indicated. "A" begins the dialogue, "B" responds, "A" responds to "B," etc. Where there is a choice of responses available, please circle the one which is more appropriate.

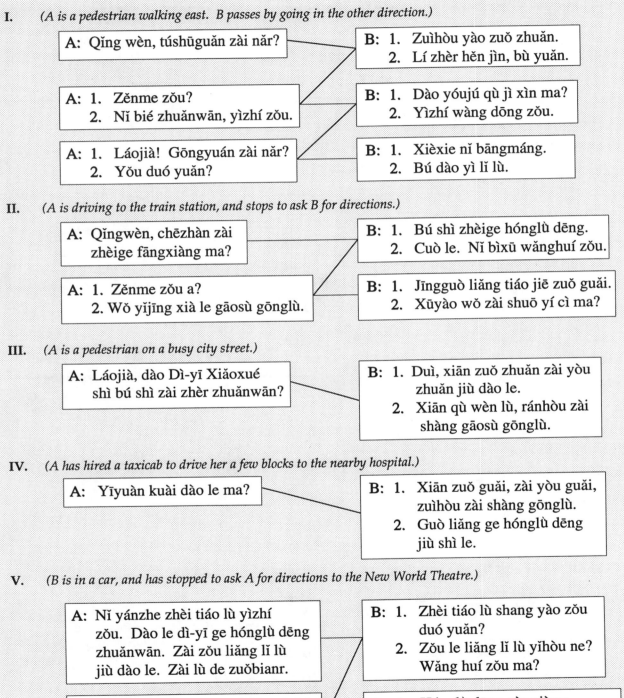

I.   *(A is a pedestrian walking east. B passes by going in the other direction.)*

A: Qǐng wèn, túshūguǎn zài nǎr?

B: 1. Zuìhòu yào zuǒ zhuǎn.
   2. Lí zhèr hěn jìn, bù yuǎn.

A: 1. Zěnme zǒu?
   2. Nǐ bié zhuǎnwān, yìzhí zǒu.

B: 1. Dào yóujú qù jì xìn ma?
   2. Yìzhí wàng dōng zǒu.

A: 1. Láojià! Gōngyuán zài nǎr?
   2. Yǒu duó yuǎn?

B: 1. Xièxie nǐ bāngmáng.
   2. Bú dào yì lǐ lù.

II.   *(A is driving to the train station, and stops to ask B for directions.)*

A: Qǐngwèn, chēzhàn zài zhèige fāngxiàng ma?

B: 1. Bú shì zhèige hónglǜ dēng.
   2. Cuò le. Nǐ bìxū wǎnghuí zǒu.

A: 1. Zěnme zǒu a?
   2. Wǒ yǐjīng xià le gāosù gōnglù.

B: 1. Jīngguò liǎng tiáo jiē zuǒ guǎi.
   2. Xūyào wǒ zài shuō yí cì ma?

III. *(A is a pedestrian on a busy city street.)*

A: Láojià, dào Dì-yī Xiǎoxué shì bú shì zài zhèr zhuǎnwān?

B: 1. Duì, xiān zuǒ zhuǎn zài yòu zhuǎn jiù dào le.
   2. Xiān qù wèn lù, ránhòu zài shàng gāosù gōnglù.

IV.   *(A has hired a taxicab to drive her a few blocks to the nearby hospital.)*

A: Yīyuàn kuài dào le ma?

B: 1. Xiān zuǒ guǎi, zài yòu guǎi, zuìhòu zài shàng gōnglù.
   2. Guò liǎng ge hónglǜ dēng jiù shì le.

V.   *(B is in a car, and has stopped to ask A for directions to the New World Theatre.)*

A: Nǐ yánzhe zhèi tiáo lù yìzhí zǒu. Dào le dì-yī ge hónglǜ dēng zhuǎnwān. Zài zǒu liǎng lǐ lù jiù dào le. Zài lù de zuǒbianr.

B: 1. Zhèi tiáo lù shang yào zǒu duó yuǎn?
   2. Zǒu le liǎng lǐ lù yǐhòu ne? Wǎng huí zǒu ma?

A: 1. Xiān zhuǎnwān, ránhòu yìzhí zǒu.
   2. Sān, sì lǐ lù zuǒyòu.

B: 1. Hónglǜ dēng nàr xiàng shénme fāngxiàng zhuǎnwān?
   2. Lù de zuǒbianr shì shénme?

Finding the post office

(David's father has written postcards to his many colleagues at home. He has no stamps.)

Father:	Dào nǎr qù mǎi yóupiào? Zhèr fùjìn yǒu yóujú ma?	*Where do I go to buy stamps? Is there a post-office nearby?*
David:	Nǐ yào yóupiào wǒ děng yìhuír bāng nǐ qù mǎi ba. Zhān hǎo le yǐhòu, bǎ xìn wǎng yóutǒng lǐ yì rēng, jiù xíng le.	*If you want stamps, I'll go buy some for you in a while. After you stick on the stamps, just toss the letters into a mailbox, and that will be that.*
Father:	Bú yòng, wǒ zìjǐ chūqù zǒuzou. Nǎr yǒu yóujú?	*That's alright (You don't need to), I'll go out myself for the walk. Where is there a post office?*
David:	Nǐ yuànyi zǒu de huà, nà yě hěn fāngbiàn. Yóujú bù yuǎn. Nǐ xiànzài jiù qù ma?	*If you want to walk, that's pretty easy (convenient) too. The post-office isn't far. Are you going right now?*
Father:	Nnng. Zěnme zǒu?	*Uh-huh. How do I get there?*
David:	Nǐ chū dàmén yǐhòu, yòu zhuǎn. Guò le liǎng ge lùkǒu, zài dì-sān ge lùkǒu zuǒ zhuǎn. Zài zǒu jǐ bù jiù huì kàndào yóujú le.	*After you go out the main exit, turn right. Go two blocks (go past two intersections) and turn left at the third intersection. Go a few more steps and you'll see the post-office.*
Father:	Zài zuǒbianr háishì yòubianr?	*On the left or right side?*
David:	Yòubianr.	*On the right.*
Father:	Hǎo ba. Gēn nǐ mā shuō yì shēng, wǒ mǎshàng jiù huílai.	*Okay, tell your mom I'll be right back.*
David:	Mā zài nǎr a?	*Where is Mom anyway?*
Father:	Hái zài cèsuǒ li ne.	*She's still in the bathroom.*

Culture notes

Hotels for foreigners in the PRC and Taiwan have rooms with private, western-style bathrooms attached. Many urban units in the PRC however, including apartments, dorm rooms and hotels for domestic consumption, do not have either an attached toilet or a bath. Public toilets and bathhouses serve as substitutes, either as part of a floor or building, or in a detached unit near the housing units. In Taiwan, attached private bathrooms are the rule for apartments and hotels, but dormitories are generally provided with common-use toilets and showers. David's parents are staying in a hotel for foreigners, so his mother has the luxury of a bathroom equipped with sink, mirror, toilet and tub attached to their room.

Structure notes

1. <u>Xiān</u> "first," <u>zài</u> "then, next," <u>ránhòu zài</u> "after that" etc. must be followed immediately by a verb or a verb phrase.

Nǐ xiān niànshū, ránhòu zài kàn diànshì.	*you + first + to study + after + then + to watch television*	*Study first, and then watch television.*
Wǒ xiān dào túshūguǎn, zài dào shūdiàn, zài dào yóujú, zuìhòu dào xuéxiào qù.	*I + first + to + library + then + to + bookstore + then + to + post office + lastly + to + school + to go*	*First I'm going to the library, then to the bookstore, then to the post office, and lastly to school.*

2. An expansion of sentence pattern 7 (**Subject + dào + place + qù**; see Unit 4e) accomodates two new elements, one involving the point from which movement originates, and the other specifying whether the movement is towards or away from the speaker.

<u>Cóng</u> "from" precedes <u>dào</u> "to," since departure from one place must occur before movement to another place can take place. If the movement is directed away from the speaker, then the final verb is <u>qù</u> "to go"; if the movement is directed toward the speaker, then the verb used is <u>lái</u> "to come."

7c. Subject + <u>cóng</u> + Place₁ + <u>dào</u> + Place₂ + <u>lái/qù</u>

Tā cóng Yīngguó lái.	*she + from + England + to come*	*She comes from England.*
Tā cóng Yīngguó dào Fǎguó qù le.	*she + from + England + to + France + to go + le*	*From England, she went to France.*
Tā cóng Fǎguó dào zhèr lái le.	*she + from + France + to + here + to come + le*	*From France, she came here.*
Tā xiǎng cóng zhèr dào Zhōngguó qù.	*she + to think + from + here + to China + to go*	*From here, she's thinking of going to China.*

3. <u>Qǐng shuō màn yìdiǎnr</u> is the shortened form of <u>Qǐng shuō de màn yìdiǎnr</u>—which follows pattern 9: **Subject + verb + <u>de</u> + adverb**. <u>Yìdiǎnr</u> following <u>màn</u> conveys the request "slower (please)," which is reminiscent of the requests <u>dà yìdiǎnr</u>, <u>xiǎo yìdiǎnr</u> etc. of Lesson 5e.

Structure exercise

Fill in each blank in the directions below with an appropriate word or phrase, based on the English equivalent.

Cóng huǒchēzhàn _____ zhèr bù hǎo zǒu. Cóng huǒchēzhàn chūlái _____ yì tiáo dà lù, děi zuǒ _____. Zǒu dào dì-sān ge _____ dēng, děi _____ zhuǎn. _____ nèige lùkǒu _____ xuéxiào yào zǒu _____ zhōngtóu. Xiān zhí zǒu, _____ liǎng ge lùkǒu zài yòu _____, mǎshàng *(right away)* děi zài zuǒ _____, _____ yí ge lùkǒu zài wǎng _____ zhuǎn yí cì. _____ yí ge dà jiēkǒu yǐhòu, zài zhí _____ wǔ lǐ lù. Cóng nèige jiēkǒu dào _____ yě yào zǒu _____ zhōng. Ránhòu, wǒmen _____ jiù _____ yòubianr.

It's not easy to get from the train station to here. When you come out from the train station it's a major road, and you have to turn left. Go to the third traffic light, and turn right. From that intersection to the school will take a half hour. First go straight, pass two intersections and turn right, then you have to turn right again right away, and then turn right again after the next intersection. After you get to a major intersection, go straight for five miles. From that intersection to here will take ten minutes. After that, our school is just on the right.

SEGMENT D

Skill: **To specify points around the world, to make comparative statements about weather.**

Wǒ hěn xiǎng dào _____ qù wánr.

Zhōngguó	*China*
Běijīng	*Beijing (Peking)*
Xī'ān	*Xian*
Gùilín	*Guilin*
Shànghǎi	*Shanghai*
Guǎngdōng	*Canton*
Táiběi	*Taipei*
Xiānggǎng	*Hong Kong*

Měiguó	*U.S.A.*
Niǔyuē	*New York*
Zhījiāgē	*Chicago*
Jiāzhōu	*California*
Jiùjīnshān (Sānfánshì)	*San Francisco*
Luòshānjī	*Los Angeles*
Huáshèngdùn	*Washington (D.C.)*

Déguó	*Germany*
Bólín	*Berlin*

Xībānyá	*Spain*
Mǎdélǐ	*Madrid*

Rìběn	*Japan*
Dōngjīng	*Tokyo*

Fǎguó	*France*
Bālí	*Paris*

Yīngguó	*England*
Lúndūn	*London*

Cháoxiǎn	*Korea*
Hànchéng	*Seoul*

Jiùjīnshān de tiānqì zěnmeyàng?	*How is the weather in San Francisco?*
Jiùjīnshān tiānqì bǐ Niǔyuē _____.	*San Francisco's weather is ____ er than New York.*

lěng	*cold*	Niǔyuē gēn Běijīng yíyàng lěng.	*New York is as cold as Beijing.*
rè	*hot*	Táiběi méiyǒu Guǎngdōng rè.	*Taipei is not as hot as Canton.*
nuǎnhuo	*warm*	Jīntiān chū tàiyáng.	*It's sunny today.*
liángkuai	*cool*	Míngtiān huì xiàyǔ.	*It will rain tomorrow.*

Dialogue Practice

The following sets of dialogues presume normal behavior, no unusual circumstances, and no misunderstandings in the contexts indicated. "A" begins the dialogue, "B" responds, "A" responds to "B," etc. Where there is a choice of responses available, please circle the one which is more appropriate.

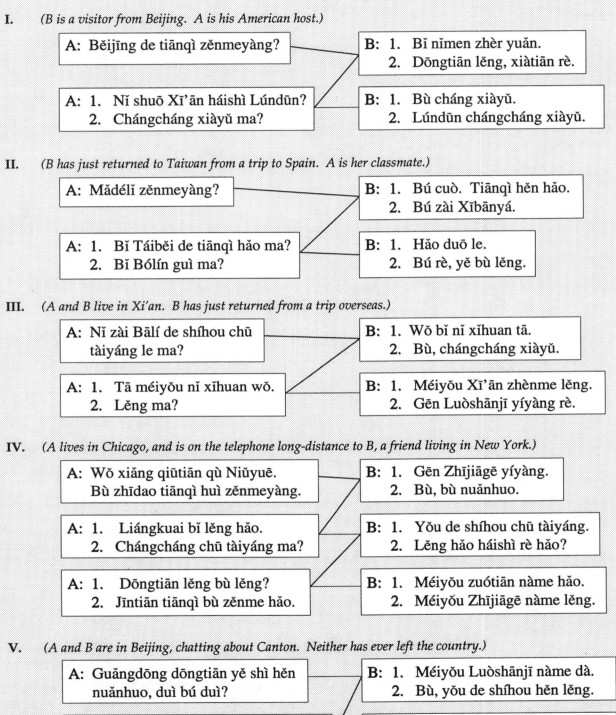

I.   *(B is a visitor from Beijing. A is his American host.)*

A: Běijīng de tiānqì zěnmeyàng?

B: 1. Bǐ nǐmen zhèr yuǎn.
    2. Dōngtiān lěng, xiàtiān rè.

A: 1. Nǐ shuō Xī'ān háishì Lúndūn?
    2. Chángcháng xiàyǔ ma?

B: 1. Bù cháng xiàyǔ.
    2. Lúndūn chángcháng xiàyǔ.

II.   *(B has just returned to Taiwan from a trip to Spain. A is her classmate.)*

A: Mǎdélǐ zěnmeyàng?

B: 1. Bú cuò. Tiānqì hěn hǎo.
    2. Bú zài Xībānyá.

A: 1. Bǐ Táiběi de tiānqì hǎo ma?
    2. Bǐ Bólín guì ma?

B: 1. Hǎo duō le.
    2. Bú rè, yě bù lěng.

III.   *(A and B live in Xi'an. B has just returned from a trip overseas.)*

A: Nǐ zài Bālí de shíhou chū tàiyáng le ma?

B: 1. Wǒ bǐ nǐ xǐhuan tā.
    2. Bù, chángcháng xiàyǔ.

A: 1. Tā méiyǒu nǐ xǐhuan wǒ.
    2. Lěng ma?

B: 1. Méiyǒu Xī'ān zhènme lěng.
    2. Gēn Luòshānjī yíyàng rè.

IV.   *(A lives in Chicago, and is on the telephone long-distance to B, a friend living in New York.)*

A: Wǒ xiǎng qiūtiān qù Niǔyuē.
    Bù zhīdao tiānqì huì zěnmeyàng.

B: 1. Gēn Zhījiāgē yíyàng.
    2. Bù, bù nuǎnhuo.

A: 1. Liángkuai bǐ lěng hǎo.
    2. Chángcháng chū tàiyáng ma?

B: 1. Yǒu de shíhou chū tàiyáng.
    2. Lěng hǎo háishì rè hǎo?

A: 1. Dōngtiān lěng bù lěng?
    2. Jīntiān tiānqì bù zěnme hǎo.

B: 1. Méiyǒu zuótiān nàme hǎo.
    2. Méiyǒu Zhījiāgē nàme lěng.

V.   *(A and B are in Beijing, chatting about Canton. Neither has ever left the country.)*

A: Guǎngdōng dōngtiān yě shì hěn nuǎnhuo, duì bú duì?

B: 1. Méiyǒu Luòshānjī nàme dà.
    2. Bù, yǒu de shíhou hěn lěng.

A: 1. Chūntiān ne?
    2. Shì Dōngjīng háishì Xiānggǎng?

B: 1. Hěn liángkuai. Cháng xiàyǔ.
    2. Dōu méiyǒu zhèr rè.

Travel aspirations

(David Wang and his parents are visiting Li's family on a Sunday afternoon. The guests are seated on a sofa in the living area; members of the family have brought in chairs and stools from other parts of the house and are gathered around them. Tea and chilled watermelon wedges have been served.)

Lǐ:	Wáng bóbo Wáng bómǔ qù le hǎo duō dìfang le.	Uncle and Auntie Wang have been to a lot of places.

(David's parents smile and nod.)

Lǐ's father:	Nǐmen qùguo Ōuzhōu, shì ma?	You've been to Europe, right?
David's father:	Shì de. Wǒmen shàngge yuè zài Bālí kāihuì.	That's right. Last month we were in Paris attending a conference.
Lǐ's mother:	Ou, Bālí wǒ yě qùguo. Wǒ shì 1985 nián qù de.	Oh, I've been to Paris too. I was there in 1985.
David's mother:	Bāo yīshēng yě shì qù kāihuì de ma?	Were you at a conference too, Dr. Bao?
Lǐ's mother:	Shì de. Kāile wǔ tiān huì. Ránhòu wǒ liúxiàlai zuòle bàn nián de yánjiū.	Yes, I attended five days of meetings. Then I stayed on to do research for six months.
David's mother:	Lǐ yīshēng yě qù le ma?	Did you go too, Dr. Li?
Lǐ's father:	Bù, wǒ méi qù. Wǒ zài jiāli zhàogù xiǎoháirmen.	No, I didn't go. I stayed home to care for the children.
Lǐ's sister:	Wáng bóbo Wáng bómǔ, nǐmen xiǎng dào Zhōngguó shénme dìfang qù wánr?	Uncle and Auntie Wang, what places in China are you going to visit?
David's father:	Wǒmen yào qù Xī'ān hé Shànghǎi. Xiǎo mèimei gēn wǒmen yíkuàir qù hǎo bù hǎo?	We are going to Xian and Shanghai. Will you come with us, little sister?
Lǐ's sister:	Hǎo a!	Okay!

(Everybody laughs.)

Culture notes

Chinese women in the PRC generally retain their own last names after marriage. In Taiwan, the equivalent of Mrs. X (X tàitai) might be used socially, but in professional contexts the premarital name is generally used. Thus Li's mother is called "Dr. Bao" by David's mother; Bao is the premarital name of Mrs. Li.

Chinese as a rule do not travel as much as most Americans. A very small percentage of Chinese from the PRC travel overseas; even travel within China, although more convenient in recent years, is a matter of some difficulty. Although overseas travel is much more common in Taiwan, it is still a mark of distinction to have been abroad—more so than in the U.S.

Structure notes

1. In <u>Jiāzhōu tiānqì zěnmeyàng</u>, <u>Jiāzhōu tiānqì</u> can be thought of as the contracted form of <u>Jiāzhōu de tiānqì</u> "California's weather, the weather of California." In that case the sentence follows the structure of pattern #2: **Subject + (<u>hěn</u>) + adjective**, where <u>Jiāzhōu de tiānqì</u> is the subject, and <u>zěnmeyàng</u> takes the place of the adjective, to be replaced in the response with something like "<u>hěn hǎo</u>."

The sentence can also be thought of as an example of **topic-comment structure**, which is very common in Chinese. The **topic** of the sentence is identified at the beginning of the sentence, and the rest of the sentence is a **comment** on that topic. <u>Jiāzhōu tiānqì hěn hǎo</u> would in that case be translated approximately as, "As for California, its weather is very good," with California being the topic and "its weather is very good" being a comment on that topic.

Other examples are:

Xiǎo Wáng tā míngtiān bù lái le.	*Xiao Wang + he + tomorrow + not + to come + le*	*Xiao Wang isn't coming tomorrow. (As for Xiao Wang, he isn't coming tomorrow.)*
Niǔyuē wǒ bú tài xiǎng qù.	*Niuyue + I + not + extremely + to feel like + to go*	*I don't really feel like going to New York. (As for New York, I don't really feel like going there.)*

2. Comparisons in Chinese are handled with the following patterns. All compare two items, labeled A and B. In pattern #13a, A is superior to B; in pattern #14, A is equal to B; and in pattern #15, A is inferior to B.

13a. A + [bù] + bǐ + B + Adjective + (de duō/ yìdiǎnr)

Basically, this pattern states that A is more (adjective) than B, by a lot (<u>de duō</u>) or by a little (<u>yìdiǎnr</u>). Thus:

Zhèige bǐ nèige hǎo.	*this one + bǐ + that one + to be good*	*This one is better than that one.*
Hóng de bǐ lǜ de hǎo de duō.	*red one + bǐ + green one + to be good + by a lot*	*Red ones are much better than green ones.*
Lǜ de bǐ lán de hǎo yìdiǎnr.	*green one + bǐ + blue one + to be good + a little*	*Green ones are a little better than blue ones.*
Nǐ de bù bǐ wǒ de hǎo.	*yours + not + bǐ + mine + to be good*	*Yours is not better than mine.*

14. A + (bù) + gēn + B + (bù) + yíyàng (+ Adjective)

<u>Gēn</u> means literally "with," and <u>yíyàng</u> means "to be the same," so the pattern asserts that A and B are the same. If an adjective is added, then the pattern states that A and B are the same in reference to the adjective. To negate the assertion, <u>bù</u> can precede either <u>gēn</u> or <u>yíyàng</u>.

Zhèige gēn nèige yíyàng.	*this one + with + that one + to be the same*	*This one is the same as that one.*
Wǒ de gēn nǐ de yíyàng hǎo.	*mine + with + yours + to be the same + to be good*	*Mine is as good as yours.*
Tā de gēn wǒ de bù yíyàng.	*his + with + mine + not + to be the same*	*His isn't the same as mine.*
Tā de yě bù gēn nǐ de yíyàng.	*his + also + not + with + yours + to be the same*	*His also isn't the same as yours.*

15. A + méiyǒu + B + Adjective

Supposing the adjective in this pattern were gāo, the resultant sentence would mean "A is not as tall as B." Literally, the pattern asserts that A is inferior to B, in terms of the quality stated in the adjective.

Nèige méiyǒu zhèige hǎo.
that one + to not have + this one + to be good
That one is not as good as this one.

Lǜ de méiyǒu hóng de hǎo.
green one + to not have + red one + to be good
The green one is not as good as the red one.

Nǐ de méiyǒu wǒ de hǎo.
yours + to not have + mine + to be good
Yours is not as good as mine.

Structure exercise

Below are three examples of comparative statements regarding the climate of points around the world.

The first example uses bǐ, indicating that the item before bǐ (labeled A in the pattern) possesses the quality expressed by the adjective to a greater degree than the item after bǐ (labeled B): thus A > B.

The second example uses gēn...yíyàng, meaning that items A and B are more or less equal in terms of the quality expressed by the adjective: or A = B.

Finally, the third example uses méiyǒu, indicating that A possesses the quality expressed by the adjective to a lesser extent than B: thus A < B.

Following these three examples, make up nine sentences of your own, based on the climatic conditions in various cities and countries.

A > B	Niǔyuē bǐ Táibéi lěng.
A = B	Luòshānjī gēn Mǎdélǐ yíyàng nuǎnhuo.
A < B	Jiùjīnshān méiyǒu Guǎngdōng rè.
A > B	_____
A = B	_____
A < B	_____
A > B	_____
A = B	_____
A < B	_____
A > B	_____
A = B	_____
A < B	_____

Nǐ cāi zài zhèige dìfāng kěyǐ
zuò shénme chē?

Answer:

Zhè shì Běijīng chēzhàn.
Kěyǐ zuò huǒchē.

SEGMENT E
Skill: To specify modes of transportation.

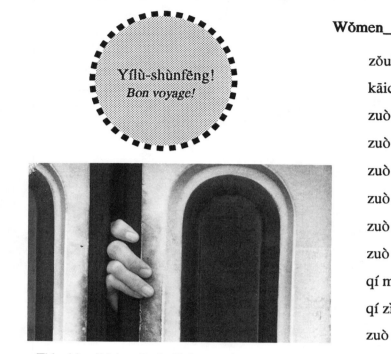

Yílù-shùnfēng!
Bon voyage!

This rider didn't make it all the way into a public bus.

Wǒmen_____qù ba.   *Let's go by_____.*

zǒulù	*walking, on foot*
kāichē	*driving a car*
zuò qìchē	*riding in a car*
zuò jìchéngchē	*riding in a taxi (Taiwan)*
zuò chūzū qìchē	*riding in a taxi (PRC)*
zuò huǒchē	*riding in a train*
zuò gōnggòng qìchē	*riding in a bus*
zuò dìtiě	*riding in a subway train*
qí mótuōchē	*riding on a motorcycle*
qí zìxíngchē	*riding on a bicycle*
zuò fēijī	*riding in an airplane*
zuò chuán	*riding in a ship, boat*

Wǒ cóng jiāli kāichē dào xuéxiào qù.	*I drive from my home to school.*
Nǐ shì zěnme lái de?	*How did you come?*
Zài nǎr shàng chē?	*Where do I board the bus (train) etc.?*
Shénme shíhou mǎi piào?	*When do I buy a ticket?*
Piàojià duóshǎo qián?	*How much is a ticket?*

shàng chē	*to board the train, bus, car*
xià chē	*to disembark the train, bus, car*
mǎi piào	*to buy a ticket*
piàojià	*the price of the ticket*

Wǒ yí ge rén qù.	*I'm going alone.*
Wǒ gēn péngyou yíkuàir qù.	*I'm going with (a) friend(s).*
Yǒu péngyou sòng wǒ qù.	*(I have) a friend (who) will take me.*

Dialogue Practice

The following sets of dialogues presume normal behavior, no unusual circumstances, and no misunderstandings in the contexts indicated. "A" begins the dialogue, "B" responds, "A" responds to "B," etc. Where there is a choice of responses available, please circle the one which is more appropriate.

I. (A has just found out that B, her neighbor, is going to Europe in two days.)

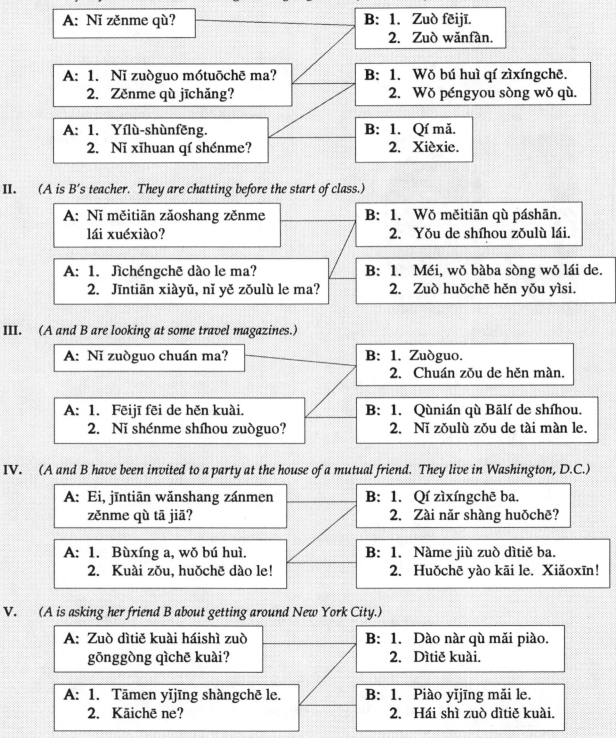

A: Nǐ zěnme qù?

B: 1. Zuò fēijī.
   2. Zuò wǎnfàn.

A: 1. Nǐ zuòguo mótuōchē ma?
   2. Zěnme qù jīchǎng?

B: 1. Wǒ bú huì qí zìxíngchē.
   2. Wǒ péngyou sòng wǒ qù.

A: 1. Yílù-shùnfēng.
   2. Nǐ xǐhuan qí shénme?

B: 1. Qí mǎ.
   2. Xièxie.

II. (A is B's teacher. They are chatting before the start of class.)

A: Nǐ měitiān zǎoshang zěnme lái xuéxiào?

B: 1. Wǒ měitiān qù páshān.
   2. Yǒu de shíhou zǒulù lái.

A: 1. Jìchéngchē dào le ma?
   2. Jīntiān xiàyǔ, nǐ yě zǒulù le ma?

B: 1. Méi, wǒ bàba sòng wǒ lái de.
   2. Zuò huǒchē hěn yǒu yìsi.

III. (A and B are looking at some travel magazines.)

A: Nǐ zuòguo chuán ma?

B: 1. Zuòguo.
   2. Chuán zǒu de hěn màn.

A: 1. Fēijī fēi de hěn kuài.
   2. Nǐ shénme shíhou zuòguo?

B: 1. Qùnián qù Bālí de shíhou.
   2. Nǐ zǒulù zǒu de tài màn le.

IV. (A and B have been invited to a party at the house of a mutual friend. They live in Washington, D.C.)

A: Ei, jīntiān wǎnshang zánmen zěnme qù tā jiā?

B: 1. Qí zìxíngchē ba.
   2. Zài nǎr shàng huǒchē?

A: 1. Bùxíng a, wǒ bú huì.
   2. Kuài zǒu, huǒchē dào le!

B: 1. Nàme jiù zuò dìtiě ba.
   2. Huǒchē yào kāi le. Xiǎoxīn!

V. (A is asking her friend B about getting around New York City.)

A: Zuò dìtiě kuài háishì zuò gōnggòng qìchē kuài?

B: 1. Dào nàr qù mǎi piào.
   2. Dìtiě kuài.

A: 1. Tāmen yǐjīng shàngchē le.
   2. Kāichē ne?

B: 1. Piào yǐjīng mǎi le.
   2. Hái shì zuò dìtiě kuài.

Farewell

(David, Li, and some friends are in Zhang's dormitory room. He is packing to go home for the recess.)

David: Zánmen míngtiān shénme shíhou shàng huǒchēzhàn?

What time shall we go to the train station tomorrow?

Zhāng: Aiya, nǐmen búyòng qù le. Wǒ yí ge rén qù jiù xíng le.

Oh, you shouldn't bother. I can go by myself.

Lǐ: Méi guānxi. Wǒmen yě qù sòng nǐ.

It's no trouble. We'll go too, to see you off.

Zhāng: Wǒ yòu bú shì kèren, zěnme hái yào sòng?

I'm not a guest, why should you see me off?

David: Xiǎo Zhāng yào zǒu le, dāngrán qù sòng. Ei, zánmen zěnme shàng huǒchēzhàn a...zuò gōnggòng qìche ma?

(Our friend) Zhang is leaving, of course we'll see you off. Hey, how will we get to the train station tomorrow...by bus?

Friend: Nà bùxíng. Tā hái yǒu xíngli ne.

That won't do. He has luggage, too.

Zhāng: Jiào liàng chūzū qìchē bú jiù xíng le ma?

If I called a cab, wouldn't that do it?

Friend: Nà tài guì le. Wǒmen qí mótuōchē sòng nǐ ba.

That's too expensive. Let's send you off on our motorcycles.

Lǐ: Tā xíngli ne?

And his luggage?

Friend: Kěyǐ bǎng zài mótuōchē hòutou!

We can strap it to the back of the motorcycle.

David: Yào xiǎoxīn ou, bú yào cuòguo le shíjiān. Xiǎo Zhāng shì ge dúshēngzǐ; tā fùmǔ zhèng děngzhe tā huíjiā ne.

You have to be careful you know, don't be late (don't miss the time). Zhang is an only child; his parents are waiting for him to come home.

Friend: Bú huì de, nǐ fàngxīn. Zánmen míngtiān yíkuàir qù, o!

We won't, relax. We'll go together tomorrow, huh.

Zhāng: Hǎo, hǎo, xièxie nǐmen. Bù hǎo yìsi la.

Alright, alright, thanks. Sorry to be such a nuisance.

Culture notes

The combination of public buses and private bicycles transport the majority of the urban population in the PRC; taxicabs and private automobiles are still economically inaccessible to most people, but motorcycles are gaining in popularity. Taiwan (Taipei) traffic is an unholy mix of taxicabs, buses, motorcyles, bicycles, private automobiles and pedestrians, all travelling helter-skelter in a variety of directions.

Between cities in both the PRC and Taiwan, ground transportation is more popular than travelling by air, for reasons of cost as well as convenience.

Whereas Zhang's friends wish to demonstrate their affection for him by seeing him off to the train station, Zhang himself is being courteous by insisting that they not take the trouble. As usual in such an exchange, the more persistent party wins; in the end Zhang gives in and accepts his friends' offer, with some demurral.

Structure notes

1. When verb phrases such as <u>zǒulù</u> "to go on foot" or <u>zuò chē</u> "to ride in a car" **precede** <u>qù</u> "to go," they indicate a **mode of transportation**. (See pattern 7d below.)

　　　　Wǒmen zuò huǒchē qù ba.　　*we + to ride + train + to go + ba*　　Let's go by train.

Conversely, when the verb phrase **follows** <u>qù</u>, it indicates not a mode of transportation but the **purpose of going**.

　　　　Wǒmen qù zuò huǒchē ba.　　*we + to go + to ride + train + ba*　　Let's go for a ride on the train.

This is reminiscent of pattern 7a **Subject + <u>dào</u> + place + <u>qù</u> + verb phrase**. For example, in the sentence <u>Wǒ dào tǐyùguǎn qù dǎ lánqiú</u> "I'm going to the gym to play basketball," <u>dǎ lánqiú</u> is the purpose of the verb <u>qù</u>, and therefore follows it.

2. <u>Wǒ cóng jiāli kāichē dào xuéxiào qù</u> utilizes the following pattern.

> **7d. Subject + <u>cóng</u> + Place$_1$ + <u>zuò</u> (vehicle) + <u>dào</u> + Place$_2$ + <u>lái/qù</u> + Purpose**

There are optional elements in this pattern—the "from" phrase, the "by means of" phrase, and the "to" phrase. When these elements are included in a sentence, they follow the sequence indicated: "from" first, "by means of" second, and "to" third. The verb can be either <u>lái</u> "to come" or <u>qù</u> "to go," depending on whether the movement is toward or away from the speaker. If there is a purpose for the movement, the statement of the purpose follows <u>lái</u> or <u>qù</u>.

Tāmen cóng Yīngguó zuò fēijī dào Měiguó lái le.	*they + from + England + to ride + airplane + to + America + to come + le*	They came from England to America by plane.
Tāmen dào Zhījiāgē qù le.	*they + to + Chicago + to go + le*	They went to Chicago.
Tāmen cóng Zhījiāgē dào Niǔyuē qù.	*they + from + Chicago + to + New York + to go*	They are going to New York from Chicago.
Tāmen cóng Niǔyuē de huǒchēzhàn zuò dìtiě dào nǐmen jiā qù kàn nǐmen.	*they + from + New York's + train station + to ride + subway + to + your home + to visit + you*	They'll take the subway from the train station in New York to your home to see you.

Structure exercise

Write sentences using each of the elements listed below to form a narrative about a hypothetical trip to China.

1. US — (ship) —> China

_____

2. Běijīng — (train) —> Xī'ān — to see the terra cotta figures (<u>bīngmǎ yǒng</u>)

_____

3. Xī'ān — (airplane) —> Guìlín — to see the scenery (<u>fēngjǐng</u>)

_____

4. Guìlín — (bus) —> Shànghǎi — to go shopping

_____

5. Airport — (taxicab) —> hotel — to rest

_____

6. Hotel — (on foot) —> restaurant — to meet friends

_____

*Zhè xiē rén zài
zuò shénme?*

Zhè shì shénme dìfāng?

Zàijiàn le ba, péngyou.

Just for fun....

Match the Chinese phrases below with the unit titles appearing throughout this textbook.

1. Hello!

      _____Zhè shì wǒmen xuéxiào.

2. Who are you?

      _____Nǐ zěnmeyàng?

3. How are you doing?

      _____Nǐ xǐhuān shénme?

4. When can we meet?

      _____Nǐ hǎo!

5. Let's go shopping.

      _____Wǒmen shàng nǎr qù?

6. What do you like?

      _____Wǒmen qù fànguǎn chī ba.

7. This is my home.

      _____Nǐ shì shéi?

8. This is my school.

      _____Wǒmen qù mǎi dōngxi ba.

9. Let's eat in a restaurant.

      _____Zhè shì wǒmen jiā.

10. Where shall we go?

      _____Wǒmen shénme shíhou jiàn?

Reference Section

The *pinyin* romanization system

The Chinese do not, of course, communicate with each other in their own language by writing in romanization—they use characters. Pinyin, literally "to spell out the sounds," is useful for foreigners accustomed to the Roman alphabet, to learn spoken Chinese. Pinyin appears regularly on Chinese billboards and street signs together with characters, and consistently in textbooks on Chinese destined for the foreign market. It is also the form in which place and people names of the PRC are written in current materials in the West, both by the mainland Chinese themselves and by others writing about the Chinese. Reference materials such as dictionaries and encyclopedias from the PRC use pinyin both as an access tool (the order of the entries is based in part on pinyin alphabetization), and to indicate pronunciation. Many Chinese word-processing programs also rely on pinyin as an input system, to interface with the alphabetic keyboard. Taiwan, however, has never used pinyin, in large part to disassociate itself from the regime on the mainland; it uses other romanizations and phonetic codes. Still, pinyin is the most widely used form of Chinese romanization available today.

The pinyin romanization system was originally developed for Russian learners. The values of individual letters therefore do not always correspond to their equivalents in English: *en* in pinyin sounds closer to *un* than *en* in English, for instance. With practice, however, students can and do become proficient.

There are basically three parts of every Chinese syllable: the tone, the initial, and the final.

The four tones.

1. The first tone: HIGH LEVEL (tāng). This is the tone obtained in English when counting quickly, as in "One-two-three-four-five-six-seven-eight-nine-ten-READY OR NOT, HERE I COME!" or in the high-pitched squeal of delight: "Hee! Hee!"

delight

2. The second tone: RISING (táng). Questions in English are generally posed with rising intonation: "Yes? Now? Me? And you?" which is equivalent to the second tone of Chinese. The rise in intonation is particularly evident if the speaker is surprised.

???????

3. The third tone: DIPPING (tǎng). The grunt of agreement ("uh-huh") that is often used in conversational English approximates the full form of the third tone in Chinese. However, in its most common form (see "modifications of tone 3" below), this Chinese tone sounds like the intonation of the first syllable of many multisyllabic English words, such as "potato, tomato, tomorrow, indeed, inform, indicative," where the voice dips to its lowest level of comfort.

agreement

4. The fourth tone: FALLING
(tàng). Where the second tone was
the rising intonation of English
questions, the fourth tone is the
falling intonation of English
assertions, particularly if they are
strenuous (as when said in anger):
"Yes! Now! You! Go!"

!!!!!!

Most Chinese words are assigned a single tone. Some have more than one, depending on context; some appear with a NEUTRAL tone (which is actually the short, mid-range intonation of the last syllable in words such as "funny, hurry, second, forever").

Words, of course, do not generally appear singly. They are preceded and followed by other words in context. The third tone changes significantly based on context.

Modifications of tone 3.

1. When it appears before tones 1, 2
or 4, tone 3 dips but does not rise
again (see "the third tone" above).

2. Before another third tone, tone 3
becomes tone 2. Thus, 3+3 = 2+3.

When words are strung together in sentences, overall intonation for the sentence or for discourse will effect the pronunciation of individual tones. They may be flattened when speaking fast, or enhanced when said with emphasis or emotion.

Word initials.

Chinese word beginnings can be represented by the following 23 letters and combinations, plus the zero initial (in which none of the following appears at the head of the word).

Labials (sounds produced by using one or both lips).

b	as in boy, but not voiced (with vocal cord vibration). More like the **p** in **spin, spot**. (bō)
p	as in **pot, police, particular**. (pō)
m	as in **mother, merry, monstrous**. (mō)
f	as in **father, frolic, frivolous**. (fō)

Dentals (sounds produced by pressing the tip of the tongue against the back of the upper teeth).

- **d**   as in desk, but not voiced. More like the t in stand, stiff, steal. (dĕ)
- **t**   as in top, tin, telephone. (tĕ)
- **n**   as in near, nuisance. (nĕ)
- **l**   as in lever, lift, legitimate. (lĕ)

Velars (sounds produced by pressing the back of the tongue against the roof of the mouth).

- **g**   as in go, but not voiced. More like the k in sky, skew, skill. (gĕ)
- **k**   as in kite, Kelly, cold. (kĕ)
- **h**   like help, hand, but with more constriction of the throat. (hĕ)

Fricatives (sounds produced by constricting the flow of air)

- **z**   as in words, goods, but not voiced. Actually closer to the -ts sound in let's, shuts. (zī)
- **c**   the -ts sound as above, followed by a puff of air; similar to let's hunt, quits home). (cī)
- **s**   as in sibling, same, soft. (sī)

- **j**   as in jeer, jeep (always preceding an "ee" or "ü" sound). (jī)
- **q**   as in cheese, cheer (always preceding an "ee" or "ü" sound). (qī)
- **x**   as in sheer, sheet (always preceding an "ee" or "ü" sound). (xī)

- **zh**   as in John, Joe (never preceding an "ee" or "ü" sound). (zhī)
- **ch**   as in charm (never preceding an "ee" or "ü" sound). (chī)
- **sh**   as in Shah, shut (never preceding an "ee" or "ü" sound). (shī)
- **r**   like run, rue, rent, but with a stronger outflow of air. (rī)

Semi-vowels

- **w**   as in war, win. (wū)
- **y**   as in yes, you. (yā)

Outline of word initials.

b	d	g	z	j	zh	unaspirated (no puff of air)
p	t	k	c	q	ch	aspirated (plus puff of air)
m	n	h	s	x	sh	
f	l				r	
				used only before "i" or "ü" sounds	never used before "i" or "ü" sounds	

Word finals.

Final sounds in Chinese are represented by the 33 letters and groups of letters indicated below.

Basic vowels

a   as in **father**, **far**.
e   as in **herd**, **serge**.
i   as in **eagle**, **feet**.
o   appears alone only after b-, p-, m-, f- and w-, where it sounds something like **war**.
u   as in **you**, **fool**, except when it follows j-, q-, x-, or y-, when it has the same value as ü (see following).
ü   as in the French t**u**, the German T**ü**r; made by saying "eee" with rounded lips. The umlaut (¨) appears when this sound value follows the initials l- and n-.

Combinations

	+a	+e	+i	+o	+u	+n	+ng
a			ai	ao		an	ang
e			ei			en	eng
i	ia	ie			iu	in	ing
			iao			ian	iang
							iong
o					ou		ong
u	ua		ui	uo/o		un	
			uai			uan	uang
ü		ue/üe				un	
						uan	

The above combinations are more or less the sum of their individual parts, except for the following.

ei   sounds quite similar to the English letter "**a**."
ie   similar to **yet**, **yes**.
iu   pronounced either as **you** or as **yo**yo, depending on context and dialect.
ian   similar to **yen**.
ui   similar to **way**.
un   pronounced "**ün**" when it follows j-, q-, x-, or y-; pronounced more like "**one**" elsewhere.
uan   pronounced "**üan**" when it follows j-, q-, x-, or y-; pronounced more like "**Juan**" elsewhere.
ue/üe   **ue** is used after j-, q-, x-, and y-, where the "u" is actually an ü sound. The umlaut appears following l- and n-.

The following pages present the sound system of Chinese in pinyin. Tones have not been indicated; many words exist in each of the four tones; some exist in only one tone.

	-a	-ai	-ao	-an	-ang	-e	-ei	-en	-eng	-r	-i	-i(r)	-i(z)
b	ba	bai	bao	ban	bang		bei	ben	beng		bi		
p	pa	pai	pao	pan	pang		pei	pen	peng		pi		
m	ma	mai	mao	man	mang	me	mei	men	meng		mi		
f	fa			fan	fang		fei	fen	feng				
d	da	dai	dao	dan	dang	de	dei		deng		di		
t	ta	tai	tao	tan	tang	te			teng		ti		
n	na	nai	nao	nan	nang	ne	nei	nen	neng		ni		
l	la	lai	lao	lan	lang	le	lei		leng		li		
g	ga	gai	gao	gan	gang	ge	gei	gen	geng				
k	ka	kai	kao	kan	kang	ke		ken	keng				
h	ha	hai	hao	han	hang	he	hei	hen	heng				
z	za	zai	zao	zan	zang	ze	zei	zen	zeng				zi
c	ca	cai	cao	can	cang	ce		cen	ceng				ci
s	sa	sai	sao	san	sang	se		sen	seng				si
j											ji		
q											qi		
x											xi		
zh	zha	zhai	zhao	zhan	zhang	zhe	zhei	zhen	zheng			zhi	
ch	cha	chai	chao	chan	chang	che		chen	cheng			chi	
sh	sha	shai	shao	shan	shang	she	shei	shen	sheng			shi	
r			rao	ran	rang	re		ren	reng			ri	
*	a	ai	ao	an	ang	e	ei	en	eng	er	yi		

	-ia	-ie	-iu	-in	-ing	-iao	-ian	-iang	-iong	-ou	-ong
b		bie		bin	bing	biao	bian				
p		pie		pin	ping	piao	pian				
m		mie	miu	min	ming	miao	mian				
f										fou	
d		die	diu		ding	diao	dian			dou	dong
t		tie			ting	tiao	tian			tou	tong
n		nie	niu	nin	ning	niao	nian	niang		nou	nong
l		lie	liu	lin	ling	liao	lian	liang		lou	long
g										gou	gong
k										kou	kong
h										hou	hong
z										zou	zong
c										cou	cong
s										sou	song
j	jia	jie	jiu	jin	jing	jiao	jian	jiang	jiong		
q	qia	qie	qiu	qin	qing	qiao	qian	qiang	qiong		
x	xia	xie	xiu	xin	xing	xiao	xian	xiang	xiong		
zh										zhou	zhong
ch										chou	chong
sh										shou	
r										rou	rong
*	ya	ye	you	yin	ying	yao	yan	yang	yong	ou	

	-u	-ui	-uo	-un	-uai	-uan	-uang	-ü	-üe	-ün	-üan
b	bu		bo								
p	pu		po								
m	mu		mo								
f	fu		fo								
d	du	dui	duo	dun		duan					
t	tu	tui	tuo	tun		tuan					
n	nu		nuo			nuan		nü	nüe		
l	lu		luo	lun		luan		lü	lüe		
g	gu	gui	guo	gun	guai	guan	guang				
k	ku	kui	kuo	kun	kuai	kuan	kuang				
h	hu	hui	huo	hun	huai	huan	huang				
z	zu	zui	zuo	zun		zuan					
c	cu	cui	cuo	cun		cuan					
s	su	sui	suo	sun		suan					
j								ju	jue	jun	juan
q								qu	que	qun	quan
x								xu	xue	xun	xuan
zh	zhu	zhui	zhuo	zhun	zhuai	zhuan	zhuang				
ch	chu	chui	chuo	chun	chuai	chuan	chuang				
sh	shu	shui	shuo	shun	shuai	shuan	shuang				
r	ru	rui	ruo	run		ruan					
*	wu	wei	wo	wen	wai	wan	wang	yu	yue	yun	yuan

Overview of cardinal numbers

yī	1	yìbǎilíngyī	101
èr	2	yìbǎilíngèr	102
sān	3	yìbǎilíngsān	103
sì	4	yìbǎilíngsì	104
wǔ	5	yìbǎilíngwǔ	105
liù	6	yìbǎilíngliù	106
qī	7	yìbǎilíngqī	107
bā	8	yìbǎilíngbā	108
jiǔ	9	yìbǎilíngjiǔ	109
shí	10	yìbǎi yìshí	110

shíyī	11	liǎngbǎi	200
shí'èr	12	sānbǎi	300
shísān	13	sìbǎi	400
shísì	14	wǔbǎi	500
shíwǔ	15	liùbǎi	600
shíliù	16	qībǎi	700
shíqī	17	bābǎi	800
shíbā	18	jiǔbǎi	900
shíjiǔ	19	yìqiān	1,000
èrshí	20	yìqiān yìbǎi yìshí yī	1,111

sānshí	30	liǎngqiān	2,000
sìshí	40	sānqiān	3,000
wǔshí	50	sìqiān	4,000
liùshí	60	wǔqiān	5,000
qīshí	70	liùqiān	6,000
bāshí	80	qīqiān	7,000
jiǔshí	90	bāqiān	8,000
yìbǎi	100	jiǔqiān	9,000
		yíwàn	10,000

Glossary of structural patterns

Pattern #		Page #
1.	Subject + *[bù]* + Equative Verb + Noun (Wǒ xìng Li. Wǒ bú xìng Wáng.)	24, 56, 140
1a.	Subject + *yě/dōu* +*[bù]* + Equative verb + Noun (Tā yě xìng Li. Tā yě bú xìng Wáng.)	28
2.	Subject + *hěn* + Adjective (Nǐ hěn gāo. Xiǎo Li bù hěn gāo. Lǎo Wáng hěn bù gāo.)	28, 34, 64, 106, 118, 122
2a.	Subject + *yě/dōu* + (*hěn*) + Adjective (Nǐmen dōu hěn gāo. Tāmen yě dōu hěn gāo. Wǒmen dōu bù gāo.)	29
2b.	Subject + Adjective + *le* (Wǒ è le. Nǐ è le ma? / Bù, wǒ bú è.)	42, 64
3.	Subject +*[bù]* + Verb + Object (Wǒ kàn shū. Tā kàn diànshì, tā bú kàn shū.)	60, 70
3a.	Subject +*[bù]* + Modal verb + Verb + Object (Nǐ xiǎng hē yǐnliào ma? / Bù, wǒ bù xiǎng hē yǐnliào. Wǒ yào hē tāng.)	52, 56
3b.	Subject + Verb + Object + *le* (Nǐ xǐzǎo le ma? / Wǒ xǐ le. Nǐ ne? / Wǒ méi xǐzǎo.)	78
3c.	Subject + *[bú]* + *zài* + Verb + Object (Nǐ zài zuò shénme? Nǐ zài xǐ yīfu ma? / Wǒ bú zài xǐ yīfu. Wǒ zài zuò fàn.)	70, 74
4.	Subject + Verb + Number + Measure + Noun (Wǒ mǎi yì běn shū.)	60, 102, 112
4a.	Subject + *[bù]* + Verb + Specifier + (Number) + Measure + Noun (Wǒ mǎi zhèi sān běn shū. Nǐ ne? / Wǒ bù mǎi nèi sān běn. Wǒ mǎi zhèi běn shū.)	106

5.   Subject + *[bú]* + *zài* + Place   93, 136, 140
      (Dìdi bú zài jiā. Tā zài xuéxiào.)

5a.   Subject + *[bú]* + *zài* + Noun + Locational noun   140
      (Māma bú zài kètīng li. Tā zài năr ne?)

5b.   Subject + *[bú]* + *zài* + Place/(Noun + Locational noun) + Verb phrase   152
      (Mèimei bú zài wòfáng li shuìjiào. Tā zài wòfáng li zuò gōngkè.)

6.   Subject + *[méi]* + Verb + *guo* + (Object)   93
      (Nǐ hēguo píjiǔ ma? / Wǒ méi hēguo.)

7.   Subject + *[bú]* + *dào* + Place + *qù*   98, 194
      (Nǐ dào fēijīchăng qù ma? / Bù, wǒ bú dào fēijīchăng qù.)

7a.   Subject + *[bú]* + *dào* + Place + *qù* + Verb phrase   164
      (Zánmen dào tǐyùguăn qù dă páiqiú ba.)

7b.   Subject + *[bú]* + *dào* + Noun + Locational noun + *qù* + Verb phrase   194
      (Zánmen dào hăibiār qù dă páiqiú ba.)

7c.   Subject + *(cóng* + Place₁) + *(dào* + Place₂) + *lái/qù*   200
      (Wǒ cóng Yīngguó lái. Wǒ dào Rìběn qù. Wǒ cóng Yīngguó dào Rìběn qù.)

7d.   Subject + *(cóng* + Place₁) + *(zuò* [vehicle]) + *(dào* + Place)   210
      + *lái/qù* + (Purpose)
      (Wǒ cóng Yīngguó zuò fēijī dào Rìběn qù xué Rìběnhuà.)

8.   Subject + *(shì)* + Adjunct + Verb + *de*   113
      (Nǐ shì năr lái de? / Wǒ shì cóng Měiguó lái de. / Nǐ shénme shíhou lái de?
      Wǒ qùnián lái de.)

9.   *(Zài)* + place + *[méi]* + *yǒu* + Noun   140, 156
      (Kètīngli méiyou diànshì, wòfáng lǐ yǒu diànshì.)

10.   Subject + *bǎ* + Object + Verb phrase   156
      <u>(Lǎo Wáng bǎ càidān ná lái le.)</u>

11.   Subject + Verb + *de* + *[bù]* + Adjective   172
      <u>(Tā shuō de hěn kuài. Nǐ shuō de bú kuài.)</u>

11a. Subject + Object + Verb + *de* + *[bù]* + Adjective   173
      <u>(Nǐ Yīngwén shuō de hěn hǎo, Rìyǔ shuō de bù hǎo.)</u>

12.   Place$_1$ + *lí* + Place$_2$ + *[bù]* + *yuǎn/jìn*   190
      <u>(Wǒ jiā lí xuéxiào hěn jìn, lí túshūguǎn yě bù yuǎn.)</u>

12a. Place$_1$ + *lí* + place$_2$ + Number + *lǐ lù*   190
      <u>(Zhōngguó lí Měiguó liùqiān lǐ lù.)</u>

13.   Subject + Adjective + *(de duō/ yìdiǎnr)*   122
      <u>(Zhèige hǎo yìdiǎr. Nèige hǎo de duō.)</u>

13a. A + *[bù]* + *bǐ* + B + Adjective + *(de duō/ yìdiǎnr)*   204
      <u>(Nǐ bǐ wǒ gāo yìdiǎr. Tā bǐ wǒ gāo de duō. Nǐ bù bǐ tā gāo.)</u>

14.   A + *gēn* + B + *yíyàng* + (Adjective)   204
      <u>(Rìwén gēn Yīngwén yíyàng nán.)</u>

15.   A + *méiyǒu* + B + *(nàme)* + Adjective   205
      <u>(Zhōngwén méiyǒu Yīngwén nán.)</u>

Chinese-English

a.   adjective
ad.   adverb
aux. v. auxiliary verb
conj.   conjunction
d.v.   directional verb
int.   interjection
m.   measure word
mod. v. modal verb
n.   noun
num.   number, numeral
part.   particle
prep.   preposition
pro.   pronoun
sp.   specifier
v.   verb
v.o.   verb–object

A

ǎi (a.) short 31
ài (v.) to love 123
aiya (int.) Aw, oh 91, 125, 192
ānpái (v.) to arrange 189
Àodàlìyà (n.) Australia 53
āyí (n.) aunt (mother's sister) 57, 97

B

ba (part.) (particle conveying a suggestion) 95, 115
bā (num.) eight 81
bǎ (m.) measure word for chairs, etc. 143
bǎ (prep.) (used in conjunction with a verb and its direct object) 156, 185, 186
bàba (n.) father, papa 57
bái (a.) white, fair 31, 103, 123
bǎi (num.) hundred 109
báicài (n.) Chinese cabbage 169
báifàn (n.) (plain) rice [Taiwan] 169
Bālí (n.) Paris 201
bàn (num.) half 71, 74
bàn (v.) do, handle 111
bǎncā (n.) board eraser 153
bāng (v.) to help 155, 199
bǎng (v.) to tie, to strap 209

bàng (m.) pound (unit of weight) 43
bāngmáng (n., v.) help, to help 197
bàngōngshì (n.) office 161
bànshì (v.) to handle matters 161
bànyè (n.) late at night, midnight 75
báo (a.) thin, light 119
bǎo (a.) full, satiated 61
bǎobao (n.) baby, term of endearment for a young child 84, 97
báo yìdiǎnr thinner, lighter (as in clothing) 119
bàozhǐ (n.) newspaper 109
Bāyuè (n.) August 81
běibianr (n.) the north 121
Běijīng (n.) Beijing (Peking) 201
Běijīng kǎoyā (n.) Peking duck 179
bēizi (n.) glass, cup 183
běn (m.) measure word for books 109, 112
běndìrén (n.) local person, native 55
bǐ (v., prep.) to compare, to be compared, in comparison 84
bié (aux. v.) do not (imperative) 115, 117, 121
Bié kèqi. Don't be (so) polite. 17
biérén (n.) other people, someone else 117, 155
bǐjìběn (n.) notebook 153
bìng (a.) sick 61
bīngxiāng (n.) refrigerator 171
bìxū (aux. v.) to have to 197
bóbo (n.) uncle 202
bófù (n.) uncle (father's older brother) 57
Bólín (n.) Berlin 201
bómǔ (n.) aunt (wife of father's older brother) 57, 202
bù (ad.) no, not 34, 60, 61
Bú cuò. I'm not bad . 17
bù dǒngshì to be immature 167
Bú duì. That's not right . 21, 123
bùgàopái (n.) bulletin board 153
bù hǎo yìsi (a.) embarassed 135, 209
Bù jí. There is no hurry. 75
bù néng (aux. v.) to be unable to 139
bù tóng (a.) dissimilar 163
Bú xiè. You're welcome . 17
bù xǐhuan (v.) to dislike 123
bùxíng (v.) to not be alright, to not work 83, 91

búyòng (v.) to be unnecessary 156, 181
bù zěnme not particularly 78
bù zěnme hǎo (a.) not too good 145
bù zhīdao (v.) to not know 37

C

cā (v.) to wipe 156
cāi (v.) to guess 36, 174
cái (ad.) only, only then, just, no more than 40, 72, 101, 139
cài (n.) dishes, courses 169
càidān (n.) menu 183
càixīn (n.) choy sum (a green vegetable) 169
cānguān (v.) to visit an institution 189
cānjiā (v.) to participate 161, 164
cānjīn (n.) napkin 183
cānjù (n.) utensils 183
cāntīng (n.) cafeteria 161
cāochǎng (n.) (playing) field 161
chá (n.) tea 183
chà (v.) to fall short 71, 74
cháng (a.) long 119
chángcháng (ad.) often 149, 152, 191
chángfāng (n.) rectangle 103
chángkù (n.) long pants 115
cháng yìdiǎnr longer 119
chǎo (v.) to quarrel 117
chǎo (v.) to scramble (stir-fry) 175
chǎofàn (n.) fried rice 169
chǎomiàn (n.) fried noodles 169
Cháoxiān/Hánguó (n.) Korea 53, 201
Cháoxiānrén (n.) a Korean person, Koreans 53
chāzi (n.) fork 183
chénglǐ (n.) downtown 191
chènshān (n.) shirt, blouse 115
chī (v.) to eat 149
chǐ (m.) foot (12 inches) 43
chǐcùn (n.) size 43
chídào (v.) to arrive late 151
chī dōngxi (v.o.) to eat something 67
chī fàn (v.o.) to eat a meal 67
chǐzi (n.) ruler 153
chǒu (a.) ugly 31
chuān (v.) to wear 115
chuáng (n.) bed 143
chuānghu (n.) window 153
chúfáng (n.) kitchen 137

chūlai (v.) to come out 135

chūmén (v.) to leave the house 149

chūnjià (n.) spring recess 157

chūntiān (n.) spring 95

chūqu/lai (v.) to go/come out 121

chū tàiyáng (v.o.) to be sunny 201

chūxiǎo (n.) lower elementary school (grades 1-3) 41

chūzhōng (n.) approximately junior high (grades 7-9) 41

cì (m.) time, occasion 49

cóng (prep.) from 53, 200

cùn (m.) inch 43

cū yìdiǎnr (a.) thicker, rougher 119

D

dà (a.) large 103, 106

dǎ diànhuà (v.o.) to talk on the telephone, to make a telephone call 127

dàgài (ad.) probably 45, 176, 180

dàhào (n.) large size 115

dài lù (v.o.) to lead the way 135

dàizi (n.) bag 109

dàlǐtáng (n.) auditorium 161

dàn (a.) bland 179

dāng (v.) to be, to act as 51

dāngmiàn (ad.) face-to-face 167

dào (m.) measure word for a course in a meal 179

dào (d.v.) to 96, 97, 164, 200

dào (v.) to arrive 95

dào (v.) to turn upside down, to turn around 156

dàodǐ (ad.) finally, after all 181

dàolǐ (n.) reason, rationale 163

dāozi (n.) knife 183

dǎpái (v.o.) to play cards 127

dǎqiú (v.o.) to play ball (general) 127

dǎsǎo (v.) to clean up 155

dàxiǎo (n.) size 103, 118

dàxué (n.) college 41

dà yìdiǎnr (a.) bigger 119

de (part.) 42, 106, 136, 146, 168

Déguó (n.) Germany 53, 201

Déguóhuà (n.) the German language 53

Déguórén (n.) a German person, Germans 53

děi (aux. v.) to have to 67, 70

děng (v.) to wait 75

Děng yíxià. Wait a moment. 75

Déwén (n.) the German language 53

Déyǔ (n.) the German language 53

diǎn (n.) a point, a tiny amount 71

diànfēngshàn (n.) electric fan 153

diànhuà (n.) telephone 37

diànshì (n.) television 67

diànyǐngyuàn (n.) movie theater 187

diǎnzhōng (n.) o'clock 71

dìbǎn (n.) floor 143

dìdi (n.) younger brother 57

dìlǐ (kè) (n.) geography (class) 157

dìqiúyí (n.) globe 153

dìtú (n.) map 153

dìxiàshì (n.) basement 137

dì-yī ge (num.) the first 157

dìzhǐ (n.) address 37

dǒng (v.) to understand 31, 103

dōngbianr (n.) the east 121

Dōngjīng (n.) Tokyo 201

Dōngnányà (Dōngnányǎ) (n.) Southeast Asia 53

Dōngnányàrén (n.) a Southeast Asian person, Southeast Asians 53

dǒngshì (v.) to be sensible 167

dōngtiān (n.) winter 95

dōngxi (n.) things 67, 101, 109, 121

dōu (ad.) both, all 28, 29, 61

dòufu (n.) tofu 169

duǎn (a.) short 119

duǎnkù (n.) short pants 115

duǎn yìdiǎnr (a.) shorter 119

duì (v.) right, correct 21, 117, 123

duì (n.) team 161

Duìbuqǐ. I'm sorry. 17

duō (a.) much, many 37, 38, 99

duō (m.) measure word for flowers 109, 112

duó dà how old 37

duó jiǔ how long 189

duóshǎo (num.) how much 37, 38, 99

Duóshǎoqian? How much money is it? 99, 102

Duō xiè. Thanks a lot. 17

dúshēngzǐ (n.) an only son 209

E

è (a.) hungry 61

Éguó (n.) Russia 53

Éguóhuà (n.) the Russian language 53

Éguórén (n.) a Russian person, Russians 53

ei (int.) 23, 55, 77, 96, 181, 193

èr (num.) two 81, 102

Èryuè (n.) February 81

érzi (n.) son 57

Éwén (n.) the Russian language 53

Éyǔ (n.) the Russian language 53

F

Fǎguó (n.) France 53, 201

Fǎguóhuà (n.) the French language 53

Fǎguórén (n.) a French person, the French 53

fāng (a.) square 103

fáng (n.) smaller rooms used as private living quarters 137

fángjiān (n.) room 137

fànguǎn (n.) restraurant 187

fāngxiàng (n.) direction 197

fàngxīn (v.) to stop worrying 209

fàngxué (v.) to dismiss school 157, 160

fángzi (n.) house 133, 143

fānqié (n.) tomato 171

fàntīng (n.) dining room 137

fànzhuō (n.) dining table 143

Fǎwén (n.) the French language 53

Fǎyǔ (n.) the French language 53

fēicháng (ad.) extraordinary, extremely, unusually 169

fēijīchǎng (n.) airport 187

fēn (m.) cent/$.01 99

fēn (m.) minute 71

fēn (m.) measure word for newspapers 109, 112

fěnhóng (a.) pink 117, 123

fěnlán (a.) powder-blue 124

fùjìn (n.) vicinity 199

fùmǔ (n.) parents 51, 189

fùqin (n.) father 57

fúwùyuán (n.) attendant 49

G

gàn (v.) to do, to engage in 49

gāngcái (ad.) just now; a few moments ago 71, 163

gāo (a.) tall 31

gǎo (v.) to cause, to do, to make 77

gàosu (v.) to tell 45

gāosù gōnglù (n.) freeway 197

gāoxiǎo (n.) upper elementary school (grades 4-6) 41

gāozhōng (n.) high school (grades 10-12) 41

ge (m.) general measure word 112, 143

gēge (n.) older brother 57

gélóu (n.) attic 137

gēn (v., conj., prep.) to follow, and, with 23, 127, 137, 191

gōngbǎojīdīng (n.) a spicy diced-chicken dish 177

gōnggòng qìchēzhàn (n.) bus
    stop 187
gōngjīn (m.) kilogram 43
gōngrén (n.) worker, laborer 49
gōngyuánli (n.) in the park 191
gōngzuò (n.) work, occupation 49
gòu (a.) enough 111, 117, 119
guā húzi (v.o.) to shave 149
guǎi (v.) to turn in a direction 197
guài (a.) strange 185
guàibude (int.) no wonder 189
guǎn (v.) to attend to, to be respon-
    sible for 121
Guǎngdōng (n.) Canton 201
guàngjiē (v.o.) to go window-
    shopping 191
guānxi (n.) connection, relationship ;
    matter, concern 45, 102
guǐ (n.) ghost 121
guì (a.) expensive 99
Guìlín (n.) Guilin 201
Guìxìng? May I ask your last name?
    21
guì yìdiǎnr (a.) more expensive 119
gùkè (n.) customer 47
guò (v.) to pass, exceed 97
guò (d.v.) across 74
guōbātāng (n.) sizzling rice
    soup 191
guójí (n.) nationality 53
guǒzhī (n.) fruit juice 183

H

hái (ad.) still, yet 97
hǎibào (n.) poster 153
hǎi bianr (n.) sea shore 191
Hái kěyǐ. It's alright. 139
háishì (ad.) still 84, 101, 121, 139,
    193
háishì (conj.) or (in questions only)
    103, 118, 123, 126, 176, 180,
    188
hǎixiān (n.) seafood 169
háiyǒu (conj.) and, in addition 139,
    145
hànbǎobāo (n.) hamburger 170
Hànchéng (n.) Seoul 201
Hánguó/Cháoxiǎn (n.) Korea 53
Hánguóhuà (n.) the Korean language
    53
Hánguórén (n.) a Korean person,
    Koreans 53
hánjià (n.) winter recess 157
Hánwén (n.) the Korean language
    53
Hányǔ (n.) the Korean language 53

hǎo (a.) well, fine, good   17, 61
hào (n.) day (in a date) 43, 81
hào (n.) number 37
hǎokàn (a.) goodlooking   31
hǎo le (v.) to have recovered 61
hàomǎ (n.) number   37
hǎowánr (a.) cute 105
hǎo yìdiǎnr (a.) better 119
hé (conj.) and, with 121, 145, 181
hē chá (vo.) to drink tea 67
hēi (a.) dark, black   31, 123
hēibǎn (n.) blackboard 153
hěn (ad.) very 28, 61, 122, 172
hé shang on the river 191
héshì (a.) appropriate 115, 118
hē shuǐ (vo.) to drink water 67
hézi (n.) box 109
Hnng. (int.) 185
hóng (a.) red 103, 123
hóng-lùdēng (n.) traffic light 197
hóngshāo (a.) red-cooked (stewed in
    soy sauce) 175
hóngshāo niúròu (n.) red-cooked
    beef 179
hòu (a.) thick, heavy   119
hòumiàn (a.) behind 143
hòutiān (n.) day after tomorrow   89
hòutou (n.) in the back, the rear   133
hòu yìdiǎnr (a.) thicker , heavier (as
    in clothing) 119
hòuyuàn (n.) back yard 137
huā (n.) flower 109
huáchuán (v.o.) to row a boat 191
huàn (v.) to change 181, 185
huàn chéng (v.) to change to 181
huáng (a.) yellow 123
huānyíng (v.) welcome 91
huàr (n.) painting 109
Huáshèngdùn (n.) Washington
    D.C. 201
huāyuán (n.) garden 137
huāyuán li (n.) in the garden 191
huàzhuāng (v.) to put on make-
    up 149
hú bianr (n.) by the lake 191
huī (a.) grey 123
huí (d.v.) back 197
huì (v.) to be able to, to know how to,
    to have a tendency to, to be
    likely to 53, 87, 127
huíjiā (v.) return home 149
Huíjiàn. See you in a while. 17
húndūntāng (n.) won-ton soup   179
huǒchēzhàn (n.) train station 187
huòzhě (conj.) or 83, 101, 120, 180,
    185

hùshi (n.) nurse 49
Húshūo! Nonsense! to lie 88, 177

J

jī (n.) chicken 169
jǐ (num.) how many 37, 43, 86, 99,
    137
jǐ (a.) to be crowded 145
jì (v.) to remember 117
jiā (n.) home 133, 137
jiājù (n.) furniture 143
jiákè (n.) jacket 115
jiāli (n.) in the home 137
jiān (a.) fried (pan-fried) 175
jiān (n.) measure word for rooms
    137
jiàn (n.) measure for clothing 115
Jiānádà (n.) Canada 53
Jiānádàrén (n.) a Canadian person,
    Canadians 53
jiǎndān (a.) to be simple 163, 185
jiǎng (v.) to speak 139
jiāngcōngjī (n.) chicken with ginger
    & green onion 169
jiānglái (n.) the future 49
jiào (v.) to be called (by given name)
    21, 24; to call 97
jiào cài (vo.) to order dishes 169
jiǎoluò (n.) corner 143
jiàoshì (n.) classroom 153, 161
jiàowù zhǔrèn (n.) dean 165
jiǎozi (n.) meat-filled dumplings,
    boiled 179
jiaòzuò (v.) to be called 180
jiāyóuzhàn (n.) gas station 187
Jiāzhōu (n.) California 201
jīchǎng (n.) airport 208
jīdàn (n.) chicken egg 169
jīdīng (n.) small cubes of
    chicken 175
jiē (n.) street, (road, etc.) 37, 197
jiē (v.) to receive 189
jiègěi (v.) to lend to 153
jiějie (n.) older sister 57
jiēkǒu (n.) intersection 197
jièlán (n.) mustard cabbage 169
jiěmèi (n.) sisters 57
jiē shang (n.) in town (on the
    street) 191
jīkuài (n.) large pieces of chicken,
    with bones 175
Jǐ kuài qian? How many dollars (is
    it)? 99, 102
jìmò (a.) lonely 139
jīn (a.) gold 123
jìn (a.) near 187

mùxūròu *(n.) pork & vegetables with crepe-like wrapper* 191

N

na *(int.) said when handing someone something* 20

ná *(v.) to take* 185

nàge *(pro.) that, that one* 103

nǎinai *(n.) paternal grandmother* 57

nálai *(v.) to bring* 183

nǎli *(pro.) where* 135

nàli *(pro.) there* 133

nàme *(pro.) so, to that extent* 139

nán *(a.) male* 105

nánbianr *(n.) the south* 121

nánkàn *(a.) unattractive* 31

nán péngyou *(n.) boyfriend* 153

nánshēng sùshè *(n.) male students' dormitory* 161

nǎr *(pro.) where* 37, 52, 53, 89

nàr *(pro.) there* 121

Nǎr de huà! *What nonsense! Who says so!* 117, 151

ne *(part.) question particle* 30, 61

něi *(sp.) which* 43, 86, 106

nèi *(sp.) that* 103, 106

nèige *(pro.) that, that one* 103, 107

něi guó *which country* 53

něi nián *which year* 43

néng *(v.) to be able to* 97

nǐ *(pro.) you* 21

nián *(n.) year* 43, 81

niàn *(v.) to study* 157

níanjí *(n.) grade/year in school* 37

niànshū *(v.) to study* 70, 80

nián yuè rì *(n.) date; year, month and day* 81, 86

Nǐ hǎo. *Hello.* 17

Nǐ hǎo ma? *How do you do?* 17

nǐmen *(pro.) you (plural)* 21

Nǐ ne? *How about you?* 17

niúnǎi *(n.) milk* 183

niúròu *(n.) beef* 169

Niǔyuē *(n.) New York* 201

niúzǎikù *(n.) blue-jeans* 115

nnng *(grunt of acknowledgement or agreement)* 68, 69, 73, 129, 158, 171

nóngmín *(n.) farmer, peasant* 49

nuǎnhuó *(a.) warm* 201

nǚ *(a.) female* 95

nǚ'ér *(n.) daughter* 57

nǚ péngyou *(n.) girlfriend* 153

nǚshēng sùshè *(n.) female students' dormitory* 161

Nǚshì *(n.) Ms.* 25

O

o *(int.)* 23, 40, 59, 90, 96, 155

ou *(int.)* 20, 209

Ōuzhōu *(n.) Europe* 53

Ōuzhōurén *(n.) a European person, Europeans* 53

P

pá *(v.) to crawl* 97

pà *(v.) to fear, to worry* 193

pái *(v.) to arrange* 159

pàichūsuǒ *(n.) police station* 187

páiqiú *(n.) volleyball* 161

pàng *(a.) fat* 31

pángbianr *(n.) beside, next to* 143

pángxiè *(n.) crab* 169

pánzi *(n.) plate* 183

páshān *(v.o.) to go hiking (in the hills)* 191

péngyou *(n.) friend* 165

piàn *(m.) measure word for slices of bread* 176

piányi *(a.) cheap, inexpensive* 99

piányi yìdiǎnr *(a.) cheaper* 119

piào jià *(n.) the price of the ticket* 207

piàoliang *(a.) pretty, handsome* 31

píjiǔ *(n.) beer* 183

píngcháng *(ad.) generally* 149, 152

píngzi *(n.) bottle* 109

pútáojiǔ *(n.) wine* 183

Q

qī *(num.) seven* 81

qí *(v.) to ride astraddle, as on bicycles and horses* 208

qǐ *(d.v.) up* 185

qiān *(num.) thousand* 99

qián *(n.) money* 81, 99

qiānbǐ *(n.) pencil* 153

qiáng *(a.) strong, powerful* 117

qiáng *(n.) wall* 143

qiántiān *(n.) day before yesterday* 89

qiántou *(n.) in front* 121

qiányuàn *(n.) front yard* 137

qiānzìbǐ *(n.) fine-line, felt-tipped pen* 153

qǐchuáng *(v.) to get out of bed* 149

qiē *(v.) to cut* 185

qǐlai *(v.) to get up, to rise up* 67

qí mótuōchē *(v.o.) to ride a motor-cycle* 207

qīng *(a.) clear* 117

qīng *(a.) light* 119

qǐng *(v.) please, to invite* 17, 49, 99

qīngcài *(n.) vegetables* 171

qīngjiégōng *(n.) custodian* 165

qīnglǐ *(v.) to tidy up* 155

Qǐngwèn... *May I ask...* 25, 197

qīng yìdiǎnr *(a.) lighter* 119

qīngzhēngyú *(n.) steamed fish* 179

qīnqì *(n.) relatives* 57

qítā *(pro.) other* 155

qiú *(n.) ball* 109

qiūtiān *(n.) fall* 95

Qīyuè *(n.) July* 81

qí zìxíngchē *(v.o.) to ride a bi-cycle* 207

qù *(d.v.) to go* 95, 207

quányú *(n.) a whole fish* 177

qùnián *(n.) last year* 95

qúnzi *(n.) skirt* 115

qù wánr *(v.) to go have fun* 191

R

ránhòu *(ad.) after that* 185, 188, 197, 200

rè *(a.) hot* 61, 201

règǒu *(n.) hot dog* 170

rén *(n.) person* 53

rènshi *(v.) to know, to be acquainted with* 147

rì *(n.) day* 81

Rìběn *(n.) Japan* 53, 201

Rìběnhuà *(n.) the Japanese language* 53

Rìběnrén *(n.) a Japanese person, the Japanese* 53

Rìwén *(n.) the Japanese language* 53

Rìyǔ *(n.) the Japanese language* 53

ròu *(n.) meat* 169

ròusī shíjìncài *(n.) slivers of pork w/ mixed vegetables* 179

ruò *(a.) weak* 31

S

sān *(num.) three* 81

sànbù *(v.) to take a walk* 67, 127, 191

Sānfánshì *(n.) San Francisco* 201

sānjiǎo *(n.) triangle* 103

sānmíngzhì *(n.) sandwich* 170

Sānyuè *(n.) March* 81

sǎodì *(v.o.) to sweep the floor* 155

sēnlín li *(n.) in the forest* 191

shāfā *(n.) sofa* 143

shài tàiyáng *(v.o.) to be in the sun* 193

shālā *(n.) salad* 170, 185

shàng *(v.) to ascend* 69, 157, 160, 209

English–Chinese

A

able to néng 97; huì 53, 87
address dìzhǐ 37
after that ránhòu 185, 188, 197, 200
after yǐhòu 75, 89, 92
afternoon, p.m. xiàwǔ 75
again zài 21, 49, 97; yòu 152
age suì; suìshu 37
air-conditioning [PRC] kōngtiáo; [Taiwan] lěngqì 153
airport fēijīchǎng 187
alone, by oneself zìjǐ yígerén 137
already yǐjīng 188, 192
altogether yígòng 99
always jǐng 117
America, the U.S. Měiguó 53, 201
American-style football Měishì zúqiú 161
Americans Měiguórén 53
and hé 121, 145, 181
and, in addition háiyǒu 139, 145
and, to follow, with gēn 23, 127, 137, 191
any, in any fashion, as one pleases suíbiàn 129, 163
anytime suíshí 91
apartment, suite (used in addresses) shì 37
approximately zuǒyòu 180, 188
April Sìyuè 81
arrange ānpái 189
arrive dào 96, 97, 164, 200
arrive late chídào 151
as you wish suíbiàn 129, 163
ascend shàng 69, 157, 160, 209
Asia Yàzhōu (Yǎzhōu) 53
Asians Yàzhōurén 53
ask for directions wèn lù 197
at/to be located zài 50, 93, 95, 133
attend or hold a conference or meeting kāihuì 203
attend to, be responsible for guǎn 121
attendant fúwùyuán 49
attic gélóu 137
auditorium dàlǐtáng 161
August Bāyuè 81
aunt (mother's sister) āyí 57, 97; (wife of father's older brother) bómǔ 57, 202

Australia Àodàlìyà 53
Aw, oh aiya 91, 141, 192

B

baby bǎobao 84, 97; wáwa 91
back yard hòuyuàn 137
bag dàizi 109
bake, grill kǎo 175
ball qiú 109
ball-point pen yuánzhūbǐ 153
bank yínháng 187
basement dìxiàshì 137
bask in the sun shài tàiyáng 193
basketball lánqiú 161
bathroom xǐzǎojiān 137
be able to néng 97
be shì 21, 24, 67
beautiful měi 31
because yīnwei 81
bed chuáng 143
bedroom wòfáng 137
beef niúròu 169
beer píjiǔ 183
before noon, a.m. shàngwǔ 89
before yǐqián 75, 89, 92
behind hòumiàn 143
Beijing (Peking) Běijīng 201
belong to (a category) shǔ 84, 85
Berlin Bólín 201
beside, next to pángbiānr 143
best friend zuì yàohǎo de péngyou 165
better hǎo yìdiǎnr 119
bigger dà yìdiǎnr 119
birthday shēngri 43, 81
black (the color) hēi (sè) 123
black hēi (de) 123
blackboard hēibǎn 153
bland dàn 179
blouse, shirt chènshān 115
blue (the color) lán (sè) 123
blue lán (de) 103, 123
blue-jeans niúzǎikù 115
board eraser bǎncā 153
board the train, bus, car shàng chē 207
boil zhǔ 175
Bon voyage! Yílù-shùnfēng! 207
book shū 67, 127
bookbag shūbāo 153
bookstore shūdiàn 187

boring wúliáo 139; méi yìsi 162, 192
born, grow shēng 43, 84, 105
both, all dōu 28, 29, 61
bottle píngzi 109
bowl wǎn 183
box hézi 109
boy, little brother xiǎodìdi 25
boyfriend nán péngyou 153
bread miànbāo 176
breakfast zǎofàn 75, 149
bring nálai 183
brothers xiōngdì 57
brown (the color), coffee-colored kāfēi (sè) 123
brush the teeth shuāyá 149
bulletin board bùgàopái 153
bunk beds shàngxià pù 121
bus stop gōnggòngqìchēzhàn 187
busy máng 61
but kěshì 90
buy a ticket mǎi piào 207
buy mǎi 103, 109
by the lake hú biānr 191
by the sea (ocean) hǎi biānr 191

C

cafeteria cāntīng 161
California Jiāzhōu 201
call jiào 97
called (by given name) jiào 21, 24
campus xiàoyuán 135
Canada Jiānádà 53
Canadians Jiānádàrén 53
candy táng 109, 176
Canton Guǎngdōng 201
careful xiǎoxīn 208, 209
cause, do, make gǎo 77
ceiling tiānhuābǎn 143
cent/$.01 fēn 99
center, middle zhōngjiàr 133
certainly, surely yídìng 180
chair yǐzi 143
change huàn 181, 185
change to huàn chéng 181
cheap, inexpensive piányi 99
cheaper piányi yìdiǎnr 119
check, bill zhàngdān 183
chest of drawers yīguì 143
Chicago Zhījiāgē 201

swimming pool yóuyǒngchí 161

T

T-shirt T-xù shān 115
table zhuōzi 143
Taipei Táiběi 201
Taiwan Táiwān 50
take a bath xǐzǎo 67, 149
take a person where they wish to go
      sòng 208, 209
take a walk sànbù 67, 127, 191
take ná 185
talk on the telephone dǎ diànhuà 127
talk shuō 21, 49, 97
tall gāo 31
tea chá 183
teacher lǎoshī 49, 165
team duì 161
telephone diànhuà 37
television diànshì 67
tell gàosu 45
ten cents/$0.10 máo 99
ten shí 81
ten thousand wàn 99
textbook kèběn 153
Thanks a lot. Duō xiè. 17
thank xièxie 17
That's not right. Bú duì. 21, 123
That's enough. Gòu le. 119
that, that one nàge 103; nèi 103, 106;
      nèige 103, 107
theater, playhouse xìyuàn 187
then, afterwards zài 197, 200
There is no hurry. Bù jí. 75
there nàli 133, nàr 121
There's no such thing. No such thing
      happened. Méiyǒu de shìr. 177
they tāmen 21
thick, heavy hòu 119
thicker, heavier (as in clothing) hòu
      yìdiǎnr 119
thin shòu 31
thin, light báo 119
things dōngxi 67, 101, 109, 121
think (feel) juéde 31
thinner, lighter (as in clothing) báo
      yìdiǎnr 119
thirsty kě 61
this zhè 67, zhèige 93
this extent, such, so zhènme 121
this month zhèige yuè 95
this one zhège, zhèige 49, 79, 99,
      103, 107
this week zhèige xīngqī 89
this year jīnnián 95

thousand qiān 99
three sān 81
Thursday Xīngqīsì 81
tidy up qīnglǐ 155
tie, strap bǎng 209
time shíhou 71
time, occasion cì 49
tired lèi 61
to be (am, are, is) shì 21, 24, 67
to be strange guài 185
to be, to act as dāng 51
to somebody's face dāngmiàn 167
today jīntiān 89, 201
tofu dòufu 169
together yíkuàir 127, 130
Tokyo Dōngjīng 201
tomato fānqié 171
tomorrow míngtiān 89
too, also yě 28, 29, 40
too, excessively tài 31, 99, 121, 139,
      179, 182
toy wánjù 109
track and field tiánjìng 161
traffic light hónglù dēng 197
train station huǒchēzhàn 187
travel agency lǚxíngshè 189
triangular sānjiǎo (de) 103
troublesome máfán 185
Tuesday Xīngqī'èr 81
turn in a direction guǎi/zhuǎn 197
turn left zuǒ zhuǎn 197
turn zhuǎnwān 197
two èr 81, 102; liǎng 99, 102, 143
type, kind yàng 109

U

ugly chǒu 31
unattractive nánkàn 31
uncle (father's older brother) bófù
      57; bóbo 202
uncle (father's younger brother)
      shūshu 57, 97
uncooked rice mǐ 171
understand dǒng 31, 103
unnecessary búyòng 156, 181
unreasonable méi dàolǐ 152
up qǐ 185
upper elementary school (grades 4-6)
      gāoxiǎo 41
upside down, to turn upside down
      dào 156
upstairs lóushàng 137
use the toilet shàng cèsuǒ 67
use yòng 154, 184, 185
usually tōngcháng 129

utensils cānjù 183

V

vegetables shūcài 169; qīngcài 171
very hěn 28, 61, 122, 172
vicinity fùjìn 119
visit an institution cānguān 189
volleyball páiqiú 161

W

Wait a moment. Děng yíxià. 75
wait děng 75
walking, on foot zǒulù 97, 207
wall qiáng 143
want yào 67, 70, 96, 109
warm nuǎnhuo 201
wash (one's) face xǐliǎn 149
wash hands xǐshǒu 149
wash the dishes xǐwǎn 149
wash the hair xǐtóu 151
Washington D.C. Huáshèngdùn 201
waste-paper basket zhǐlǒu 153
watch television kàn diànshì 67, 115
we wǒmen, zánmen 21, 127
weak ruò 31
wear chuān 115
weather tiānqì 201
Wednesday Xīngqīsān 81
week lǐbài, xīngqī 81
weight, body tǐzhòng 43
welcome huānyíng 91
well, fine, good hǎo 17, 61
west xībianr 133
What does it (this) mean? Shénme
      yìsi? 31
What nonsense! Who says so! Nǎr de
      huà! 117, 151
What shall we do? How shall we
      handle it? Zěnme bàn? 180
what kind shénmeyàng 103
what shénme 21, 52, 123, 127
What's wrong? What happened?
      Zěnme le? 77, 90, 151, 163, 193
when shénme shíhòu 52
where nǎli 135; nǎr 37, 52, 53, 89
which country něiguó 53
which něi 43, 86, 106
which year něi nián 43
white, fair bái 31, 103, 123
Who knows! Shéi zhīdào! 95
who, whom shéi 21, 52, 109, 133
whole fish quányú 177
why wèishénme 52, 81, 86
window chuānghu 153
window shopping guàngjiē 191

wine pútáojiǔ 183
winter dōngtiān 95
winter recess hánjià 157
wipe cā 156
won-ton soup húndūntāng 179
work, occupation gōngzuò 49
wow wa 101, 139, 155
write a letter xiěxìn 127

X

Xi'an Xī'ān 201

Y

year nián 43, 81
year, month, date nián yuè rì 81
yellow (the color) huáng (sè) 123

yesterday zuótiān 89
you (plural) nǐmen 21
you nǐ 21
You're welcome. Bú xiè. 17
young xiǎo 25
younger brother dìdi 57
younger sister mèimei 57

Z

zero líng 100